W9-AQO-592

☐ THE AGE OF PROTEST

THE
AGE
OF
PROTEST

EDITED BY

WALT ANDERSON
San Fernando Valley State College

 GOODYEAR PUBLISHING COMPANY, INC.
Pacific Palisades, California

© 1969 BY GOODYEAR PUBLISHING COMPANY, INC.
Pacific Palisades, California

Library of Congress Catalog Card Number 79-77543

Current Printing (last digit):
10 9 8 7 6 5 4 3 2

Printed in the United States of America

☐ PREFACE: TOWARDS A THEORY OF PROTEST

I participated in what may well turn out to have been an historic occasion, the first "teach-in" at the University of Michigan. This originated as a protest movement against the escalation of the war in Vietnam, by a group of Michigan faculty, mostly younger men. It developed from a simple protest into what turned out to be a unique educational experience in which between two and three thousand students literally sat down and talked and argued all night. The movement spread rapidly to other campuses and organized a national teach-in which was held in Washington in May. It now begins to look like almost a national mobilization of university teachers and students. In a way, the forerunner of this movement was the remarkable mobilization of faculty members on university campuses against

Kenneth E. Boulding, "Towards a Theory of Protest," BULLETIN OF THE ATOMIC SCIENTISTS, *October, 1965. Reprinted by permission.*

Goldwater, which represented political arousement on a scale which has rarely, if ever, been seen before in these supposedly cloistered circles.

Nobody, unfortunately, is much concerned to study the effects of all this, some of which may be quite different from what the people who are aroused by the arousal intend. I am constantly impressed by the ironies of social systems, where action often produces quite the reverse of the consequences which are intended. On the other hand, presumably, the better our knowledge of social systems, the more likely are we to avoid any unintentional consequences. It is important, therefore, for protesters to have some theory of protest, and to be sensitive to those circumstances in which protest is effective in achieving its intended consequences, and those circumstances in which it is not.

Let me venture, then, on a few tentative suggestions for a possible theory of protest, in the form of some tentative propositions.

1. Protest arises when there is strongly felt dissatisfaction with existing programs and policies of government or other organizations, on the part of those who feel themselves affected by these policies but who are unable to express their discontent through regular and legitimate channels, and who feel unable to exercise the weight to which they think they are entitled in the decision-making process. When nobody is listening to us and we feel we have something to say, then comes the urge to shout. The protester is the man in the advertisement who does not read the *Philadelphia Bulletin,* but who has something very important to say that clearly isn't in it. Furthermore, as he apparently has no access to the *Bulletin,* all he can do is to stand in the middle of its complacent readers and scream.

2. Protest is most likely to be successful where it represents a view which is in fact widespread in the society, but which has somehow not been called to people's attention. The protest of the man who does not read the *Philadelphia Bulletin* is likely to be highly successful, as he is usually trying to call attention to events which obviously ought to be in the *Bulletin,* being intrinsically newsworthy. Societies, like solutions, get supersaturated or supercooled; that is, they reach a situation in which their present state is intrinsically unstable, but does not change because of the absence of some kind of nucleus around which change can grow. Under these circumstances, protest is like the seed crystal or the silver iodide in the cloud. It precipitates the whole system toward a position which it really ought to be in

anyway. We see this exemplified in the relative success of the protest movements in civil rights. Here we have a situation, as Myrdal saw very clearly in *The American Dilemma,* in which certain fundamental images of the American society were inconsistent with its practices, and where, therefore, the protesters could appeal to an ideal which was very widely held. Wherever there is hypocrisy, there is strong hope of change, for the hypocrite is terribly vulnerable to protest. On the other hand, in the absence of protest, the supersaturated society may go on for a long time without change, simply because of what physicists call the nucleation problem.

3. Where the society is not supersaturated, a protest movement has a much rougher time. It then has to move the society toward the new position, from which change can then crystallize out, and this is a much more difficult task than crystallizing change in a society that is ready for it. Furthermore, protest as a social form, which may be very effective and indeed necessary in crystallizing a supersaturated society, may be quite ineffective in moving a society which is not saturated for change toward a point where it is saturated. That is, the techniques for creating the pre-conditions of change may be very different from the techniques required for crystallizing it. Where a society is divided and ambivalent, a protest movement designed to push it in one direction may easily arouse movements of counter-protest designed to resist the movement or to push it in the other direction. This is something to which protesters rarely give sufficient attention. Because they are themselves emotionally aroused, they tend to think that almost everybody must be in a similar frame of mind, which may not be true at all. It is quite possible, for instance, for protest movements to arouse counter-protests much larger than the original protests, and, hence, the net result of the protest is to move the system away from the direction in which the protesters want it to move. The Goldwater campaign was a good example of this. Goldwater was nominated as a Republican candidate as a result of a protest movement among discontented conservatives. The result, however, was the arousal of a much larger movement of counter-protest among those who were frightened and dismayed by Goldwater, which resulted in a quite unprecedented defeat.

4. The dynamic process of social systems is not entirely random, and this means that any particular social system is more likely to go in some directions than it is in others. Obviously, a protest movement which is trying to push the social system in a direction in which it

has a high probability of going anyway is more likely to be successful than one that is trying to push the social system in a direction that has a low probability. Unfortunately, it is by no means easy to assess the various probabilities of change; nevertheless, we can surely know something about it. At least we can be pretty sure, for instance, that movements toward absolute hereditary monarchies today have a pretty slim chance of success. We can identify certain cumulative processes in the history of social systems, such as the growth of knowledge, the widening of integrative systems, and so on, which have a certain long-run irreversibility about them, even if they may have short-run setbacks. Systems move, however painfully, toward payoffs. As we learn to understand the payoffs, we can identify those protest movements which have the best chance of success. On the other hand, it is not the "real" payoffs which determine human behavior, but the imagined ones, and there can often be a strong divergence between the two, at least in the short-run, and this short-run can be painfully long.

5. We might, perhaps, distinguish between protest movements and educational movements, the one designed to crystallize a change for which a society is ready, the other to push the society toward a change for which it is not yet ready. The techniques of these two movements may be very different. A protest movement needs to be shrill, obstreperous, undignified, and careless of the pattern of existing legitimacy which it is seeking to destroy in the interest of a new pattern which is waiting to emerge. Educational movements have to be low-keyed, respectful of existing legitimacies—tying into them wherever possible, and chary of arousing counter-protest. A good example of this in race relations is the work of the NAACP, which unquestionably laid the educational ground-work for the recent protest movement in civil rights. When the movement for protest arrives, however, the educational institution is often pushed aside, and perhaps properly so, as inappropriate in the circumstances. On the other hand, protest movements for which society has not been prepared by education, or which are seeking for improbable change, are virtually doomed to failure, like the IWW. The movement for social security in this country is an interesting example of one in which the educational process dominates it almost completely, and where the role of protest is almost negligible.

6. Even when a situation is ripe for a protest movement, it can go astray and be ineffective if it takes an inappropriate form. The

form of a protest should be closely related to the object of protest. This is why, for instance, on the whole, the sit-ins have been very successful, whereas marches and parades are usually less so. It can be particularly disastrous to the protest movement if the protest takes a form which arouses a counter-protest over the form itself, and not over the object of protest. Any object of protest can easily be lost in argument and counter-argument over the question as to whether the form of the protest is legitimate or appropriate.

7. Protest movements are also likely to be weakened if the object of protest is not clear, or if there are many different objects, some of them incompatible, combined in the same protest. Thus, the strike in industrial conflict is usually a rather effective form of protest, particularly when it is directed toward a change that would have come anyway, because it is appropriate to the objective, and the objective itself is usually very clear. Political protest, by contrast, is apt to be diffuse; its objectives are unclear and often inconsistent. Political protest movements almost always run into the problem of strange bedfellows, and the less clear the objectives of protest, the less likely is anybody to fulfill them.

Kenneth E. Boulding

☐ CONTENTS

☐ THE AGE OF PROTEST

☐ INTRODUCTION

The title of this book has been chosen in the conviction that protest is the definitive and characteristic political act of this period in history. This conviction may well be confirmed by the historians, but we cannot wait for their verdict before we examine what protest *is*. It is urgently necessary that we find out what is going on in modern society that subjects it to so many forms of resistance from within, and what the consequences of protest are likely to be—consequences for those who protest, for the objects of protest, for the spectators and, finally, for the society that the act of protest aims to change.

The contents of this book are almost without exception the writings of people who are themselves involved in protest or to some extent sympathetic to the movements they study or report. This book is not meant to be a pro and con symposium on whether protest should or should not exist. It exists, and I hold that in all its forms—potent or futile, noble or silly, mature or irresponsible—it represents a true human voice that deserves to be listened to and understood. This attitude does not presuppose that all protest is morally or legally right.

There have been valuable psychological and sociological studies of protest, but disappointingly little from the discipline of political science. It is surprising that so few political scientists acknowledge the extent to which protest has become part of the common vocabulary of political behavior—how many Americans, for instance, often those same respectable Americans who disapprove of riots and peace marches, break out placards and parade in protest against school policies, supermarket prices, city government decisions, and the like. The counter-protest demonstration in support of government or institutional authority has also become commonplace. More and more people at some time in their lives experience protest *as protesters*. Where once the electorate waited for the next election, or wrote to their newspapers or government officials, or did nothing at all, increasingly they turn to the techniques of protest.

There are many questions, and many kinds of questions, to be asked about protest. Consider the matter of aggressiveness: There is something to be learned about an act of protest by discovering how eagerly the protester approached the confrontation—did he seek it out, or did it seek him out? The latter possibility is eloquently personified in the character of Sir Thomas More in Robert Bolt's *A Man For All Seasons*. More does not pursue martyrdom—in fact uses all his wit to avoid it—but is ultimately brought to a point where he feels he must resist. Even then, he is accused by his daughter, visiting him in prison, of having chosen to be a hero:

MARGARET: In any State that was half good, you would be raised up high, not here, for what you've done already. It's not your fault the State's three-quarters bad. Then if you elect to suffer for it, you elect yourself a hero.

MORE: That's very neat. But look now. . . . If we lived in a State where virtue was profitable, common sense would make us good, and greed would make us saintly. And we'd live like animals or angels in the happy land that *needs* no heroes. But since in fact we see that avarice, anger, envy, pride, sloth, lust and stupidity commonly profit far beyond humility, chastity, fortitude, justice and thought, and have to choose, to be human at all . . . why then perhaps we *must* stand fast a little—even at the risk of being heroes.[1]

For all its historical setting, *A Man For All Seasons* (which was winning Oscars in Hollywood in the same month that Captain Howard Levy was being tried before a court-martial in South Carolina) is an authentic product of the age of protest.

If More's resistance is placed at one end of the scale of aggressiveness, there is no lack of deliberately sought-out confrontations to place at the other end: In 1968, Columbia University and the Democratic Convention in Chicago provided two instances of aggressive protest, where demonstrations were successfully organized to arouse the greatest amount of public interest. But even in these cases, we must recognize that no protest is effective unless it gains momentum by catching up some people who, while not initially intending to become protesters, find themselves at some point compelled to take sides. This is the polarization process central to radical doctrine. The familiar charge of authorities that a protest was started by "outside agitators" may in some cases be quite correct—but the question of why and how other people became involved is far more significant.

There are other ways to measure acts of protest. Perhaps the most important scale is that of effectiveness: Does a protest achieve its aims, is it ineffective, or does it in fact lose ground—create an overreaction and worsen the conditions the protesters had hoped to improve? Viewed from another perspective, do protesters *want* to achieve their stated aims? Is a given protest a rational, goal-oriented act, or is it as Nat Hentoff has suggested, sometimes self-therapy? Another question: Are the protesters making demands to benefit themselves or someone else? This is basic to an understanding of the internal organization of any movement which contains such components as students and faculty, draftable and draft-exempt, or black and white.

One of the most fascinating questions of all about protest, and one for which no substantial answer has so far been offered, is historical: What has happened, in ten years or so, to alter so dramatically the political behavior of Americans? Why wasn't there a student revolt in Berkeley during the loyalty oath controversy of

[1] Robert Bolt, *A Man For All Seasons* (New York: Random House, Inc., 1962).

1950? Why didn't Negroes boycott buses in Montgomery before 1955? Is protest a surface thing, a minor change of political style magnified by television and the press, or does it signal a deep shift in social consciousness, a basic alteration in the way people relate to their institutions?

In studying underlying causes, we need to consider the possibility that protest is related to the sheer size of the country. Given the expectations of Americans reared to believe that in a democracy the government is theirs, responsive to their opinions, the actual experience of being one citizen in a country of some 200 million must inevitably be frustrating. Who has not known the feeling of resolving that some governmental decision *must* be changed, then being overwhelmed by the realistic awareness of how futile it would be to try to change it. In a society where such expectations and frustrations coexist, a certain amount of protest may provide a healthy equilibrium—perhaps conservatives and revolutionaries should both consider the possibility that protest may not lead to revolution, but may on the contrary prevent it. Some psychiatrists contend that a neurosis has survival value to the neurotic in that it saves him from becoming psychotic; a similar hypothesis might be of value to those who are concerned about a sick society.

Nearly thirty years ago, economist Joseph A. Schumpeter explained political *apathy* in terms of the individual's inability to change the course of events:

One has one's phrases, of course, and one's wishes and daydreams and grumbles; especially, one has one's likes and dislikes. But ordinarily they do not amount to what we call a will—the psychic counterpart of purposeful responsible action. In fact, for the private citizen musing over national affairs there is no scope for such a will and no task at which it could develop. He is a member of an unworkable committee, the committee of the whole nation, and this is why he expends less disciplined effort on mastering a political problem than he expends on a game of bridge.[2]

The same explanation could be applied today to political *activism,* and specifically to the frequency of recourse to acts of protest by those who *do* develop a will.

One of the most striking facts about contemporary politics is the frequency with which one encounters, all along the spectrum, a com-

[2] Joseph A. Schumpeter, *Capitalism, Socialism and Democracy* (New York: Harper & Row, Publishers, 1942), p. 261.

mon belief in the need for some degree of decentralization, re-humanization, for new kinds of democratic opportunities at the community level. This is evident in the New Left preoccupation with "counter-institutions" such as the free university, in the black power demand for local autonomy, in the cautious efforts of government agencies to give control of programs to the people actually affected by them, in the conservative reaction against federal bureaucracy and the erosion of states' rights. That same belief takes on a special meaning for people who become involved in acts of protest; they often seem to be trying desperately, not to destroy institutions, but to become a part of them.

The selections that follow vary widely in style and content. There are studies, essays, papers, reports by professional journalists, and firsthand accounts by protesters. Some items were chosen mainly because of subject matter, others because of some personal quality that gives a view of its own of what it is like to live in an age of protest. Examples of the latter are Eldridge Cleaver's *Letter from Jail* and *Moments in a Southern Town,* written by a young civil rights worker named Peter de Lissovoy.

There are, in all, twenty-five selections in this book. Many students and teachers will read only certain portions, but whenever possible the book should be read in its entirety—because all of the pieces fit together and the *Gestalt* they form is a picture, at once ominous and inspiring, of America in the second half of the twentieth century.

☐ INDICTMENTS

To understand protest at all one must know something of what there is to protest against, what can be found objectionable in the existing social order. These first four selections, therefore, are criticisms, putting into words something of what the protester puts into action.

The occasion of Paul Goodman's indictment of the military-industrial complex was an invitation in 1967 from the military-industrial itself, or an important segment of it, to address a meeting on planning for the 1970's. The speech was in itself something of a confrontation —the social critic facing a largely hostile audience—and deserves to be regarded as an act of protest in its own right.

Theodore Roszak's criticism of the values of academia also comes from within the walls—Dr. Roszak teaches history at the California State College at Hayward.

The National Advisory Commission on Civil Disorders was appointed by President Johnson in 1967, and headed by Gov. Otto

Kerner of Illinois. The committee's report—of which *The Basic Causes* is one chapter—created a national furor with its charge that "white racism" played a major part in creating the conditions which led to discontent among American Negroes.

Herbert Marcuse has become one of the leading spokesmen for radical youth. He is, at the age of 70, teaching philosophy at the University of California at San Diego. In *The New Forms of Control* he discusses the increasing comfort—and decreasing freedom—of life in modern industrial society.

A CAUSERIE AT THE MILITARY-INDUSTRIAL

Paul Goodman

The National Security Industrial Association (NSIA) was founded in 1944 by James Forrestal, to maintain and enhance the beautiful wartime communication between the armament industries and the government. At present it comprises 400 members, including of course all the giant aircraft, electronics, motors, oil, and chemical corporations, but also many one would not expect: not only General Dynamics, General Motors, and General Telephone and Electronics, but General Foods and General Learning; not only Sperry Rand, RCA, and Lockheed, but Servco and Otis Elevators. It is a wealthy club. The military budget is $84 billion.

At the recent biennial symposium, held on October 18 and 19 in the State Department auditorium, the theme was "Research and Development in the 1970's." To my not unalloyed pleasure, I was invited to participate as one of the seventeen speakers and assigned the topic "Planning for the Socio-Economic Environment." Naturally I could make the usual speculations about why I was thus "co-opted." I doubt that they expected to pick my brains for any profitable ideas. But it is useful for feeders at the public trough to present an image of wide-ranging discussion. It is comfortable to be able to say, "You see? these far-outniks are impractical." And business meetings are dull and I am notoriously stimulating. But the letter of invitation from Henri Busignies of ITT, the chairman of the symposium committee, said only, "Your accomplishments throughout your distinguished career eminently qualify you to speak with authority on the subject."

What is an intellectual man to do in such a case? I agree with the Gandhian principle, always cooperate within the limits of honor, truth, and justice. But how to cooperate with the military industrial club! during the Vietnam war 1967! It was certainly not the time to reason about basic premises, as is my usual approach, so I decided simply to confront them and soberly tell them off.

Fortunately it was the week of the demonstration at the Pentagon, when there would be thousands of my friends in Washington. So I tipped them off and thirty students from Cornell and Harpur drove down early to picket the auditorium, with a good leaflet about the evil environment for youth produced by the military corporations. When they came, the white helmets sprang up, plus the cameras and reporters. In the face of this dangerous invasion, the State Department of the United States was put under security, the doors were bolted, and the industrialists (and I) were not allowed to exit—on the 23rd Street side. Inside, I spoke as follows:

R & D FOR THE SOCIO-ECONOMIC ENVIRONMENT OF THE 1970'S

I am astonished that at a conference on planning for the future, you have not invited a single speaker under the age of thirty, the group that is going to live in that future. I am pleased that some of the young people have come to pound on the door anyway, but it is too bad that they aren't allowed to come in.

This is a bad forum for this topic. Your program mentions the "emerging national goals" of urban development, continuing education, and improving the quality of man's environment. I would add another essential goal, reviving American democracy; and at least two indispensable international goals, to rescue the majority of mankind from deepening poverty, and to insure the survival of mankind as a species. These goals indeed require research and experimentation of the highest sophistication, but not by you. You people are unfitted by your commitments, your experience, your customary methods, your recruitment, and your moral disposition. You are the military industrial of the United States, the most dangerous body of men at the present in the world, for you not only implement our disastrous policies but are an overwhelming lobby for them, and you expand and rigidify the wrong use of brains, resources, and labor so that change becomes difficult. Most likely the trends you represent will be interrupted by a shambles of riots, alienation, ecological catastrophes, wars, and revolutions, so that current long-range planning, including this conference, is irrelevant. But if we ask what *are* the technological needs and what ought to be researched in this coming period, in the six areas I have mentioned, the best service that you people could perform is rather rapidly to phase yourselves out, passing on your relevant knowledge to people better qualified, or reorganizing yourselves with entirely different sponsors and commitments, so that you learn to think and feel in a different way. Since you are most of the R & D that there is, we cannot do without you as people, but we cannot do with you as you are.

In aiding technically underdeveloped regions, the need in the foreseeable future is for an intermediate technology, scientifically sophisticated but tailored to their local skills, tribal or other local social organization, plentiful labor force, and available raw materials. The aim is to help them out of starvation, disease, and drudgery without involving them in an international cash nexus of an entirely different order of magnitude. Let them take off at their own pace and in their own style. For models of appropriate technical analyses, I recommend you to E. F. Schumacher, of the British Coal Board, and his associates. Instead, you people—and your counterparts in Europe and Russia—have been imposing your technology, seducing native elites mostly corrupted by Western education, arming them, indeed often using them as a dumping ground for obsolete weapons. As Dr. Busignies pointed out yesterday, your aim must be, while maintaining leadership, to allow very little technical gap, in order to do business. Thus, you have involved these people in a wildly inflationary economy, have driven them into instant urbanization, and increased the amount of disease and destitution. You have disrupted ancient social patterns, debauched their cultures, fomented tribal and other wars, and in Vietnam yourselves engaged in genocide. You have systematically entangled them in Great Power struggles. It is not in your interest, and you do not have the minds or the methods, to take these peoples seriously as people.

The survival of the human species, at least in a civilized state, demands radical disarmament, and there are several feasible political means to achieve this if we willed it. By the same token, we must drastically de-energize the archaic system of nation-states, e.g. by internationalizing space exploration, expanding operations like the International Geophysical Year, de-nationalizing Peace Corps and aid programs, opening scientific information and travel. Instead, you—and your counterparts in Europe, Russia, and China—have rigidified and aggrandized the states with a Maginot-line kind of policy called Deterrence, which has continually escalated rather than stabilized. As Jerome Wiesner has demonstrated, past a certain point your operations have increased insecurity rather than diminished it. But this has been to your own interest. Even in the present condition of national rivalry, it has been estimated, by Marc Raskin who sat in on the National Security Council, that the real needs of our defense should cost less than a fourth of the budget you have pork-barreled. You tried, unsuccessfully, to saddle us with the scientifically ludicrous Civil Defense program. You have sabotaged the technology of inspection for disarmament. Now you are saddling us with the antimissile missiles and the multi-warhead missiles (MIRV). You have corrupted the human adventure of space with programs for armed platforms in orbit. Although we are the most heavily armed and the most naturally protected of the Great Powers, you have seen to it that we spend a vastly greater amount and perhaps a higher proportion of our wealth on armaments than any other nation.

This brings me to your effect on the climate of the economy. The wealth of a nation is to provide useful goods and services, with an emphasis first on necessities and broad-spread comforts, simply as a decent background for un-economic life and culture; an indefinitely expanding economy is a rat-race. There ought to be an even spread regionally, and no group must be allowed to fall outside of society. At present, thanks to the scientific ingenuity and hard work of previous generations, we could in America allow a modest livelihood to everyone as a constitutional right. And on the other hand, as the young have been saying by their style and actions, there is an imperative need to simplify the standard of living, since the affluent standard has become frivolous, tawdry, and distracting from life itself. But you people have distorted the structure of a rational economy. Since 1945, half of new investment has gone into your products, not subject to the market nor even to Congressional check. This year, 86 per cent of money for research is for your arms and rockets. You push through the colossally useless Super-Sonic Transport. At least 20 per cent of the economy is directly dependent on your enterprises. The profits and salaries of these enterprises are not normally distributed but go heavily to certain groups while others are excluded to the point of being out-caste. Your system is a major factor in producing the riots in Newark. *(At this remark there were indignant protests.)*

Some regions of the country are heavily favored—especially Pasadena and Dallas—and others disadvantaged. Public goods have been neglected. A disproportionate share of brains has been drained from more useful invention and development. And worst of all, you have enthusiastically supported an essentially mercantilist economics that measures economic health in terms of abstract Gross National Product and rate of growth, instead of concrete human well-being. Both domestically and internationally, you have been the bellwether of meaningless expansion, and this has sharpened poverty in our own slums and rural regions and for the majority of mankind. It has been argued that military expenditure, precisely because it is isolated and wasteful, is a stabilizer of an economy, providing employment and investment opportunities when necessary; but your unbridled expansion has been the chief factor of social instability.

Dramatically intervening in education, you have again disrupted the normal structure. Great universities have come to be financed largely for your programs. Faculties have become unbalanced; your kind of people do not fit into the community of scholars. The wandering dialogue of science with the unknown is straitjacketed for petty military projects. You speak increasingly of the need for personal creativity, but this is not to listen to the Creator Spirit for ideas, but to harness it to your ideas. This is blasphemous. There has been secrecy, which is intolerable to true academics and scientists. The political, and morally dubious co-opting of science, engineering, and social science has disgusted and alienated many of the best students. Further, you have warped the method of education, beginning with the primary grades. Your need for narrowly expert personnel has led to processing the young to be test-passers, with a gross exaggeration of credits and grading. You have used the wealth of public and parents to train apprentices for yourselves. Your electronics companies have gone into the "education industries" and tried to palm off teaching machines, audio-visual aids, and programmed lessons in excess of the evidence for their utility. But the educational requirements of our society in the foreseeable future demand a very different spirit and method. Rather than processing the young, the problem is how to help the young grow up free and inventive in a highly scientific and socially complicated world. We do not need professional personnel so much as autonomous professionals who can criticize the programs handed to them and be ethically responsible. Do you encourage criticism of your programs by either the subsidized professors or the students? *(At this, Mr. Charles Herzfeld, the chairman of the session, shouted "Yes!" and there was loud applause for the interruption, yet I doubt that there is much such encouragement.)* We need fewer lessons and tests, and there ought to be much less necessity and prestige attached to mandarin requirements.

Let us turn to urbanism. *Prima facie,* there are parts of urban planning—construction, depollution, the logistics of transportation—where your talents ought to be peculiarly useful. Unfortunately, it is your companies who have oversold the planes and the cars, polluted the air and water, and balked at even trivial remedies, so that I do not see how you can be morally trusted with the job. The chief present and future problems in this field, however, are of a different kind. They are two. The long-range problem is to diminish the urbanization and suburban sprawl altogether, for they are economically unviable and socially harmful. For this, the most direct means, and the one I favor, is to cut down rural emigration and encourage rural return, by means of rural reconstruction and regional cultural development. The aim should be a 20 per cent rural ratio instead of the present 5 per cent. This is an aspect of using high technology for simplification, increasing real goods but probably diminishing the Gross National Product measured in cash. Such a program is not for you. Your thinking is never to simplify and retrench, but always to devise new equipment to alleviate the mess that you have helped to make with your previous equipment.

Secondly, the immediately urgent urban problem is how to diminish powerlessness, anomie, alienation, and mental disease. For this the best strategy is to decentralize urban administration, in policing, schooling, social welfare, neighborhood renewal, and real-estate and business ownership. Such community development often requires heightening conflict and risking technical inefficiency for intangible gains of initiative and solidarity. This also is obviously not your style. You want to concentrate capital and power. Your systems analyses of social problems always tend toward standardization, centralization, and bureaucratic control, although these are not necessary in the method. You do not like to feed your computers indefinite factors and unknown parameters where spirit, spite, enthusiasm, revenge, invention, etc., will make the difference. To be frank, your programs are usually grounded in puerile theories of social psychology, political science, and moral philosophy. There is a great need for research and trying out in this field, but the likely cast of characters might be small farmers, Negro matriarchs, political activists, long-haired students, and assorted sages. Not you. Let's face it. You are essentially producers of exquisite hardware and good at the logistics of moving objects around, but mostly with the crude aim of destroying things rather than reconstructing or creating anything, which is a harder task. Yet you boldly enter into fields like penology, pedagogy, hospital management, domestic architecture, and planning the next decade—wherever there is a likely budget.

I will use the last heading, improving the quality of man's environment, as a catch-all for some general remarks. In a society that is cluttered, overcentralized, and overadministered, we should aim at simplification, decentralization, and de-control. These require highly sophisticated research to determine where, how, and how much. Further, for the first time in history, the scale of the artificial and technological has dwarfed the natural landscape. In prudence, we must begin to think of a principled limitation on artifice and to cut back on some of our present gigantic impositions, if only to insure that we do not commit some terrible ecological blunder. But as Dr. Smelt of Lockheed explained to us yesterday, it is the genius of American technology to go very rapidly from R & D to application; in this context, he said, prudence is not a virtue. A particular case is automation: which human functions should be computerized or automated, which should not? This question—it is both an analytic and an empirical one—ought to be critical in the next decade, but I would not trust IBM salesmen to solve it. Another problem is how man can feel free and at home within the technological environment itself. For instance, comprehending a machine and being able to repair it is one thing; being a mere user and in bondage to service systems is another. Also, to feel free, a man must have a rather strong say in the close environment that he must deal with. But these requirements of a technology are not taken into account by you. Despite Dr. Smelt, technology *is* a branch of moral philosophy, subordinate to criteria like prudence, modesty, safety, amenity, flexibility, cheapness, easy comprehension, repairability, and so forth. If such moral criteria became paramount in the work of technologists, the quality of the environment would be more livable.

Still a further problem is how to raise the scientific and technical culture of the whole people, and here your imperialistic grab of the R & D money and of the system of education has done immeasurable damage. You have seen to it that the lion's share has gone to your few giant firms and a few giant universities, although in fact very many, perhaps more than half of, important innovations still come from independents and tiny firms. I was pleased that Dr. Dessauer of Xerox pointed this out this morning. If the money were distributed more widely, there would probably be more discovery and invention, and what is more important, there would be a larger pool of scientific and competent people. You make a fanfare about the spinoff of a few socially useful items, but your whole enterprise is notoriously wasteful—for instance, five billions go down the drain when after a couple of years you change the design of a submarine, sorry about that. When you talk about spinoff, you people remind me of the TV networks who, after twenty years of nothing, boast that they did broadcast the McCarthy hearings and the Kennedy funeral. *(This remark led to free and friendly laughter; I do not know whether at the other industry or at their own hoax.)* Finally, concentrating the grants, you narrow the field of discovery and innovation, creating an illusion of technological determinism, as if we *had* to develop in a certain style. But if we had put our brains and money into electric cars, we would now have electric cars; if we had concentrated on intensive agriculture, we would now find that this is the most efficient, and so forth. And in grabbing the funds, you are not even honest; 90 per cent of the R & D money goes in fact to shaping up for production, which as entrepreneurs you should pay out of your own pockets.

No doubt some of these remarks have been unfair and ignorant. *(Frantic applause.)* By and large they are undeniable, and I have not been picking nits.

These remarks have certainly been harsh and moralistic. We are none of us saints, and ordinarily I would be ashamed to use such a tone. But you are the manufacturers of napalm, fragmentation bombs, the planes that destroy rice. Your weapons have killed hundreds of thousands in other Vietnams. I am sure that most of you would concede that much of what you do is ugly and harmful, at home and abroad. But you would say that it is necessary for the American way of life, at home and abroad, and therefore you cannot do otherwise. Since we believe, however, that that way of life itself is unnecessary, ugly, and un-American *(shouts of "Who are* **we?***")*—we are I and those people outside—we cannot condone your present operations; they should be wiped off the slate.

Most of the 300 in the audience did not applaud these remarks, but there was quite strong applause from a couple of dozen. Afterward these sought me out singly and explained, "Thanks for having the courage" or more significantly, "Those kids outside are right. My son is doing the same thing in Boston—Ohio State—etc."

The chairman of the session, Charles Herzfeld of ITT, felt obliged to exclaim, "The remark about our committing genocide in Vietnam is obscene. He does not say what is really intolerable there, the Viet Cong single out college graduates for extermination."! !

More poignantly, the director of the symposium, a courteous and intelligent man, apologized to the gathering for having exposed them to me, which must have been a wrench for him to say. He had of course seen my text beforehand.

We went out by the exit onto the other avenue, and I was able to rejoin the more amiable company of the young people, who were now sitting with their backs pressed against the auditorium doors, still among the white helmets. I answered their questions about the proceedings and we dispersed. That night NBC-TV showed a picture of the pickets, and next morning I got a story in the *Post*.

WHERE IS IT AT? Unquestionably the week of Resistance demonstrations was successful and made its point, that thousands are now willing to go to jail or get their heads broken to stop the Vietnam war. There were no disappointments: Turning in the draft-cards, resistance at the induction centers and staging areas and against Dow and Navy recruiters, the crowd in Washington and the melee at the Pentagon, all proved strong enough.

We are witnessing a test of legitimacy, and in my opinion the government position is now untenable. Despite a few exotic slogans, there is a groundswell of American populism, including sporadic populist violence as in 1890 and 1933, but mainly solidly secure in the belief that it is itself the democratic voice and LBJ is a usurper. As was not reported in the press, the night vigil on the Pentagon steps on October 22 sang *The Star-Spangled Banner*. It was probably a mistake for the President to have exposed so many troops to the young resisters who were mostly peaceful but obviously spunky and sometimes persuasive.

The climate is beginning to feel like the eve of the French withdrawal from Algeria, including the same coalition of the young, the intellectuals, and the Algerians (Negroes). The question remains, is the American structure so rich and technologically powerful that its government can dispense with legitimacy? I don't know. And while the NLF and the North Vietnamese have been hanging on and continuing to counter-attack (and their people and our people are dying), American opinion has finally begun to veer sharply toward getting out. The hawk spokesmen have become divided and confused.

There is a persistent rumor in Washington that the President (or the hidden government) is about to cast the die and approve the prepared invasion of North Vietnam in December. If so, a hundred thousand youth and many many others will resist non-violently or violently and there will be martial law and concentration camps. I will not speculate further along this atomic line.

But there is evidence that shrewder counsel might prevail; to write off this odious war, adopt a somewhat less adventurous foreign policy, put a little more money into the cities, divert some of the military industrial enterprise into Outer Space and "long-range planning," and come to a solid understanding with the Russians. I think this is the meaning of the rapidly increasing dovishness in Congress and the sudden conversion of the Republicans who threaten to nominate Percy or Gavin. The strategy is similar to the New Deal: when the going gets too rough domestically, accommodate and go on to build a grander corporate structure that is, in some respects, better—temporarily. For this plan, however, Johnson would have to go, since it now seems impossible for him to sound a retreat from Vietnam without getting shot by the irate father of a young man who died in vain. Whether we would then get Robert Kennedy or a moderate Republican is probably unimportant.

Needless to say, this is not the outcome that the radical young are after. They fear, justifiedly, that if we stop the war, most of the Americans will again fall morally and politically asleep. Yet they, like the rest of us, do want to stop the Vietnam war; there are few indeed who are so fanatical for world upheaval as to want that particular evil to continue so that good may come. In my opinion, also, they will have to learn that one is not going to re-structure modern society with a fraction of the 10 per cent Negro population, nor even with the "Third World" ruled by Ben Bellas, Nassers, Maos, Nkrumahs, Sukarnos, or their successors. This is not the stuff of new humanism. For instance, those who objected to being processed at Berkeley will have to think seriously about Chairman Mao's little red book. And those who want to make love not war but who also want to imitate Che Guevara in American cities, must ask themselves what adequate guerrilla tactics would be in a high technology, namely to poison the water, wreck the subways, and cause power failures in New York and Chicago; is this what they intend?

But I do not think the young themselves will fall asleep. They have been through remarkable experiences and have found one another. There is the potentiality of a kind of youth international. Most important, the present power-systems of the world are indeed unfit for modern conditions, and this will become increasingly apparent. If the young continue to be in conflict, to try out innovations, and to study professionally what ought to be done with our technology and ecology, mores and authority-structure, and the fact of one world, they will gradually shape for themselves a good inheritance to come into. Considering the tremendous power and complexity of the systems they want to displace, twenty years is a short time to devise something better.

THE COMPLACENCIES
OF THE ACADEMY

Theodore Roszak

Pascal thinks that men pursue their business and their sciences with such single-mindedness in order to escape the most important questions which every moment of loneliness and true leisure would urge upon them—questions concerning the Why, Whence, and Whither of life. But curiously enough, not even the most obvious question occurs to our scholars: what benefit their labor, their haste, and their painful ecstasies can possibly have? . . . But if, as men of science, you go about science in the same manner in which brokers go about the tasks which life's daily necessities impose upon them, then what is to become of a culture condemned to await the hour of its birth and its salvation amidst this excited, breathless, aimless, fidgeting infatuation with science and learning? [1]

—Friedrich Nietzsche

The "men of science" who were on the receiving end of Nietzsche's typically abrasive contempt when he issued the above challenge nearly a century ago were his own colleagues in the German universities. But he might have been speaking with undiminished force to the present generation of American scholars and scientists. And would the account they could give of themselves be any less pathetic than the account German science and scholarship has had to tender in our time? No doubt there are fine distinctions that can be made between the concentration camp and the strategic hamlet, the gas oven and the thermonuclear missile. But with how much pride can

---

[1] Quoted in *The Abuse of Learning: The Failure of the University* by Frederic Lilge (New York, 1948), pp. 92-3.

any of us undertake the exercise in moral pedantry it would require to draw these distinctions?

It is by no means an historical coincidence that both American and German academics should prove vulnerable to the barb of Nietzsche's insight. For much of the character of higher learning in America was established in the post-Civil War period by a generation of scholars and scientists who had received their advanced training in the German academies. For men like Josiah Royce, G. Stanley Hall, Henry Baxter Adams, the German university with its lecture method, its seminars, its laboratories, and its rigorous Teutonic conception of *Wissenschaft* was what higher education was all about—or certainly ought to be all about. Universities such as Heidelberg, Leipzig, Göttingen and Berlin became the academic New Jerusalem; their American disciples brought home their style and standards like exotic treasures and redesigned higher education in America to serve as a suitable setting for them.

To be sure, the zeal of that generation of academics—the creators of the "graduate school," of aristocratic scholarly communities like Johns Hopkins and Clark, of the American learned societies—helped to save the American university from becoming a very philistine place indeed. For the academic world which they confronted in the latter nineteenth century was rapidly being submerged in that peculiarly American vulgarization of higher learning known as "service." "Service," as it was, and still is, interpreted by the administrative, financial, and political forces that govern American higher education, meant the indiscriminate adaptation of the university to the interests of the private or public groups that supported it. It meant, for example, offering "professional study" and even degrees in boy-scouting, fire insurance, home economics, and hotel management. (Such courses were available in schools of the caliber of Cornell, Chicago, and Wisconsin.) It meant, in brief, conferring the prestige of higher learning on whatever kinds of technical information and vocational training, whatever modes of socialization and entertainment, the community wanted from the campus.

The conflict between service and scholarship in American higher education was not destined to be resolved wholly in favor of either side—at least not at the vast majority of the more important state and private universities. Instead, the conflict has gradually worked itself into an impasse. And, in our typically "pragmatic" way, the impasse has been given a name and has become a substitute for a solution. The name is "the multiversity"—the school which teaches, in Robert Hutchins' words, "anything we can get anybody to pay for." Including, let it be said, valid subjects. For if the "service station" concept of higher education has survived, and indeed prospered, over the past three generations, the principled academic has at least managed to carve out and fortify a niche for himself in the busy labyrinth of the contemporary campus. As Laurence R. Vaysey shows in his excellent description of the clash of educational ideals in *The Emergence of the American University* (Chicago, 1965), such was the compromise that scholarly research and liberal culture finally settled for in the major state and private universities. In the graduate schools, in the colleges of arts and letters, in their portion of the general education requirements, the academics have achieved a kind of disgruntled coexistence with the home economists, the educationists, the engineers, the business administrators, and the vast contingent of those who train and entertain in the guise of teaching.

This historic competition between vulgar and elitist notions of higher education continues to structure much of the discussion that goes on in the multiversities about the ideals of education, as well as a great amount of faculty politics. The proponents of the multiversity still parade under the banner of "democracy"; the scholars still champion the virtues of disinterested intellect. But the truth is that their dialogue has become merely a peevish one, a debate between half-men who have lost touch with the essential meaning both of "democracy" and "intellect" and who are equally guilty of a cultural failure that is beyond the power of both to comprehend.

For what have these two academic traditions led to finally? On the one hand, the ideal of service has led to a collaboration between the universities, the corporations, and the government so indiscriminate that the American military establishment has no more difficulty in procuring academics to carry out any project—bar none—than its counterparts in totalitarian societies. Ranking physicists and engineers specialize in thermonuclear weaponry, and leading schools like MIT and the University of California at Berkeley derive a major part of their budgets from "service" of this kind. Biologists at the University of Pennsylvania have worked under secret contracts to develop chemical-biological weaponry. As part of the Army's Project Camelot, social scientists have pooled their expertise in order to help our military plan counterinsurgency activities in

Latin America. In order to provide the USIA with cold-war propaganda of a scholarly cut, the University of Southern California has set up, with the generous support of a radical right-wing industrialist, a Research Institute on Communist Strategy and Propaganda.

And so on. And so on. A full listing of such activities—including the prestigious employment academics have sought at military think-tanks like the RAND Corporation—could go on for dozens of pages. But the picture is clear enough: in the name of service, universities and university men have willingly collaborated in all the corruptions into which our governments's exaggerated sense of omnipotence has led us. The concept of service, the willingness to do whatever society will pay for, has culminated in the virtually complete abandonment of moral discrimination—the indispensable element of wisdom. Until at last, the multiversity, morally speaking, resembles nothing so much as the highly adaptable brothel in Jean Genêt's *The Balcony*.

Meanwhile, what have Nietzche's "excited, breathless, aimless, fidgeting" scholars come to in contemporary America? The answer is equally melancholy. For up until the recent flurry of campus protest against the war in Vietnam, the American academic scene has produced a virtually unbroken record of social irrelevance and moral complacency.

Certainly the opportunities for a strong show of intellect and conscience have not been lacking in America. The "balance of terror"—which comes down to an exquisitely rationalized social commitment to the strategy of genocide—has entrenched itself in the psychology and morality, as well as the economy, of our society. The threadbare ideals and rhetoric of an anachronistic nationalism continue to dominate our politics. The ominous imbalance of wealth between the world's rich and poor nations continues to increase. The control of democratic institutions over decision-making elites continues to weaken. But about all of these forces that threaten the spiritual, and indeed the physical, survival of civilization, the scholarly community has little to say.

Nor do American academics lack occasions for educating the general public. At least once a year, each of the learned societies that control the careers and standards of professional academics holds regional and national conferences. Very rarely, of course, do these conferences gain any public visibility, but this is not because the press is unwilling to provide coverage. On the contrary, a paper like *The New York Times* goes out of its way to find anything of public relevance that is discussed at these meetings. Thus, at the 1965 meeting of the American Historical Association, the *Times* reported fully on a paper dealing with the problem of violence in the civil rights struggle and on one concerning the relations of Pope Pius XII with anti-Nazi conspirators. At the 1965 meeting of the American Political Science Association, a *Times* reporter, clearly at the end of his resources, went about the corridors pressing political scientists for their cautious and pedestrian opinions on the Johnson administration. Following the 1965 conference of the American Sociological Association, the *Times* finally appeared to lose patience and, taking up some critical remarks made by the Association's president, went on to chastise the sociologists for offering so little that had any relevance to the problems of our times. Complaining strongly (for the *Times*) about the "mores of the academic world where demonstrations of abstract technical expertise—preferably of a mathematical nature—merit special status," the editorial went on to ask if the function of sociology is "to get particular individuals academic promotions, profitable grants of doubtful use, or is it to make pioneering contributions to the understanding of the nature and operation of a complex society undergoing rapid change"?

Clearly the conferences of learned societies are meant to serve other functions than that of communicating with the society-at-large. Their structure and tone derive from much the same purposes that shape the trade conventions of, say, the Association of Plumbing Contractors or the Association of Hotel Managers, where new and specialized knowledge is passed about, old friends get together, and valuable commercial contracts are made. Still it is odd, to say the least, that the conferences of learned societies in the humanities and social sciences should transpire so routinely and unobtrusively in our society. There is, after all, not a single one of the professions of higher learning that is not ultimately connected with that aggregation of ideals which distinguishes civilized life from barbarism. Indeed, few of us who teach in the universities would consider a student adequately educated who had not been asked to ponder the examples of Socrates and Abelard, Galileo and Spinoza, Voltaire and Pasteur, among all the other figures who fought to dignify the life of the mind and to assert the pre-eminence of the moral virtues. But what do the examples of these great forebears mean to academics themselves? What does it imply when those who are peculiarly charged with the cultivation and defense of intellectual and humane values come together year after year, ostensibly to make a collective assertion of their identity as teachers and scholars, but in reality with little more socially significant purpose in mind than can be found at a convention of hotel managers? Do they believe that civilized values in our day require no special cultivation or defense and that there are other and better things to do than to use these assemblies as forums for vigorous public discussion of public issues? Or do they believe that no matter what may be wrong with America, it is not at all the teacher's responsibility to address himself to its correction?

Let us examine a contrasting situation. The matters discussed and voted upon at the annual convention of the AFL-CIO are apt to be front-page news. No Presidential administration would dare let such a convention meet without entering thickly into its politics and attempting to influence its resolutions on public questions. But has any administration ever troubled itself to send representatives to meetings of the American Historical Association or the Modern Language Association with a view to "winning over" the conference? The prospect is absurd.

One may object that the AFL-CIO is after all a voting bloc of immense size and is courted as such by political leaders. The learned societies, being so inconsequential in their voting strength, receive no political attention. But this objection will not do. Obviously, the learned societies are in no position to compete as a "bloc vote" with other forces in our society. Nor would that be an appropriate form of competition for them. But they *are* societies of opinion-makers—or at least potentially so. They are composed of learned and articulate men whose words and deeds affect millions of students and could be of considerable influence with the voting public. Their opinions, if not their votes, should carry weight in Washington. The embarrassment of the Johnson administration at Robert Lowell's refusal in 1965 to accept a White House award is an example of how sensitive official society is to the thoughtful dissent of one intellectual. The press coverage given to the testimony of academics such as Henry Steele Commager at the hearings on Vietnam of the Senate Foreign Relations Committee is another example of potential influence. If the Johnson administration does not trouble itself for the opinions of academics—except of those who support its policies—it is simply because the opinions are not there in the first place. Academic societies are politically irrelevant and are treated as such—what academic societies do and say is, in the end, "academic."

This public irrelevance, this narrow professionalism of scholarship in the humanities and social sciences, makes its difficult to take seriously much of the conventional campus competition between "academics" and "nonacademics," between "technicians" and "humanists." For is not the scholar's lack of moral responsiveness really equivalent to the technician's lack of moral discrimination? Is the scholar who indulges in fastidious but morally undirected research into Shakespearean sonnets or nineteenth-century European diplomatic history any less of a mere technician than the typical electronics engineer? For what is it that significantly distinguishes the humanist from the technician, if it is not the willingness to ask: What is this knowledge *for?* Where does it lead?

Since such questions of purpose, direction, and value are no more fashionable among scholars today than among technicians, it is no wonder that the servants of learning and the servants of the warfare state have by and large been able to arrange a subtle and pervasive *entente* on the campuses.

The world-as-it-is has become increasingly generous to its academics. It is only natural, perhaps, that academics are more willing than ever to prepare students to take their places passively in the world-as-it-is. The baccalaureate and doctorate provide admission into the ranks of an elite professional class distributed through the corporations, the military, and the government bureaucracies. The "humanities" serve the Great Society by providing the university graduate with a finer taste in music, literature, art, films: that is, a little cultural icing for the economic cake. Both humanist and technician can take pride in their joint product: let us say, an Aerospace computer programmer. Off the job, he is a man of easy culture. He listens appreciatively to his local "good music" station; his library is filled with paperback editions of Plato, Tolstoy, Shakespeare; his walls are graced with Modigliani and Braque prints. He remembers his Humanities IA and his English Lit. 44B, and they decorate his life. On the job, he complacently and ingeniously perfects the balance of terror.

To be sure, the issue of social responsibility is beginning to receive attention on the campuses, but serious discussion is taking place mainly among the students, graduate students, and junior

faculty. Those on the commanding heights of the learned professions are doing little more than cautiously prowling about the
margins of a question that is at least twenty years overdue for
urgent consideration—and contenting themselves, finally, with that
strange kind of pride academics seem to be able to take in "recognizing" a problem but not in solving it.

Thus, at the 1965 conference of the American Sociological Association, Pitirim Sorokin, in his presidential address, announced that
it is time "to get beyond the phase of fact-finding to the creative,
generalizing period that is now due." Or we have the example of
Morris Bishop, president in 1965 of the MLA, lamenting the fact
that there simply isn't any longer enough literature to provide work
for all the scholars now on the scene. (But his solution is to suggest
some further study of the literature of Zoology or aviation!) Or we
have Kenneth Boulding telling the1965 meeting of the American
Economic Association in no uncertain terms that ". . . the whole
economics profession, indeed, is an example of that monumental
misallocation of intellectual resources which is one of the most
striking phenomena of our times." Boulding's complaint was that
the economists have been "obsessed with macro-economics, with
piddling refinements in mathematical models, and with the monumentally unsuccessful exercise in welfare economics which has preoccupied a whole generation with a dead end, to the almost total
neglect of some of the major problems of our day." Did his remarks
make any difference? Judging by the contents of those issues of the
American Economic Journal published subsequent to his remarks:
not in the least. For the image of economics we find there is still
that of a chaotic mass of neat little conundrums for technicians to
"kick around." But perhaps Boulding's criticism is being seriously
"talked up" around the profession and will come to something . . .
eventually.

Despite all the protest and unrest on the campuses, then, one
must still say of the academics what C. Wright Mills said of them
almost a decade ago in *The Causes of World War III:* [2]

They live and work in a benumbing society without living and working
in protest and in tension with its moral and cultural insensibilities. They
use the liberal rhetoric to cover the conservative default. They do not

[2] C. Wright Mills, *The Causes of World War III* (New York: Simon &
Schuster, Inc., 1958), p. 145. Reprinted by permission. © 1958, Simon &
Schuster, Inc.

make available the knowledge and the sensibility required by publics, if publics are to hold responsible those who make decisions "in the name of the nation." They do not set forth reasons for human anger and give it suitable targets.

There are many more today who would associate themselves with that accusation. But the accusation remains in force; the cultural default Mills attacked persists. And the reason for its persistence still requires close study. For despite the fact that more academics now than perhaps ever before in American history are beginning to respond to the tug of social conscience, the problem we are confronted with is not simply a matter of overcoming a certain timidity or sluggishness on the part of individual scholars. The problem has an *institutional* dimension; it has to do with the total configuration of relationships in which the individual academic finds himself: his training, his habits of work, his patterns of friendship and allegiance. That is to say, it has to do with the fact that the academic man exists mainly within the environment of his own profession.

In a recent critique of higher education, Paul Goodman chided the universities for failing to be "communities of scholars" and the academics for yielding control of the schools to administrators of an organization-man mentality. The situation Goodman describes smacks of usurpation and despotism. But it is not experienced as such by most academics. What the administrators have taken over—actually with the full consent of most faculty members—is simply the running of the particular campuses on which the professions are practiced. The campus is *not* understood to be the "community" to which a scholar belongs. Rather he belongs to a particular department and profession. It is in the department that a scholar makes his career; it is before a professional audience that every "serious" scholar performs and is judged.

In reality, the profession of History, say, is simply the sum total of all the history departments at all the colleges and universities in the country. The profession has no national organization of any significance—beyond, perhaps, the editorial board of its leading journal. Nonetheless, its informal networks of information, evaluation, and employment exist, and their standards count in the career of every historian who wants to succeed. In the mind of "academic man" there is a vision rather like Jacob's ladder: a great *cursus honorum,* which runs from an instructorship at Punxatawney State

Teacher's Normal up to the dizzying heights of a full professorship at Harvard, Columbia, Berkeley. A knowledgeable academic can probably peg the relative standing on that ladder of every one of his colleagues.

Thus for most academics the locus of their allegiance is the department—and beyond the department, the profession. Everything in between, which includes the coordination and running of the campuses on which departments are encamped, is very largely left to the administrator. For, given the prevailing standards of the learned professions, what the administrators are concerned with— mainly local and "interdepartmental" affairs—has relatively little influence on the career of the academic.

This is, of course, the reason why academics—especially ambitious academics at the "best" schools—have so much trouble with the bothersome business of education. Students belong to the particular campus on which they are studying. Educating them provides no professional visibility, and therefore designing an educational environment for them is left primarily to the administrators. This problem shows up especially in the handling of general education. General education, being broad and integrative, does not run readily through the narrow channels of the standard professional disciplines. Nor can one make a career in the important schools as a "generalist." So what careerist in his right mind would want to teach courses in general education? When the Columbia University faculty abandoned the sophomore year of its Contemporary Civilization survey, it explained its decision by observing that "the members of the staff do not regard the course as a challenge to their professional skill. . . ."

As with education, so too with the obligation of the campus to its community: unless community problems can create professionally acceptable research, they are merely local issues. Academics may become seriously concerned with such problems, but the faculty departments, which are primarily professional entities, usually pay little attention to what a man does in the way of education or community activity. When the English department at, say, the University of California, comes to make its decisions about hiring and firing, promotions and tenure, the voting members will be much more concerned about the impression their appointments will create in the English department at Harvard than in the local student body or the local community. This is what the "community of scholars" means as most academics understand that term.

From the moment that a student decides upon an academic career and undertakes graduate work, he becomes part of this "community." He must play the game by its rules or else abandon the board. His graduate studies, his dissertation, his ability to find a position at a "name" school—all of these are tokens in the game on which his teachers have gambled a certain amount of their professional prestige. If he is to find a job (indeed, in many cases, if he is even to be made aware that a prospective job exists), if he is to achieve tenure and promotions, if he is to survive and prosper, and especially if he is to acquire any amount of glory, then he must be obedient to the expectations of the professional powers that control these rewards. And he, in turn, will finish by enforcing the same expectations on the apprentices he ushers into the guild.

How, one wonders, have the professions managed to establish their authority so persuasively in the American university? David Riesman offers one illuminating answer. He reminds us that the academic life can very rapidly declass those who enter it, drawing them out of family, regional, and ethnic backgrounds. This is bound to be the case with the student who comes from lower-class origins, from a minority group, or from a rural community. For those who are thus dislocated, the profession becomes "the scholar's country"—replete with its own jealous "nationalism." As Riesman remarks, "The fervency of this nationalism reflects the sacrifices the scholar has made to become a scholar, what he has had to surrender of earlier social-class origins and ambitions." The profession becomes, then, an anchorage, a place to belong. But if academic life declasses, it can also re-class—into something that feels like and often even pays like the great American upper-middle class, from which many of the scholar's students (at the "better" schools at least) are apt to come.

The de-classing capacity of academic life (what Riesman calls its "universalizing quality") is, I think, a desirable feature. It is, potentially, a liberating experience. But the re-classing that usually follows is apt to be disastrous. It is at this point that the academic is integrated into the higher levels of the national society, with all that this means in the way of conformity to parochial loyalties. The universities, governed so ponderously by government and corporate wealth, finance and enforce the integration, and as we have already seen, few academics, whether scholars or technicians, exert themselves to avoid the tempting rewards. The American upper-middle class is a comfortable place to find oneself—especially when one

adds just the right admixture of jet-set elegance for the highly successful academic: research grants with foreign travel, visiting lecture-
ships, prestigious conferences, and perhaps even invitations to help
out in Washington. It is a marvelous institution that can offer a
young man who may have started with nothing but brains such an
opportunity to rise so high in the Great Society.

Undoubtedly the social forces that structure the academic professions are powerful. But the fact that a temptation is offered does not
excuse the acceptance of it. Nor does the fact that a social pressure
is very strong mean that those it acts upon are totally without the
freedom to resist it. It would be pathetic, indeed, if those who have
given themselves to the life of the mind were to plead that they
were powerless to reform their own professional environment, powerless even to save their own souls by the brave attempt to achieve
reform. But the plea becomes outrageous when the forces to which
men surrender exert their greatest power, not by terror or repression,
but by offering the bribes of prestige and comfort.

The pursuit and communication of knowledge—whether it be
concerned with the sociology of the Pentagon or the aesthetics of
Chaucer—is, or ought to be, a noble enterprise. The rhetoric that
academics are in the habit of expending on this point is, indeed,
almost dizzying. I suspect every one of us carries around a fat selec-
tion of favorite clichés about the "beauty," the "moral worth," and
the "dignity" of the "search for truth"; for example, Carl Becker's
statement that "the value of history is, indeed, not scientific, but
moral; . . . it prepares us to live more humanely in the present,
and to meet rather than to foretell, the future." Very well, then: if
the quest for knowledge is indeed a noble enterprise and so ennobles
those who undertake it, what is the measure of a man's nobility?
Is it not, in very large measure, his sensitivity to what is ignoble—
to all that is base, false, ugly, barbaric? Is it not his willingness to
speak out bravely against those forces that debase our lives and
threaten the survival of civilized life?

Let us suppose, then, that an instructor in American history takes
an active part in organizing a thoughtful, well-conceived campaign
against capital punishment in his state. He musters the students to
the cause and succeeds in engaging public officials and people generally in a searching debate of crime and punishment. He has not made
a more genuine *intellectual* contribution than if he had written a
definitive study on the decline of cotton factorage in the American
South for the period of 1865-1894?

Or, again, suppose that a psychology instructor, feeling that the politics of his community has gone slack, undertakes to run for Congress, with an eye to stimulating serious public discussion of pressing local problems. His campaign is responsible from start to finish, and he forces his opposing candidates to take clear-cut stands they would otherwise have avoided like the plague. How shall we assess the man's *intellectual* behavior? Is it more or less valuable than an exhaustive study of olfaction in the unrestrained rat?

Suppose an English instructor devotes a large amount of his time to organizing "freedom schools" in the slums and conducting a creative writing workshop there. Should we, for purposes of promotion and tenure, count his *intellectual* efforts as highly as if he had produced a critical study of Golding's translation of Ovid's *Metamorphoses?*

Suppose an anthropology instructor busies himself organizing a teach-in on the Vietnam war. Perhaps he even travels to Vietnam for the Inter-Universities Committee and then writes a solid analysis of the effects of the war on the rural population for the *Atlantic Monthly* or *The New Republic.* Is his work worth more or less—*intellectually* speaking—than a study of unity and diversity in the celebration of cattle curing rites in a north Indian village?

No doubt many academics will say that since these men are involved in "action" as distinct from "thought," why do they deserve any academic consideration at all? Isn't the academic's function to "think" rather than "act"? This is the question that frequently arose in discussions among the members of the now-defunct Council for Correspondence, which made probably the most significant single effort in the postwar period to organize academics into a political force. The reply to it is, I think, to ask how much sense it makes to regard "thinking" and "doing" as separate, if not incompatible, activities. Analysis and discussion, where they are politically relevant, become political *acts*—and it is this that we have specified as the peculiar social responsibility of intellectuals. To think, to speak, to teach, to write: all these *are* forms of doing. They ought properly to be seen as integral components of action and as an indispensable part of the political process. Without doing any more, an academic may help make the life of his society richer and nobler. But what if he wants to go further? If a man's thought should carry over into more overt forms of action, such as those we mentioned above, are we to regard it as somehow automatically debased? Surely not. For in a healthy personality "thought" and "action" merge gracefully along a single spectrum, and there is no natural barrier that prevents a man from undertaking some task of public leadership or organization in order to realize in fact what his understanding tells him must be done. Indeed, action—say, in the dramatic form of civil disobedience—may be the only way of forcing an intellectual dialogue upon reluctant and secretive authorities. In such situations, the unwillingness to act, to "make trouble," may imply that one is less than serious about the intellectual position he holds.

One can imagine all sorts of other questions being raised about our hypothetical instructors. But the truth is that only at the barest handful of schools in America today would their citizenly conduct be given any weight whatever in making "professional" decisions about them. No matter how intellectually sound or morally courageous that conduct might be, no matter of what benefit it might be to students or community, it would normally be discounted out-of-hand in evaluating the man.

Why should this continue to remain true when almost every aspect of American life has become a matter of open concern? Is it because we feel that anybody can "be political"—and so it isn't much of an achievement to do these things? But there are wise and foolish, profound and superficial ways to "be political," just as there are wise and foolish, profound and superficial exercises in scholarship. A Warren Harding might indeed be a fool. But a Thomas Jefferson, a Norman Thomas, an A. J. Muste, or to bring the point closer to our own time, an H. Stuart Hughes running for the Senate in Massachusetts—are men who have made intellect central to their politics. To be deeply and wisely political is a rare and commendable achievement—and one that often takes a great deal more courage than "pure research."

Should citizenly conduct be discounted because one fears that politically engaged academics won't be able to train graduate students in scholarly techniques and may fail in their duty of discovering knowledge? One is reminded here of the embittered objection a University of California professor raised in late 1965 against the student activists on campus. They were, he charged, seeking to "politicize" the university. Indeed they were. And why not? If one accepts that it is the function of intellectuality to make knowledge work in the defense of civilized values, then we may be dealing here with men who are indeed more capable than most "training" intellectuals. They may be able to do precisely what our present forms of graduate instruction never do: namely, to force a man to reflect on the function and purpose of his professional commitment.

What we contend here is that the training of teachers and scholars and the pursuit of research—as these activities are presently handled —result in a great deal of mindless specialization and irrelevant pedantry that ought not to be credited with intellectual respectability. There is probably not a single field of the social sciences and humanities that does not already boast a larger body of "knowledge" than can be "popularized"—and so assimilated into the cultural mainstream of our society—within the next fifty to one hundred years. Is it more "knowledge" of this surplus kind, expertly gleaned by precise techniques, that we exclusively require? Or, in the protracted emergency in which our civilization finds itself, shouldn't priority be given to a scholar's ability to link his special knowledge or moral insight to our social needs? In assessing a scholar's intellectual quality, shouldn't we be prepared to ask what the man's thought or the example of his actions has been worth in the defense of civilized values? If these are not the only questions to be raised in evaluating an academic, they ought at least to be among the first.

What we ask here of individual academics ought to be demanded of the professions generally. Suppose the professions were to be evaluated by putting to them the following question: In what intellectual areas have the leading institutions of our society—and especially the government—learned to tread lightly for fear of arousing collective critical resistance by the academic community? The answer would not be an encouraging one. Where the humanities and social sciences are concerned (and often enough the natural sciences, too), the government knows that it can, whenever it needs to, get away with any kind of slapdash propaganda. It confronts, in these areas, no organized critical authority—beyond that, perhaps, of the more conscientious journalists. Among the academics, it will find only scattered dissenters, many of whom may only be able to reach minority audiences; and the dissenters are easily offset by the influence of the academic "experts" who implement or defend government policies and are often enough figures of great prestige in our otherwise apolitical learned professions.

It does not take much imagination to see how vastly enriched our society's politics would be by citizenly "service" from the professions. We do not have an intellectually respectable politics in America, very largely because the single largest intellectual interest group in our society—the learned professions—has opted out of politics, except where it defends the status quo. It has felt no professional obligation to relate the life and work of its members to the problems of justice and survival which dominate our times. It does not insist that intellect embrace a dimension of citizenship. But if the major institutions of our society were made aware that the things they do and the things they say were being carefully scrutinized by a public of knowledgeable and conscientious academics, if the opinions of professional thinkers and teachers became a constant and recognized part of public controversy, that controversy, at the very least, could be elevated to the level of a rational dialogue, instead of remaining the province of shabby slogans, cynical propaganda, and engineered consensus. One may grant that the rights and wrongs of great public issues do not always yield to simple and unequivocal solutions. But rational solutions become impossible where, as in contemporary America, policy-making remains a mystery of state sealed off from a lethargic public by vested interest and esoteric expertise.

So long as our politics retain this character, there is very little that academics—whether they are humanists or scientists, specialists or generalists, scholars or technicians—have any right to be proud of. They may indeed be cultivating a luxuriant garden of knowledge and theory, and cultivating it with fastidious skill and taste. But the obscene shadows of misguided power and thermonuclear extinction brood over that garden and all the world surrounding it. And any conception of intellect that leads men to ignore that fact is ultimately futile and cowardly.

THE BASIC CAUSES

*Report of the National Advisory Commission
on Civil Disorders*

The record before this Commission reveals that the causes of recent racial disorders are imbedded in a massive tangle of issues and circumstances—social, economic, political, and psychological—which arise out of the historical pattern of Negro-white relations in America.

These factors are both complex and interacting; they vary significantly in their effect from city to city and from year to year; and the consequences of one disorder, generating new grievances and new demands, become the causes of the next. It is this which creates the "thicket of tension, conflicting evidence, and extreme opinions" cited by the President.

Despite these complexities, certain fundamental matters are clear. Of these, the most fundamental is the racial attitude and behavior of white Americans toward black Americans. Race prejudice has shaped our history decisively in the past; it now threatens to do so again. White racism is essentially responsible for the explosive mixture which has been accumulating in our cities since the end of World War II. At the base of this mixture are three of the most bitter fruits of white racial attitudes:

Pervasive discrimination and segregation. The first is surely the continuing exclusion of great numbers of Negroes from the benefits of economic progress through discrimination in employment and education, and their enforced confinement in segregated housing and schools. The corrosive and degrading effects of this condition and the attitudes that underlie it are the source of the deepest bitterness and at the center of the problem of racial disorder.

Black migration and white exodus. The second is the massive and growing concentration of impoverished Negroes in our major cities resulting from Negro migration from the rural South, rapid population growth and the continuing movement of the white middle class

Reprinted from the REPORT OF THE NATIONAL ADVISORY COMMISSION ON CIVIL DISORDERS *(Washington, D.C.: U. S. Government Printing Office, 1968), pp. 203-6.*

to the suburbs. The consequence is a greatly increased burden on the already depleted resources of cities, creating a growing crisis of deteriorating facilities and services and unmet human needs.

Black ghettos.   Third, in the teeming racial ghettos, segregation and poverty have intersected to destroy opportunity and hope and to enforce failure. The ghettos too often mean men and women without jobs, families without men, and schools where children are processed instead of educated, until they return to the street—to crime, to narcotics, to dependency on welfare, and to bitterness and resentment against society in general and white society in particular.

These three forces have converged on the inner city in recent years and on the people who inhabit it. At the same time, most whites and many Negroes outside the ghetto have prospered to a degree unparalleled in the history of civilization. Through television—the universal appliance in the ghetto—and the other media of mass communications, this affluence has been endlessly flaunted before the eyes of the Negro poor and the jobless ghetto youth.

As Americans, most Negro citizens carry within themselves two basic aspirations of our society. They seek to share in both the material resources of our system and its intangible benefits—dignity, respect and acceptance. Outside the ghetto many have succeeded in achieving a decent standard of life, and in developing the inner resources which give life meaning and direction. Within the ghetto, however, it is rare that either aspiration is achieved.

Yet these facts alone—fundamental as they are—cannot be said to have caused the disorders. Other and more immediate factors help explain why these events happened now.

Recently, three powerful ingredients have begun to catalyze the mixture.

Frustrated hopes.   The expectations aroused by the great judicial and legislative victories of the civil rights movement have led to frustration, hostility, and cynicism in the face of the persistent gap between promise and fulfillment. The dramatic struggle for equal rights in the South has sensitized Northern Negroes to the economic inequalities reflected in the deprivations of ghetto life.

Legitimation of violence.   A climate that tends toward the approval and encouragement of violence as a form of protest has been created by white terrorism directed against nonviolent protest, including instances of abuse and even murder of some civil rights workers in the South; by the open defiance of law and federal authority by state and local officials resisting desegregation; and by some protest groups engaging in civil disobedience who turn their backs on nonviolence, go beyond the Constitutionally protected rights of petition and free assembly, and resort to violence to attempt to compel alteration of laws and policies with which they disagree. This condition has been reinforced by a general erosion of respect for authority in American society and reduced effectiveness of social standards and community restraints on violence and crime. This in turn has largely resulted from rapid urbanization and the dramatic reduction in the average age of the total population.

Powerlessness. Finally, many Negroes have come to believe that they are being exploited politically and economically by the white "power structure." Negroes, like people in poverty everywhere, in fact lack the channels of communication, influence and appeal that traditionally have been available to ethnic minorities within the city and which enabled them—unburdened by color—to scale the walls of the white ghettos in an earlier era. The frustrations of powerlessness have led some to the conviction that there is no effective alternative to violence as a means of expression and redress, as a way of "moving the system." More generally, the result is alienation and hostility toward the institutions of law and government and the white society which controls them. This is reflected in the reach toward racial consciousness and solidarity reflected in the slogan "Black Power."

These facts have combined to inspire a new mood among Negroes, particularly among the young. Self-esteem and enhanced racial pride are replacing apathy and submission to "the system." Moreover, Negro youth, who make up over half of the ghetto population, share the growing sense of alienation felt by many white youth in our country. Thus, their role in recent civil disorders reflects not only a shared sense of deprivation and victimization by white society but also the rising incidence of disruptive conduct by a segment of American youth throughout the society.

Incitement and encouragement of violence. These conditions have created a volatile mixture of attitudes and beliefs which needs only a spark to ignite mass violence. Strident appeals to violence, first heard from white racists, were echoed and reinforced last summer in the inflammatory rhetoric of black racists and militants. Throughout the year, extremists crisscrossed the country preaching a doctrine of black power and violence. Their rhetoric was widely reported in the mass media; it was echoed by local "militants" and organizations; it became the ugly background noise of the violent summer.

We cannot measure with any precision the influence of these organizations and individuals in the ghetto, but we think it clear that the intolerable and unconscionable encouragement of violence heightened tensions, created a mood of acceptance and an expectation of violence, and thus contributed to the eruption of the disorders last summer.

The police. It is the convergence of all these factors that makes the role of the police so difficult and so significant. Almost invariably the incident that ignites disorder arises from police action. Harlem, Watts, Newark and Detroit—all the major outbursts of recent years— were precipitated by routine arrests of Negroes for minor offenses by white police.

But the police are not merely the spark. In discharge of their obligation to maintain order and insure public safety in the disruptive conditions of ghetto life, they are inevitably involved in sharper and more frequent conflicts with ghetto residents than with the residents of other areas. Thus, to many Negroes police have come to symbolize white power, white racism, and white repression. And the fact is that many police do reflect and express these white attitudes. The atmosphere of hostility and cynicism is reinforced by a widespread perception among Negroes of the existence of police brutality and corruption, and of a "double standard" of justice and protection—one for Negroes and one for whites.

THE NEW FORMS OF CONTROL

Herbert Marcuse

A comfortable, smooth, reasonable, democratic unfreedom prevails in advanced industrial civilization, a token of technical progress. Indeed, what could be more rational than the suppression of individuality in the mechanization of socially necessary but painful performances; the concentration of individual enterprises in more effective, more productive corporations; the regulation of free competition among unequally equipped economic subjects; the curtailment of prerogatives and national sovereignties which impede the international organization of resources. That this technological order also involves a political and intellectual coordination may be a regrettable and yet promising development.

The rights and liberties which were such vital factors in the origins and earlier stages of industrial society yield to a higher stage of this society: they are losing their traditional rationale and content. Freedom of thought, speech, and conscience were—just as free enterprise, which they served to promote and protect—essentially *critical* ideas, designed to replace an obsolescent material and intellectual culture by a more productive and rational one. Once institutionalized, these rights and liberties shared the fate of the society of which they had become an integral part. The achievement cancels the premises.

To the degree to which freedom from want, the concrete substance of all freedom, is becoming a real possibility, the liberties which pertain to a state of lower productivity are losing their former content. Independence of thought, autonomy, and the right to political opposition are being deprived of their basic critical function in a society which seems increasingly capable of satisfying the needs of the individuals through the way in which it is organized. Such a society may justly demand acceptance of its principles and institutions, and reduce the opposition to the discussion and promotion of alternative policies *within* the status quo. In this respect, it seems to make little difference whether the increasing satisfaction of needs is accomplished by an authoritarian or a non-authoritarian system. Under the conditions of a rising standard of living, non-conformity with the system itself appears to be socially useless, and the more so when it entails tangible economic and political disadvantages and threatens the smooth operation of the whole. Indeed, at least in so far as the necessities of life are involved, there seems to be no reason why the production and distribution of goods and services should proceed through the competitive concurrence of individual liberties.

Freedom of enterprise was from the beginning not altogether a blessing. As the liberty to work or to starve, it spelled toil, insecurity, and fear for the vast majority of the population. If the individual were no longer compelled to prove himself on the market, as a free economic subject, the disappearance of this kind of freedom would be one of the greatest achievements of civilization. The technological processes of mechanization and standardization might release individual energy into a yet uncharted realm of freedom beyond necessity. The very structure of human existence would be altered; the individual would be liberated from the work world's imposing upon him alien needs and alien possibilities. The individual would be free to exert autonomy over a life that would be his own. If the productive apparatus could be organized and directed toward the satisfaction of the vital needs, its control might well be centralized; such control would not prevent individual autonomy, but render it possible.

This is a goal within the capabilities of advanced industrial civilization, the "end" of technological rationality. In actual fact, however, the contrary trend operates: the apparatus imposes its economic and political requirements for defense and expansion on labor time and free time, on the material and intellectual culture. By virtue of the way it has organized its technological base, contemporary industrial society tends to be totalitarian. For "totalitarian" is not only a terroristic political coordination of society, but also a non-terroristic economic-technical coordination which operates through the manipulation of needs by vested interests. It thus precludes the emergence of an effective opposition against the whole. Not only a specific form of government or party rule makes for totalitarianism, but also a specific system of production and distribution which may well be compatible with a "pluralism" of parties, newspapers, "countervailing powers," etc.

Today political power asserts itself through its power over the machine process and over the technical organization of the apparatus. The government of advanced and advancing industrial societies can maintain and secure itself only when it succeeds in mobilizing, organizing, and exploiting the technical, scientific, and mechanical productivity available to industrial civilization. And this productivity mobilizes society as a whole, above and beyond any particular individual or group interests. The brute fact that the machine's physical (only physical?) power surpasses that of the individual, and of any particular group of individuals, makes the machine the most effective political instrument in any society whose basic organization is that of the machine process. But the political trend may be reversed; essentially the power of the machine is only the stored-up and projected power of man. To the extent to which the work world is conceived of as a machine and mechanized accordingly, it becomes the *potential* basis of a new freedom for man.

Contemporary industrial civilization demonstrates that it has reached the stage at which "the free society" can no longer be adequately defined in the traditional terms of economic, political, and intellectual liberties, not because these liberties have become insignificant, but because they are too significant to be confined within the traditional forms. New modes of realization are needed, corresponding to the new capabilities of society.

Such new modes can be indicated only in negative terms because they would amount to the negation of the prevailing modes. Thus economic freedom would mean freedom *from* the economy—from being controlled by economic froces and relationships; freedom from the daily struggle for existence, from earning a living. Political freedom would mean liberation of the individuals *from* politics over which they have no effective control. Similarly, intellectual freedom would mean the restoration of individual thought now absorbed by mass communication and indoctrination, abolition of "public opinion" together with its makers. The unrealistic sound of these propositions is indicative, not of their utopian character, but of the strength of the forces which prevent their realization. The most effective and enduring form of warfare against liberation is the implanting of material and intellectual needs that perpetuate obsolete forms of the struggle for existence.

The intensity, the satisfaction and even the character of human needs, beyond the biological level, have always been preconditioned. Whether or not the possibility of doing or leaving, enjoying or destroying, possessing or rejecting something is seized as a *need* depends on whether or not it can be seen as desirable and necessary for the prevailing societal institutions and interests. In this sense, human needs are historical needs and, to the extent to which the society demands the repressive development of the individual, his needs themselves and their claim for satisfaction are subject to overriding critical standards.

We may distinguish both true and false needs. "False" are those which are superimposed upon the individual by particular social interests in his repression: the needs which perpetuate toil, aggressiveness, misery, and injustice. Their satisfaction might be most gratifying to the individual, but this happiness is not a condition which has to be maintained and protected if it serves to arrest the development of the ability (his own and others) to recognize the disease of the whole and grasp the chances of curing the diseases. The result then is euphoria in unhappiness. Most of the prevailing needs to relax, to have fun, to behave and consume in accordance with the advertisements, to love and hate what others love and hate, belong to this category of false needs.

Such needs have a societal content and function which are determined by external powers over which the individual has no control; the development and satisfaction of these needs is heteronomous. No matter how much such needs may have become the individual's own, reproduced and fortified by the conditions of his existence; no matter how much he identifies himself with them and finds himself in their satisfaction, they continue to be what they were from the beginning —products of a society whose dominant interest demands repression.

The prevalence of repressive needs is an accomplished fact, accepted in ignorance and defeat, but a fact that must be undone in the interest of the happy individual as well as all those whose misery is the price of his satisfaction. The only needs that have an unqualified claim for satisfaction are the vital ones—nourishment, clothing, lodging at the attainable level of culture. The satisfaction of these needs is the prerequisite for the realization of *all* needs, of the unsublimated as well as the sublimated ones.

For any consciousness and conscience, for any experience which does not accept the prevailing societal interest as the supreme law of thought and behavior, the established universe of needs and satisfactions is a fact to be questioned—questioned in terms of truth and falsehood. These terms are historical throughout, and their objectivity is historical. The judgment of needs and their satisfaction, under the given conditions, involves standards of *priority*—standards which refer to the optimal development of the individual, of all individuals, under the optimal utilization of the material and intellectual resources available to man. The resources are calculable. "Truth" and "falsehood" of needs designate objective conditions to the extent to which the universal satisfaction of vital needs and, beyond it, the progressive alleviation of toil and poverty, are universally valid standards. But as historical standards, they do not only vary according to area and stage of development, they also can be defined only in (greater or lesser) *contradiction* to the prevailing ones. What tribunal can possibly claim the authority of decision?

In the last analysis, the question of what are true and false needs must be answered by the individuals themselves, but only in the last analysis; that is, if and when they are free to give their own answer. As long as they are kept incapable of being autonomous, as long as they are indoctrinated and manipulated (down to their very instincts), their answer to this question cannot be taken as their own. By the same token, however, no tribunal can justly arrogate to itself the right to decide which needs should be developed and satisfied. Any such tribunal is reprehensible, although our revulsion does not do away with the question: how can the people who have been the object of effective and productive domination by themselves create the conditions of freedom?

The more rational, productive, technical, and total the repressive administration of society becomes, the more unimaginable the means and ways by which the administered individuals might break their servitude and seize their own liberation. To be sure, to impose Reason upon an entire society is a paradoxical and scandalous idea—although one might dispute the righteousness of a society which ridicules this idea while making its own population into objects of total administration. All liberation depends on the consciousness of servitude, and the emergence of this consciousness is always hampered by the predominance of needs and satisfactions which, to a great extent, have become the individual's own. The process always replaces one system of preconditioning by another; the optimal goal is the replacement of false needs by true ones, the abandonment of repressive satisfaction.

The distinguishing feature of advanced industrial society is its effective suffocation of those needs which demand liberation—liberation also from that which is tolerable and rewarding and comfortable

—while it sustains and absolves the destructive power and repressive function of the affluent society. Here, the social controls exact the overwhelming need for the production and consumption of waste; the need for stupefying work where it is no longer a real necessity; the need for modes of relaxation which soothe and prolong this stupefication; the need for maintaining such deceptive liberties as free competition at administered prices, a free press which censors itself, free choice between brands and gadgets.

Under the rule of a repressive whole, liberty can be made into a powerful instrument of domination. The range of choice open to the individual is not the decisive factor in determining the degree of human freedom, but *what* can be chosen and what *is* chosen by the individual. The criterion for free choice can never be an absolute one, but neither is it entirely relative. Free election of masters does not abolish the masters or the slaves. Free choice among a wide variety of goods and services does not signify freedom if these goods and services sustain social controls over a life of toil and fear—that is, if they sustain alienation. And the spontaneous reproduction of super-imposed needs by the individual does not establish autonomy; it only testifies to the efficacy of the controls.

Our insistence on the depth and efficacy of these controls is open to the objection that we overrate greatly the indoctrinating power of the "media," and that by themselves the people would feel and satisfy the needs which are now imposed upon them. The objection misses the point. The preconditioning does not start with the mass production of radio and television and with the centralization of their control. The people enter this stage as preconditioned receptacles of long standing; the decisive difference is in the flattening out of the contrast (or conflict) between the given and the possible, between the satisfied and the unsatisfied needs. Here, the so-called equalization of class distinctions reveals its ideological function. If the worker and his boss enjoy the same television program and visit the same resort places, if the typist is as attractively made up as the daughter of her employer, if the Negro owns a Cadillac, if they all read the same newspaper, then this assimilation indicates not the disappearance of classes, but the extent to which the needs and satisfactions that serve the preservation of the Establishment are shared by the underlying population.

Indeed, in the most highly developed areas of contemporary society, the transplantation of social into individual needs is so effective that the difference between them seems to be purely theoretical. Can one really distinguish between the mass media as instruments of information and entertainment, and as agents of manipulation and indoctrination? Between the automobile as nuisance and as convenience? Between the horrors and the comforts of functional architecture? Between the work for national defense and the work for corporate gain? Between the private pleasure and the commercial and political utility involved in increasing the birth rate?

We are again confronted with one of the most vexing aspects of advanced industrial civilization: the rational character of its irrationality. Its productivity and efficiency, its capacity to increase and spread comforts, to turn waste into need, and destruction into construction, the extent to which this civilization transforms the object world into an extension of man's mind and body makes the very notion of alienation questionable. The people recognize themselves in their commodities; they find their soul in their automobile, hi-fi set, split-level home, kitchen equipment. The very mechanism which ties the individual to his society has changed, and social control is anchored in the new needs which it has produced.

The prevailing forms of social control are technological in a new sense. To be sure, the technical structure and efficacy of the productive and destructive apparatus has been a major instrumentality for subjecting the population to the established social division of labor throughout the modern period. Moreover, such integration has always been accompanied by more obvious forms of compulsion: loss of livelihood, the administration of justice, the police, the armed forces. It still is. But in the contemporary period, the technological controls appear to be the very embodiment of Reason for the benefit of all social groups and interests—to such an extent that all contradiction seems irrational and all counteraction impossible.

No wonder then that, in the most advanced areas of this civilization, the social controls have been introjected to the point where even individual protest is affected at its roots. The intellectual and emotional refusal "to go along" appears neurotic and impotent. This is the socio-psychological aspect of the political event that marks the contemporary period: the passing of the historical forces which, at the preceding stage of industrial society, seemed to represent the possibility of new forms of existence.

But the term "introjection" perhaps no longer describes the way in which the individual by himself reproduces and perpetuates the external controls exercised by his society. Introjection suggests a variety of relatively spontaneous processes by which a Self (Ego) transposes the "outer" into the "inner." Thus introjection implies the existence of an inner dimension distinguished from and even antagonistic to the external exigencies—an individual consciousness and an individual unconscious *apart from* public opinion and behavior.[1] The idea of "inner freedom" here has its reality: it designates the private space in which man may become and remain "himself."

Today this private space has been invaded and whittled down by technological reality. Mass produciton and mass distribution claim the *entire* individual, and industrial psychology has long since ceased to be confined to the factory. The manifold processes of introjection seem to be ossified in almost mechanical reactions. The result is, not adjustment but *mimesis:* an immediate identification of the individual with *his* society and, through it, with the society as a whole.

This immediate, automatic identification (which may have been characteristic of primitive forms of association) reappears in high industrial civilization; its new "immediacy," however, is the product of a sophisticated, scientific management and organization. In this process, the "inner" dimension of the mind in which opposition to the status quo can take root is whittled down. The loss of this dimension, in which the power of negative thinking—the critical power of Reason—is at home, is the ideological counterpart to the very material process in which advanced industrial society silences and reconciles the opposition. The impact of progress turns Reason into submission to the facts of life, and to the dynamic capability of producing more and bigger facts of the same sort of life. The efficiency of the system blunts the individual's recognition that it contains no facts which do not communicate the repressive power of the whole. If the individuals find themselves in the things which shape their life, they do so, not by giving, but by accepting the law of things—not the law of physics but the law of their society.

I have suggested that the concept of alienation seems to become questionable when the individuals identify themselves with the existence which is imposed upon them and have in it their own development and satisfaction. This identification is not illusion but reality. However, the reality constitutes a more progressive stage of alienation. The latter has become entirely objective; the subject which is alien-

---

[1] The change in the function of the family here plays a decisive role: its "socializing" functions are increasingly taken over by outside groups and media. See my *Eros and Civilization* (Boston: Beacon Press, 1955), p. 96 ff.

ated is swallowed up by its alienated existence. There is only one dimension, and it is everywhere and in all forms. The achievements of progress defy ideological indictment as well as justification; before their tribunal, the "false consciousness" of their rationality becomes the true consciousness.

This absorption of ideology into reality does not, however, signify the "end of ideology." On the contrary, in a specific sense advanced industrial culture is *more* ideological than its predecessor, inasmuch as today the ideology is in the process of production itself.[2] In a provocative form, this proposition reveals the political aspects of the prevailing technological rationality. The productive apparatus and the goods and services which it produces "sell" or impose the social system as a whole. The means of mass transportation and communication, the commodities of lodging, food, and clothing, the irresistible output of the entertainment and information industry carry with them prescribed attitudes and habits, certain intellectual and emotional reactions which bind the consumers more or less pleasantly to the producers and, through the latter, to the whole. The products indoctrinate and manipulate; they promote a false consciousness which is immune against its falsehood. And as these beneficial products become available to more individuals in more social classes, the indoctrination they carry ceases to be publicity; it becomes a way of life. It is a good way of life—much better than before—and as a good way of life, it militates against qualitative change. Thus emerges a pattern of *one-dimensional thought and behavior* in which ideas, aspirations, and objectives that, by their content, transcend the established universe of discourse and action are either repelled or reduced to terms of this universe. They are redefined by the rationality of the given system and of its quantitative extension.

The trend may be related to a development in scientific method: operationalism in the physical, behaviorism in the social sciences. The common feature is a total empiricism in the treatment of concepts; their meaning is restricted to the representation of particular operations and behavior. The operational point of view is well illustrated by P. W. Bridgman's analysis of the concept of length: [3]

---

[2] Theodor W. Adorno, *Prismen. Kulturkritik und Gesellschaft.* (Frankfurt: Suhrkamp, 1955), p. 24 f.

[3] P. W. Bridgman, *The Logic of Modern Physics* (New York: Macmillan, 1928), p. 5. The operational doctrine has since been refined and qualified. Bridgman himself has extended the concept of "operation" to include the

We evidently know what we mean by length if we can tell what the length of any and every object is, and for the physicist nothing more is required. To find the length of an object, we have to perform certain physical operations. The concept of length is therefore fixed when the operations by which length is measured are fixed: that is, the concept of length involves as much and nothing more than the set of operations by which length is determined. In general, we mean by any concept nothing more than a set of operations; *the concept is synonymous with the corresponding set of operations.*

Bridgman has seen the wide implications of this mode of thought for the society at large: [4]

To adopt the operational point of view involves much more than a mere restriction of the sense in which we understand 'concept,' but means a far-reaching change in all our habits of thought, in that we shall no longer permit ourselves to use as tools in our thinking concepts of which we cannot give an adequate account in terms of operations.

Bridgman's prediction has come true. The new mode of thought is today the predominant tendency in philosophy, psychology, sociology, and other fields. Many of the most seriously troublesome concepts are being "eliminated" by showing that no adequate account of them in terms of operations or behavior can be given. The radical empiricist onslaught thus provides the methodological justification for the debunking of the mind by the intellectuals—a positivism which, in its denial of the transcending elements of Reason, forms the academic counterpart of the socially required behavior.

Outside the academic establishment, the "far-reaching change in all our habits of thought" is more serious. It serves to coordinate ideas and goals with those exacted by the prevailing system, to enclose them in the system, and to repel those which are irreconcilable with the system. The reign of such a one-dimensional reality does not mean that materialism rules, and that the spiritual, metaphysical, and bohemian occupations are petering out. On the contrary, there is a great deal of "Worship together this week," "Why not try God," Zen, existentialism, and beat ways of life, etc. But such modes of protest and transcendence are no longer contradictory to the status quo and

---

"paper-and-pencil" operations of the theorist (in Philipp J. Frank, *The Validation of Scientific Theories* [Boston: Beacon Press, 1954], Chap. II). The main impetus remains the same: it is "desirable" that the paper-and-pencil operations "be capable of eventual contact, although perhaps indirectly, with instrumental operations."

[4] P. W. Bridgman, *The Logic of Modern Physics, loc. cit.,* p. 31.

no longer negative. They are rather the ceremonial part of practical behaviorism, its harmless negation, and are quickly digested by the status quo as part of its healthy diet.

One-dimensional thought is systematically promoted by the makers of politics and their purveyors of mass information. Their universe of discourse is populated by self-validating hypotheses which, incessantly and monopolistically repeated, become hypnotic definitions or dictations. For example, "free" are the institutions which operate (and are operated on) in the countries of the Free World; other transcending modes of freedom are by definition either anarchism, communism, or propaganda. "Socialistic" are all encroachments on private enterprises not undertaken by private enterprise itself (or by government contracts), such as universal and comprehensive health insurance, or the protection of nature from all too sweeping commercialization, or the establishment of public services which may hurt private profit. This totalitarian logic of accomplished facts has its Eastern counterpart. There, freedom is the way of life instituted by a communist regime, and all other transcending modes of freedom are either capitalistic, or revisionist, or leftist sectarianism. In both camps, non-operational ideas are non-behavioral and subversive. The movement of thought is stopped at barriers which appear as the limits of Reason itself.

Such limitation of thought is certainly not new. Ascending modern rationalism, in its speculative as well as empirical form, shows a striking contrast between extreme critical radicalism in scientific and philosophic method on the one hand, and an uncritical quietism in the attitude toward established and functioning social institutions. Thus Descartes' *ego cogitans* was to leave the "great public bodies" untouched, and Hobbes held that "the present ought always to be preferred, maintained, and accounted best." Kant agreed with Locke in justifying revolution *if and when* it has succeeded in organizing the whole and in preventing subversion.

However, these accommodating concepts of Reason were always contradicted by the evident misery and injustice of the "great public bodies" and the effective, more or less conscious rebellion against them. Societal conditions existed which provoked and permitted real dissociation from the established state of affairs; a private as well as political dimension was present in which dissociation could develop into effective opposition, testing its strength and the validity of its objectives.

With the gradual closing of this dimension by the society, the self-limitation of thought assumes a larger significance. The interrelation between scientific-philosophical and societal processes, between theoretical and practical Reason, asserts itself "behind the back" of the scientists and philosophers. The society bars a whole type of oppositional operations and behavior; consequently, the concepts pertaining to them are rendered illusory or meaningless. Historical transcendence appears as metaphysical transcendence, not acceptable to science and scientific thought. The operational and behavioral point of view, practiced as a "habit of thought" at large, becomes the view of the established universe of discourse and action, needs and aspirations. The "cunning of Reason" works, as it so often did, in the interest of the powers that be. The insistence on operational and behavioral concepts turns against the efforts to free thought and behavior *from* the given reality and *for* the suppressed alternatives. Theoretical and practical Reason, academic and social behaviorism meet on common ground: that of an advanced society which makes scientific and technical progress into an instrument of domination.

"Progress" is not a neutral term; it moves toward specific ends, and these ends are defined by the possibilities of ameliorating the human condition. Advanced industrial society is approaching the stage where continued progress would demand the radical subversion of the prevailing direction and organization of progress. This stage would be reached when material production (including the necessary services) becomes automated to the extent that all vital needs can be satisfied while necessary labor time is reduced to marginal time. From this point on, technical progress would transcend the realm of necessity, where it served as the instrument of domination and exploitation which thereby limited its rationality; technology would become subject to the free play of faculties in the struggle for the pacification of nature and of society.

Such a state is envisioned in Marx's notion of the "abolition of labor." The term "pacification of existence" seems better suited to designate the historical alternative of a world which—through an international conflict which transforms and suspends the contradictions within the established societies—advances on the brink of a global war. "Pacification of existence" means the development of man's struggle with man and with nature, under conditions where the competing needs, desires, and aspirations are no longer organized by vested interests in domination and scarcity—an organization which perpetuates the destructive forms of this struggle.

Today's fight against this historical alternative finds a firm mass basis in the underlying population, and finds its ideology in the rigid orientation of thought and behavior to the given universe of facts. Validated by the accomplishments of science and technology, justified by its growing productivity, the status quo defies all transcendence. Faced with the possibility of pacification on the grounds of its technical and intellectual achievements, the mature industrial society closes itself against this alternative. Operationalism, in theory and practice, becomes the theory and practice of *containment*. Underneath its obvious dynamics, this society is a thoroughly static system of life: self-propelling in its oppressive productivity and in its beneficial coordination. Containment of technical progress goes hand in hand with its growth in the established direction. In spite of the political fetters imposed by the status quo, the more technology appears capable of creating the conditions for pacification, the more are the minds and bodies of man organized against this alternative.

The most advanced areas of industrial society exhibit throughout these two features: a trend toward consummation of technological rationality, and intensive efforts to contain this trend within the established institutions. Here is the internal contradiction of this civilization: the irrational element in its rationality. It is the token of its achievements. The industrial society which makes technology and science its own is organized for the ever-more-effective domination of man and nature, for the ever-more-effective utilization of its resources. It becomes irrational when the success of these efforts opens new dimensions of human realization. Organization for peace is different from organization for war; the institutions which served the struggle for existence cannot serve the pacification of existence. Life as an end is qualitatively different from life as a means.

Such a qualitatively new mode of existence can never be envisaged as the mere by-product of economic and political changes, as the more or less spontaneous effect of the new institutions which constitute the necessary prerequisite. Qualitative change also involves a change in the *technical* basis on which this society rests—one which sustains the economic and political institutions through which the "second nature" of man as an aggressive object of administration is stabilized. The techniques of industrialization are political techniques; as such, they prejudge the possibilities of Reason and Freedom.

To be sure, labor must precede the reduction of labor, and industrialization must precede the development of human needs and satisfactions. But as all freedom depends on the conquest of alien necessity, the realization of freedom depends on the *techniques* of this conquest. The highest productivity of labor can be used for the perpetuation of labor, and the most efficient industrialization can serve the restriction and manipulation of needs.

When this point is reached, domination—in the guise of affluence and liberty—extends to all spheres of private and public existence, integrates all authentic opposition, absorbs all alternatives. Technological rationality reveals its political character as it becomes the great vehicle of better domination, creating a truly totalitarian universe in which society and nature, mind and body are kept in a state of permanent mobilization for the defense of this universe.

☐ THE UNIVERSITIES

Traditionally students have been active advocates of social change —the unusual lack of such activity was cause for much concern and discussion in the 1950's—and thus universities have traditionally been centers of protest movements.

As long as a university itself was somewhat neutral politically, it might be merely a staging area from which demonstrations would emerge, and would escape becoming in itself the object of protest. But American universities in the 1960's have not been so fortunate: Protests have not merely been launched *from* them against the establishment—but *at* them directly because they *are* the establishment. The well-meant efforts of educators to make universities relevant to society have ultimately resulted in the universities' becoming the objects of protest, and also of such major counter-protest political movements as the Ronald Reagan campaign for the governorship of California in 1966, which made Berkeley its key issue, and the George

Wallace campaign for the Presidency in 1968, which rode on a wave of resentment of student activism and "bearded professors."

Although the Berkeley Free Speech Movement was unique to that institution, precipitated by a dispute over rules peculiar to that campus and that university's role as a public-supported institution, it has become the archetype of student revolt.

Sol Stern's report on the FSM—which first appeared in 1965—stresses the role of the university's liberal president, Clark Kerr. A sequel to the FSM, archetypal in itself as an illustration of the precarious position of the conciliating liberal in an age of protest, was Kerr's dismissal from the presidency at the request of Governor Reagan in 1967.

The Columbia student rebellion of 1968 was, according to students Dotson Rader and Craig Anderson, more deliberately planned. Although Berkeley is a state-supported institution and Columbia a private one, there are many parallels in that both are prestigious "liberal" schools, and both are deeply involved in defense-oriented research projects. Columbia's proximity to Harlem illustrates one reason why it may be unnecessary for modern universities to *choose* to be relevant—they are, rather, thrust into relevance by conditions beyond their control.

Gianfranco Corsini, literary editor of *Paese Sera* in Rome, comments on the new wave of student protest abroad and reveals how the conflict within American society is projected onto Europe—so that, at the same time that students in Italy or France or Germany may protest against American foreign policy, they take as their role models Mario Savio or Mark Rudd, and as their anthem, *We Shall Overcome*.

A DEEPER DISENCHANTMENT

Sol Stern

The University of California is probably the most impressive and prestigious state university in the country. It boasts a world-famous faculty that includes a half dozen Nobel Prize winners and its many departments are all considered "first rate." It is the "compleat" university. There is something there for everyone: a sprawling, pleasant campus, top-notch recreational facilities (including an outdoor country-club and swimming pool nestled in the Berkeley hills), a huge library, and excellent medical facilities. A constant flow of illustrious and exciting speakers and performers appear on the campus: everyone from U Thant to the Budapest String Quartet to Joan Baez. The resident student gets all this, plus his education, for approximately one hundred dollars a semester.

The city of Berkeley itself is *the* pleasant place to live. With its coffee houses and art movies, its almost perfect climate, its proximity to such places as San Francisco, Big Sur and Yosemite, Berkeley would appear to be the "compleat" college town.

Despite all the academic glitter and the bountiful social life Berkeley offers, there is deep and bitter resentment among many students about their life at the university. It is a resentment that starts from the contradiction between the public image and reputation of the university and their actual day-to-day experiences as students. For these students recognize that all that is exciting and stimulating about Berkeley comes from the frills and extras of university life; the formal university-learning experience is generally a deadening one.

The new undergraduate learns quickly that of all the functions of the Great University his own education is perhaps the least important. He has almost no contact with the famous professors he has heard about. They, for their part, seek ways to escape the "burden" of teaching to be able to devote full time to the pursuit of their professions (which are not defined to include teaching). Graduate teaching assistants do most of whatever face-to-face teaching the under-

Sol Stern, "A Deeper Disenchantment," LIBERATION, *February, 1965, pp. 15-20. Reprinted by permission.*

graduate encounters. For the most part, however, the undergraduate learns that his success at school depends on his ability to master a four-year system of lectures, reading lists and examintions that have little to do with genuine learning. A student organization, SLATE, publishes a *Supplement to The General Catalogue,* every semester, which advises the undergraduate on ways to beat the "system" and get a reasonable education in spite of it. Whether the undergraduate is morally revolted by the system, or whether he shrugs it off as merely another facet of the lifesmanship he must master, it is as a "system" that his education is commonly perceived and becomes a central part of the undergraduate folklore.

Many graduate students share a more special malaise. They have already made something of a commitment to academic and university life, but it is a commitment beclouded with ambiguities and doubts. The graduate students, in their closer proximity to the professors and the specialized disciplines, have also become privy to the intellectual dishonesties and political scheming that go on at the upper levels of Academia. There is a wide-spread belief that they are prisoners in a system of professional rewards and penalties, determined by those very professors whose manipulations they observe at first hand. It is a system they have no power to change and leaves them only the option of playing the academic game according to the rules or getting out.

This alienation in the midst of the apparent good life finds symbolic expression at a campus gathering place known as "the Terrace"—an outdoor pavilion of the Student Union cafeteria, where one can bask in sunshine most of the year and enjoy a majestic view of San Francisco Bay. Many of the more active and concerned students gather here for the usual rounds of student gossip and political banter. Their range of political opinion and affiliation is extremely wide; they include every variety of revolutionary and reformist socialist, radicals and liberal democrats, civil-rights activists, anarchists, pacifists and even an occasional Goldwaterite. When the talk is of national and international politics the arguments are heated, but when the talk turns to what can only be described as "university politics" there is a sudden change of perspective. A common note of cynicism enters the dialogue. Common enemies are easily identifiable: they are the university bureaucracy, the graduate school system, the political schemers among the faculty. Most often and most pointedly the enemy is the president of the university, Clark Kerr.

It tells us much about the mood of these students that the man who is most clearly viewed as the enemy carries all the traditional credentials of the modern political liberal. In his speeches and writings, Clark Kerr is indeed always on the side of the angels: for academic freedom, for free speech, for freedom of inquiry. He has received the highest award of the American Association of University Professors for his efforts on behalf of academic freedom. Yet if Kerr is a bonafide card-carrying liberal he also typifies much of what the students consider the failure of American liberalism during the Cold War era. Official establishment liberalism offers nothing to these students because it has lost its passion and crusading spirit. It has become manipulative, crafty and cautious. In domestic and international politics it has become identified with *realpolitik* and opportunism.

Kerr, for all his liberal rhetoric and reputation, represents only the cold bureaucrat who could never command these students' confidence. His style and physical bearing do not help him in this respect. He looks ever so much like the officious bank president. His public appearances are carefully managed and he seems never to allow himself any spontaneous gesture or show of emotion. Even on those occasions when he is working for a liberal reform, as he did recently in getting the Board of Regents to lift its ban on Communist speakers on campus, his style tends to infuriate the students. For he does not act by moral persuasion nor out of great principle but as the behind the scenes manipulator, the committee man, the politician.

But more than matters of personality and style mark Kerr as an appropriate symbol for the bureaucratic "system." Kerr has also become the foremost spokesman and ideologist for the new bureaucratic style in American higher education. In his Godkin Lectures, at Harvard in 1963, he first coined the term "multiversity" to describe the model American university of the future. This "multiversity" will increasingly service the established institutions of business, government, labor, and the national defense effort. In Kerr's own words, "the university is being called upon . . . to respond to the expanding claims of national service; to merge its activity with industry as never before."

Now all of this is not so terribly new or provocative. Many educators have commented upon and lamented this trend. But it is different with Kerr: he cheerfully accepts the trend as the inexorable path of development and draws the appropriate conclusions. For if the "multiversity" is to become more and more attuned to the needs of industry and national defense, then the requirements of tough-minded bureaucracy and management must have first claims on those who lead the "multiversity." The "Managerial Revolution" has come to the campus; now the most important stratum of the university is not the faculty, nor the students, nor any single educational Idea, but rather the manager and administrator. The "multiversity" is a "mechanism held together by administrative rules and powered by money." To guide this mechanism through its many complex functions, the university president must be guided primarily by the tools and arts of manipulation and mediation.

At the University of California Clark Kerr has indeed appeared as that model administrator-manager. As both the author of this scenario of the future and the leading player in it, Kerr has made himself the perfect target for all the resentment that the development of the "multiversity" arouses. That is why the students regard Kerr's liberalism as irrelevant. It is also why "multiversity" takes on, in conversations on the terrace, all of the emotional connotations of the term "1984."

Perhaps what has been most infuriating to the students on the terrace is the fact that all the physical evidence about them seemed to point inescapably to the power of Clark Kerr's vision of the future. The University of California was becoming more and more like the model "multiversity." Moreover, the average student, despite his private anxieties and resentments, did not appear to be in the mood for any rebellion against the role assigned to him by the "multiversity." Nor did the faculty appear terribly upset about the consequences of the "multiversity"; they seemed rather to be enjoying the increased emoluments it was bringing them in the form of grants, consultation fees, and most important of all, freedom from teaching.

During the course of the free-speech struggle last fall, the students at the terrace learned that they did have resources available to fight back against the "multiversity." They were not yet reduced altogether to private and impotent grumblings. They learned how they could stake out an area of autonomy and take some of the initiative out of the hands of the administrators and managers.

When the issue of free speech was first raised, it did not seem that all the above sentiments would be brought to bear. It was after all a move not uncharacteristic of the old-fashioned university that precipitated the free-speech struggle. At the beginning of the fall semester the administration enforced an old but never used rule which had the effect of prohibiting the use of the campus by students for soliciting of funds and recruiting for political activities. Representatives of nineteen student political organizations then formed themselves as an ad hoc group to press for a removal of these restrictions. So far there was nothing in this that suggested the beginning of a student rebellion. Student protest is accounted for by the theorist of the "multiversity." Indeed, it is one of the characteristic talents of the new administrator-manager of the "multiversity" that he is able to contain and divert student protests so that they do not interfere with the efficient functioning of the university machine.

What did give a clue that this was more than the ordinary student protest was the refusal of the students to play their roles entirely according to those "administrative rules" which keep the university bureaucracy functioning smoothly. From the beginning the students showed a unique and surprising determination to assert their autonomy. Whenever the university administration attempted to use the "normal" channels as a means of diverting them, the students were ready to take the dispute outside those channels for a more direct confrontation with the administration. A unique quality of audacity marked this protest. *Life* magazine was forced to recognize it, with a slight tinge of awe, as a "Tough Campus Revolt."

This toughness showed itself almost immediately. The students' first response to the new administrative regulations was direct and simple. They ignored them. Taking the position that the restrictions were a violation of their constitutional rights, they left it to the administration to try to enforce them. They set up their tables on the campus and continued to recruit and collect money. When the administration tried to bring disciplinary action against five of the students who had been manning the tables, six hundred students signed statements saying that they, too, had been guilty of violating the rules. When the Dean summoned the five students to his office, three hundred showed up and demanded to be seen too.

Finally the Dean announced that eight students had been suspended for various activities in protesting the new rules. The students again had a ready response. They set up their tables directly in front of the administration building. The administration replied by having one of those manning a table arrested and placed in a campus police car (he had gone limp and a car had to be summoned to take him away). At this point a group of students spontaneously threw themselves in front of the car and blocked its path. Soon they were joined by hundreds of others and within an hour the police car was surrounded by a solid phalanx of one thousand bodies.

This spontaneous demonstration developed rapidly into a massive sit-in and rally around the police car that lasted thirty-two hours. As it grew and grew, student speakers mounted the embattled police car, using it as a podium from which to address the throng and state the demands the administration must meet to end the demonstration. At the end of the second day, five hundred helmeted police stood by with their night sticks, ready to wade in and disperse the students. Serious violence was averted only at the last minute as a settlement was reached between the student leaders and Clark Kerr. The crowd heard and approved the terms of the agreement and then dispersed voluntarily. Audacity had won the students a number of points. The suspensions of the eight leaders would be reviewed by a faculty committee, the university agreed not to press charges against the arrested student, and the rules on political activity would be submitted to a study committee on which students would be represented.

Much was learned during this first skirmish with the administration: the students realized that audacity and directness could move the bureaucracy where normal channels failed. Now the students turned to organizing themselves more effectively. The ad hoc group of the political organizations was turned officially into the Free Speech Movement, and an executive committee of fifty and a steering committee of twelve were set up. Intensive organizing among the student body was conducted to gather more support, and new groups were urged to send representatives to the movement (or FSM, as it was now generally called). An FSM Newsletter was published and leaflets by the score were put out to explain FSM's position and the latest developments to the student body. A massive and well documented report was put together by graduate students, tracing the history of past administration attempts to limit student political rights.

After six weeks of student petitions, testimony at committees, and more rallies and demonstrations, the administration bent a little more. The eight suspended students were reinstated and the ban on soliciting and recruiting for political action was lifted. One major point remained at issue, however. The university now reserved the right to discipline individuals and organizations for advocacy on the campus of illegal acts off the campus (presumably such acts as civil-rights sit-ins). This was an extremely important point, for the students were generally of the opinion that the original restrictions had been im-

posed as a result of pressures from local business interests, particularly
William Knowland's *Oakland Tribune,* which were anxious to see the
Berkeley campus cut off as a source for militant civil-rights activities.

At this point, however, the FSM was split on tactics for the first
time. Many were for resuming the dramatic direct-action methods
used earlier in the term. Others felt that the issues were not clear-cut
enough to demand such a course. As the FSM floundered, the administration gave it back its *raison d'être.* The administration now
decided that it was going to bring disciplinary action against four of
the student leaders for their actions during the demonstrations around
the police car some two months before. This was seen by the students
as nothing less than an attempt to break the movement by cutting off
its head.

Thus on December 2nd, over one thousand students marched into
the administration building, taking over all four of its floors. They
announced that they were prepared to sit there until the administration
had called off its action against their leaders. In the meantime, the
powerful organization of graduate students, which had been formed
during the free-speech struggle, announced its intention to call a
university-wide strike in a few days in support of the FSM demands.

It is significant that the next act in the steadily escalating crisis
came not from any campus official, but from the Governor of the
State, Pat Brown. He ordered the arrests of the students. This was
done not because any clear breach of the peace had occurred (the
students were orderly and disciplined and were not blocking any of
the building's entrances or pathways), but essentially as a result of
the incessant pressures of the press and elements in the community
who saw in the student rebellion a threat to their own well-being.
The next morning, with hundreds of state troopers surrounding the
administration building and refusing even to allow any faculty members inside to observe the arrests, Clark Kerr held a press conference
to support the Governor's action for the maintenance of Law and
Order. The "multiversity" as a service center for society had now been
confirmed in a rather ironic and twisted way—the administrator had
become spokesman and messenger for the police power of the state.

On leading the students into the administration building the day
before, Mario Savio, the leader of the FSM, had uttered the classic
words of the movement:

There is a time when the operation of the machine becomes so odious,
makes you so sick at heart that you can't take part; you can't even tacitly

take part, and you've got to put your bodies upon the levers, upon all the apparatus and you've got to make it stop. And you've got to indicate to the people who own it, that unless you're free the machine will be prevented from working at all.

This was a sentiment that now seemed to be shared by a majority of the student body, to whom the operation of the machine was now revealed as extremely odious. No longer was it merely a question of certain administrative rules that were at issue, but the whole stumbling and faceless bureaucracy that had stood by as political pressures forced a virtual police occupation of the campus.

So the students did indeed bring the machine to a grinding halt. A strike plan went into effect immediately and scores of picket lines were thrown around the classroom buildings. Many faculty members now supported the strike. A philosophy professor announced to the students gathered at a rally that he was calling off all his classes, as he could not in conscience conduct classes while the campus was under police occupation.

Most of the education that took place in the next few days came outside the classrooms, in the innumerable knots and crowds of students and faculty that sprang up everywhere on the campus. They argued and discussed the nature of democracy, the rule of law, and civil disobedience. The FSM organized classes off the campus at their "Free University of California." It was truly an amazing scene. Nothing less than a revolution, though a gentle one, seemed to be taking place.

In the meantime, the administration was acting characteristically. President Kerr announced that he was going off to Chicago on business—but then stayed on the campus to negotiate and mediate quietly behind the scenes. Sensing the enormity of the crisis, Kerr decided to go before the students on the third day of the strike; it was the first time he had addressed the students directly during the whole dispute.

A special university convocation was called to hear Kerr present a compromise proposal for ending the dispute, which had been drawn up by the department chairmen. The convocation was held at the university's outdoor Greek Theatre; it was an appropriate setting for a drama that was a farce and tragedy all at the same time. Eighteen thousand members of the university community filed into the theatre as in some feudal assembly, each to his appointed place: first the students in the rear, then the faculty up closer to the stage, then the

Department Chairmen seated up on both sides of the stage; finally the President himself made his appearance and took a seat in the center of the stage. It was a processional that had been followed before and is common practice on most university campuses. But coming at a time when the students had brought the university machinery to a halt, it must have seemed like the final absurdity of the administrative ethos.

The students whose action had forced the calling of the convocation were not to be allowed representation. Both the leaders of the FSM and the President of the Student Government had asked to be allowed to speak and were denied. President Kerr read his "peace plan" without even mentioning the existence of the FSM. It was as if to dramatize the missing factor that Mario Savio walked up on the stage and toward the microphone as the chairman was announcing that the meeting was adjourned. Before Savio could speak, two campus policemen rushed up from behind and dragged him bodily from the stage. To the thousands of students who witnessed this incident and roared their disapproval, it was another outrageous example of the crudities that the processes of the "multiversity" lead to.

Clark Kerr's peace plan only alienated the students further. He had learned nothing from the experiences of the past few months and seemed incapable of leading or teaching in such a situation. The strike went on, and was ended only the next day when the Academic Senate voted overwhelmingly to support almost all the demands of the students and pledge to work for their adoption by the Board of Regents. The students now put away their picket signs, stirred and exhilarated by the support they had received from the faculty and the prospect of total victory.

The issue of political expression at the campus is, at the time of writing, not yet settled. The regents of the State of California are a collection of all the practicality that the leaders of the state's political and economic system have to offer. Perhaps it ought not to have been expected that they would deal with a set of requests formulated under the pressures of a student rebellion, as a question of principle. At their first meeting on the subject they tried to fob-off all the parties concerned. To the citizens of the state, they pledged their determination to preserve Law and Order on the campus; to the students, they pledged their devotion to the First and Fourteenth Amendments to the Constitution. Finally there were more committees set up to study the problems of political advocacy on the campus.

Whatever the final outcome, it is clear that the meaning of these events lies deeper than the use of the Berkeley campus for political activity. The students themselves, slightly amazed at the proportions of the movement they had touched off, also looked about for meanings.

It was widely understood that some deeper disenchantment lay behind the free-speech fight. A campus minister had written to the school newspaper that he saw behind the student rebellion a reaction to "the modern isolation and alienation of the spirit" and that the students were trying to restore a lost sense of "community." "Alienation" and "community"; these words were much heard from the students during their rallies and demonstrations. The computer, too, somehow became a symbol of the "system" that the students were objecting to. "Are you a student or an IBM card?" Thus read one of the FSM leaflets urging students to support the strike.

Yet this revolt was not just a blind lashing out at the machine—a modern Luddite rebellion. The IBM card and "the bureaucracy" were symbols, but behind the symbols stood men. And among the students there was a widespread feeling that the men who ran the system here at Berkeley, those who rationalized it and those who spoke for it, had betrayed them. That these men spoke with the rhetoric of sophisticated liberalism was only more appalling. Here on the campus, Clark Kerr and others like him were bowing to and abetting all the forces of mindless bureaucracy and alienation. One must admit that even Clark Kerr had known and spoken of the alienation of students. In his Godkin Lectures he had recognized that the student was often confused and lonely and without purpose, in the "Knowledge Factory." But for Kerr, the source of this alienation lay not with any policies of men, nor with any institution. Like the "multiversity" itself, alienation was an immutable, inevitable consequence of the growing complexity of modern society.

Thus Kerr and many other observers could not fully understand the nature of this revolt against the university administration and against Kerr himself. Were not all the rallies and demonstrations and sit-ins slightly irrational, like tilting against history itself? Sometimes, to Kerr and others, these events, being irrational and inexplicable, had to have some sinister force behind them. Thus Kerr at one point spoke of outside agitators, Maoists, Castroites, and other such devils stirring up the students. A professor at the university, Lewis Feuer, in an article which otherwise showed understanding of the terrible effects of the "multiversity" also had to explain much of the student revolt as being instigated by a collection of Maoist-beatnik-sexual libertine pseudo-students who were all looking for some synthetic revolution to make up for the emptiness which they felt in their lives. Finally, everyone spoke of the unreasonableness of the students. They were rejecting all the "normal channels" for settling disputes; they showed a contempt for Law and Order. They were, according to Clark Kerr, attempting to disrupt the orderly processes of the university and impose anarchy of the campus.

To the students however all the talk about "reasonableness," "orderly processes" and "normal channels" seemed but a facade behind which a "higher irrationality" was being practiced by the administrators, the bureaucrats and the politicians. These men defined "orderly processes" and "reasonableness" as all that was consistent with the on-going system. To Clark Kerr, for example, it was presumably "reasonable" that the university engage in contracted research for the Defense Department, "reasonable" for the university to allow its facilities to be used by the Marine Corps to recruit students, but it was "unreasonable" for the students to recruit civil-rights workers to disrupt the flow of commerce in the outside community.

Behind all the talk of "orderly processes" was a demand that the students accommodate themselves to a style of protest that would have frozen them to the very administrative apparatus that they were trying to change. It was this administrative style that was as much a source of the students' alienation as "the complexity of modern society." Correspondingly, it was the style of the student protest that most upset so many of the important people of the state and the university. The students had set up their own counter-community, independent of the university system. Their own standards of justification prevailed and they kept their own counsel, not paying too much attention to the pleas for "realistic" approaches that came from their elders, many of whom were jaded ex-radicals.

In acting as they did the students achieved some unique results. They took the first genuine steps toward that sense of community everybody was always vainly searching for. It was widely remarked that there was more face-to-face communication among the faculty and between faculty and students during the days of the strike than there had ever been before. The classroom had been replaced by the open and unstructured forum. In those innumerable spontaneous sessions between professors and students, important educational experiences unfolded. There was a give and take and an openness that could not have occurred in the classroom. The professors faced the students without their academic regalia, without their grade books, without the prospects of giving or withholding a recommendation. There was much talk during those days of a "Free University of California." Unlike Clark Kerr's "multiversity" it was an idea and a model of a future university that *the students* would have liked to create and participate in—one that would more often act in opposition to the powers-that-be in the society outside.

In all this a new mood seemed to grip the students. The "multiversity," with all its horrendous consequences, was not historically inevitable as the technological determinists were continuously announcing, but would come because men with power abetted it. The new technology should have brought with it greater opportunities for community and more meaningful purpose in life. The problem was how to make those in power and in the entrenched bureaucracy use those opportunities for decent purposes. To bring such pressure, it became necessary to shake up the bureaucrats and dramatize the gap between them and the students by creating new and audacious styles of protest.

One does not wish to exaggerate or romanticize what the students at Berkeley did. The "multiversity" is still omnipresent and students must go back and play by its rules. Yet it must not be forgotten that behind the facade of orderly and pleasant campuses there are deep currents of unrest and dissatisfaction. White, middle-class students in the North also need a liberation movement, for they have no community in which they exercise citizenship. They feel imprisoned and oppressed by a smiling and genial bureaucracy.

The issues at Berkeley are deeper than civil rights and civil liberties. These issues merely provided the form of this first serious revolt against modern liberal bureaucracy. When and if the "pocket" problems of civil rights and poverty are solved, this society will still have to deal with a crisis that is more basic to the lives of most of its citizens. It is this that concerns the students at Berkeley, and in response to that crisis they created an important little wedge against the creeping totalitarianism that threatens all of us.

REBELLION AT COLUMBIA

Dotson Rader and Craig Anderson

Sunday night, April 28, Frank Michel stood on the balcony of Mathematics Hall, under a large sign that read, "Rudd Hall, Liberated Zone #5," and looked across the crowded yard toward Low Library, the central administration building, to the lighted windows of the president's office where other protesting students sat in the windows singing and shouting slogans ("Columbia goes from jerk to jerk— Eisenhower to Grayson Kirk"), and yelled to a group of disgruntled jocks below, "We've beaten you bastards! We've won!"

Frank Michel was one of the small group of students, led by Tom Hayden, who had stormed Math Hall on Thursday night and secured it for the liberation. He had been in the building ever since, working with 200 other protesting students, building barricades, pulling up the tiles on the lower floors, greasing stairways, putting plastic bags and vaseline in strategic places to serve as anti-gas protection. He was tired and happy. He was on the committee in charge of feeding over 600 students twice a day in the five liberated buildings. Other committees handled defense and medical details (there was a doctor on duty at all times in each of the buildings). Saturday the Math Building, considered the most radical of the five units, had organized itself into a commune and voted to prohibit drinking, pot, acid and sex.

On the lower campus the black students had opened the doors of Hamilton Hall and stood on the steps outside, behind a protective line of faculty members from the radical caucus of the ad hoc committee. They sang peace songs and greeted students bringing them food and money. They posted a sign renaming Hamilton Hall "Malcolm X Hall" and declared it a part of Harlem. They, too, had won.

Inside the president's office in Low Library students were completing the task of photostating the files of Grayson Kirk. They sat

Dotson Rader and Craig Anderson, "Rebellion at Columbia." Reprinted by permission of THE NEW REPUBLIC, © *1968, Harrison-Blaine of New Jersey, Inc.*

on the floor around the desk with huge piles of documents arranged by their political, financial or educational content. Material relating to the IDA and CIA was the first to be copied. Then private correspondence from the Trustees and from noted political figures (Maxwell Taylor, Eisenhower, Fulbright, Lyndon Johnson) was photostated.

Gathered around the sundial, the central meeting place on the Columbia campus where protest rallies are traditionally held, over 800 students sat on blankets and huddled around lighted candles and lamps and waited. For they had decided that if the police were ordered against the demonstrators in the buildings that Sunday night they would interpose themselves between the students and the police. Nearby, the ad hoc faculty committee, some 300 professors, argued through the night. They knew that after the crisis the faculty would emerge as the controlling power at the university. The debate now was over the mechanics for exercising that power.

Months before, at an SDS conference in Maryland, the decision had been reached to take physical control of a major American university this spring. Columbia was chosen because of its liberal reputation, its situation in New York and the fact that it was an Ivy League school. SDS felt it was important at this time to disrupt a private, prestige, tactically vulnerable university. Columbia's relations with the West Harlem community, which borders it on two sides, had steadily deteriorated over the years. The decision to begin construction of a gymnasium in Harlem's Morningside Park had united the community against the university. It had evicted hundreds of people from buildings around the university in order to allow for expansion of the campus (and to lower the crime rate in the area).

Columbia was also vulnerable to major disruption because its faculty had become increasingly disenchanted with the leadership of Grayson Kirk and Vice President David Truman, Kirk's chosen successor. Kirk, as spokesman for a conservative Board of Trustees, had steadfastly refused to consider the establishment of a Faculty Senate or to create new constitutional procedures enabling the faculty to exercise power over academic and disciplinary matters. The faculty had already split with the administration over its handling of student protests earlier in the year and over its reluctance to increase the size of Columbia College and to admit to the undergraduate colleges a greater percentage of Negroes.

Originally the two issues to be raised were a general amnesty and a discontinuation of the gym. The amnesty was necessary because

SDS had it on reliable authority that its six leaders, on probation for earlier demonstrations, would not be allowed to return to Columbia at the end of this academic year and that the charter of the organization would be revoked during the summer. The gym was made an issue because it would coalesce the black radicals behind the protest.

The question of the university's affiliation with the Institute for Defense Analyses was the last to be included in the list of grievances. It was added because the week of April 22 would bring thousands of anti-war protesters to New York and the IDA issue would tie the activities of the radical students on campus to the larger concern of stopping the Vietnam war.

But the three issues were pretexts. The point of the game was power. And in the broadest sense, to the most radical members of the SDS Steering Committee, Columbia itself was not the issue. It was revolution, and if it could be shown that a great university could literally be taken over in a matter of days by a well organized group of students then no university was secure. Everywhere the purpose was to destroy institutions of the American Establishment, in the hope that out of the chaos a better America would emerge.

With their three issues, SDS were able to bring into their camp a large following of students concerned with the quality of life at Columbia and with its relations with the Harlem community. But after the protest began and the days wore on and the violent intentions of some of the leadership became evident, more moderate students in the liberated buildings began voting instructions to the Central Committee to moderate both their demands and their tactics. One of the members of the defense committee in Math Hall, when approached by moderate students in opposition to his instruction to the commune that it use clubs and gasoline against the police, retorted, "You fucking liberals don't understand what the scene's about. It's about power and disruption. The more blood the better."

Tuesday afternoon, April 23, approximately a hundred radical students, led by Mark Rudd, chairman of SDS, had marched to Morningside Park to protest the building of the gym. They began pulling down the fences that protected the construction site. The police were called and Rudd led the students away, leaving the police and the administration with the impression that the day's protest was over. Instead of dispersing, Rudd directed the SDS demonstrators in an attack upon Hamilton Hall, a classroom and administration building of Columbia College. The Acting Dean of the College, Henry S. Coleman, was trapped in his office and the building sealed. The building was secured by four o'clock. At four-thirty, Tom Hayden, former national chairman of SDS and a leader of poverty projects in Newark and Chicago, arrived at Hamilton Hall as planned. It was Hayden's decision that produced the withdrawal of white students from Hamilton, leaving the building in sole possession of the blacks. Mark Rudd and the Steering Committee opposed Hayden's decision, yet tactically it was one of the most astute decisions the radicals were to make. It effectively prevented the university from acting against the seizure of Hamilton Hall. (Rap Brown, Wednesday, was the first in a chorus of black radicals who would inform the university that if the police moved against the black students the university would be burned to the ground.)

Later that day, with Low Library occupied, the administration attempted to split the radicals by negotiating separately with Hamilton Hall. They offered the blacks total amnesty (something they felt they could not offer generally because the Trustees demanded some of the students be punished), 25 new scholarships specifically for Negro students, and a termination of gym construction. The blacks refused.

Shortly after midnight Thursday the police were called to campus. Vice President David Truman went to the ad hoc committee and informed it the police had been asked to restore order on campus. His announcement was greeted by shouts of "Shame! Shame!" and "Resign!" Evicted by the faculty from the hall the Vice President fled back into Low Library pursued by a score of angry, shouting professors.

One hour later plainclothes police forcibly entered Low Library, using their night sticks to break through the crowd of professors who had blockaded the entrance to the building. Many teachers were hurt. One of the teaching assistants had to be hospitalized at St. Luke's with a head injury. SDS had won a clubbed and outraged faculty to its side.

By early Saturday morning the administration, faced with $11 million in cancelled pledges and hundreds of threatened resignations (among them Eric Bentley's), appeared to capitulate to SDS demands. With the possibility of violence rising hourly with the growing crowds outside the gates and more and more non-students being spirited on to campus to join the students in the buildings (Dwight MacDonald and Stephen Spender were two of the non-students who joined the protest inside the liberated halls), and with the faculty and student body united in opposition to the administration's use of police force, the president appeared to have little choice. He agreed that the gymnasium would not be built. Within a year he would resign as president for reasons of health and the university would sever its ties with the IDA. An amnesty would be granted in fact if not in name. (The administration was unmoving in its conviction that it could not publicly announce a general amnesty, but Kirk stated to the Steering Committee that no one would receive more than a reprimand.) The Steering Committee agreed not to liberate any more buildings and not to forcibly resist a police raid, if one became necessary. It is on the question of the police raid that the administration and the Steering Committee came to a surprising understanding. It was agreed that one might be necessary if alumni and trustee pressure on the president became so great that he had to protect his own position by affirmative action. SDS, still wanting a public announcement of general amnesty, agreed to allow a bust of the white held buildings if such a statement of amnesty were politically impossible and if, in order to protect its own power over its organization, a bust was necessary to give the appearance that the committee resisted, refusing compromise, to the bitter end. In any case the university would give the Steering Committee sufficient warning to allow students who did not want arrest to leave the buildings in time. No gas would be used.

Until Sunday afternoon the Steering Committee did not inform the liberated buildings of the "no bust" promise. It waited, in part, to keep the threat of a bust as a means of uniting its supporters; also, it was not sure it could trust the president. When it got around to telling the students no bust was coming, it added the words, "at least until Tuesday."

Tuesday it came. At 1:30 A.M., when Police Commissioner Leary was assured that Harlem was asleep, 2,000 police, many of them plainclothesmen, 50 mounted horsemen, swept across Columbia, surrounded the liberated buildings, and methodically cleared them one by one. Hamilton Hall was the first to be raided. Police entered without weapons, barehanded, and the blacks meekly followed a lieutenant through the tunnels into a paddy wagon. The president's office was cleared in less than 30 minutes. Police violence was unprovoked and unlimited. A pregnant girl was dragged by the hair down

Avery's steps. Professors were beaten senseless. In Mathematics, the students were dragged down six flights of concrete steps, leaving blood so thick the cops were slipping in it. With the halls cleared, plain-clothesmen turned on thousands of innocent bystanders on the university lawn. Hundreds were injured. A male student, thrown to the ground, had his eye gouged by a plainclothesman. Horsemen on Broadway rode into terrified crowds, trampling spectators. For two and a half hours, faculty watching through the windows, and wounded students still unremoved from the buildings, witnessed the police destroying furniture, urinating on rugs, dumping files on the floor.

The reaction was swift and emphatic. By that Tuesday afternoon the SDS-called strike had won the majority. The faculty, outraged, moved to increase its power. In direct confrontation with university directives the Committee on Instruction of the college unilaterally ordered classes closed for the week. A Joint Faculties Assembly (prohibited by university regulations) was established, and its executive committee began issuing directives on all university activity.

Frank Michel yelled, "We won!" If polarization and paralysis of a great university is victory, then indeed they did win.

BERKELEY ON THE TIBER

Gianfranco Corsini

In the spring of 1967, Italians watching the government-controlled TV news were suddenly confronted with a scene that might have been familiar to an American audience, but was new here. Except for the neo-Roman architecture of the Fascist-built University of Rome, the sit-in taking place in the main square of this "citadel of culture" could easily have been mistaken for a scene filmed on the Berkeley campus. The students were mourning the death of Paolo Rossi, victim of a neo-Fascist assault on the militant dissenters at the university, and when the speeches to the silent crowd were over, the air was suddenly filled with the singing of *We Shall Overcome*—

Gianfranco Corsini, "Berkeley on the Tiber," THE NATION, *June 10, 1968, pp. 749-52. Reprinted by permission.*

in English. In their time of crisis, the first protest song to come to the minds of thousands of Italian students was the anthem of the American civil rights movement. But in a sense this choice of song was appropriate, for the biggest student uprising ever to take place in this country started with borrowed tactics and borrowed slogans.

There is no doubt that the request for "student power," stressed by this unprecedented national movement, was originally motivated, to quote *Newsweek,* "by the desire to reform an archaic system of higher education" and to obtain "a voice in university administration." The emphasis was definitely on "power," and the working committees of the students who occupied main universities detailed their aims in a series of remarkable documents, now available in several books. The manifestoes of "participatory education" are obviously based on the specific needs of the outmoded Italian educational system. There has also been a symbolic banning of stuffy old books as a protest against the authoritarian notion of culture as "wealth possessed and distributed by the university institutions." It was accordingly suggested that the students be provided with more topical counter-courses (lectures), which turned out to be on matters such as revolution in South America, black power, Wilhelm Reich and the sexual revolution, new trends in psychoanalysis, the doctrines of Herbert Marcuse. In the mimeographed documents one can find a bibliography of preliminary reading which includes Hal Draper's *The Berkeley Revolution,* Paul Goodman's *Growing Up Absurd,* Stokely Carmichael's *Black Power,* the *Autobiography of Malcolm X,* and Marcuse's *One Dimensional Man,* all available in Italian translations.

The anti-textbooks of the new student elite in Italy, 1968, also include works by Guevara, Debray, and Ho Chi Minh, but the massive presence of American authors is particularly instructive for anyone who would grasp the principal motivations of the Italian—and to a certain extent European—student movement. The "specter that haunts" the strongholds of European "culture" seems to speak in English, with a strong American accent. The world-wide rejection of established values and institutions, which also animates the Italian student movement, springs from two parallel "ideological" sources that merge here in a new mixture. On the one hand it includes a revaluation of the Marxist "world view"; on the other, it responds to the more empirical suggestions of American "dissent."

Emphasis varies from country to country, but in Continental dimensions the movement can be interpreted as a protest against the existing society, a critique of the main features of its affluence, and the rejection of its accelerating process of Americanization. Thus America provides both villain and hero. At the very moment when Italian and French and German students join in a massive attack upon neo-capitalism, neo-colonialism and neo-imperialism (as represented by the American socio-economic structure, the American intervention in Vietnam, and the American failure to give equal rights to its black citizens), they also borrow the intellectual weapons of their struggle from the arsenal of American "dissent." The American "myth" that we have known in the past is dying out, and a new American myth is growing in its place.

The present student rebellion is making Europeans aware of a major change in the relation between Europe and the United States; and for the second time within twenty-five years this relation is totally reversed. The American myth of "freedom and opportunity" which inspired the young Italian dissenters struggling against fascism in the late thirties and early forties lost its persuasion in the McCarthy era, and gave way to final rejection in the fifties, as documented by the later works of Pavese or Vittorini. The "discovery" of American "culture" which had begun to shake the old foundations of the European humanistic tradition was followed too closely by the disillusion of the cold war. Intellectual Europe began to shrink back into the comfortable boundaries of its heritage.

But European society has been changing almost at the pace of American society, fast enough to become soon aware that isolation was impossible. Oddly enough, it was then the American "sociological imagination" of the late fifties and early sixties that awakened some European intellectuals to the alarming symptoms of their own advancing mass society. By that time Europe had begun to wonder where its "lonely crowds" were going, who was its "power elite," when the "other" Europe would be found, or why its "inner persuaders" were twisting reality to fit their aims.

At that point a new European generation, still unequipped for self-criticism (except through the conventional channels of the Communist Parties in France and Italy, but without even those in England and Germany), found some inspiration in the new American symbol of the dissenter. The new American hero of a thousand faces looked like the Berkeley student or the SNCC activist, Allen Ginsberg or Malcolm X; Sergeant Yossarian or Noam Chomsky; Paul Goodman or Herbert Marcuse. Each one of them represented the "other

America," as they call it here, and at the same time the "other man" that a whole generation was waiting to see emerge from the general mess. The strength of the new hero was that, though free of the sins of the Christian-colonial tradition, he was yet the unmistakable product of the technological age. Born into it, he proved the possibility of rejection from within. After all, he seemed to suggest that if there could be "another America" there could also be "another Europe"; hence his credibility in defiance of the simple, old-fashioned negations of dogmatic Marxism.

The new radicalism, then, developed where the old radicalism was still a strong component of political life; at the same time, in other areas (Germany or England) it aimed in a way to replace the old. This accounts for the ideological shadings to be found among the various European student movements. In Germany, where there is no strong left-wing opposition, the influence of the American radical students seems particularly close, whereas in France or Italy the new radicalism still finds itself deeply rooted in the Marxist movement. Also significant in these two countries is the participation of radical Catholic groups which tend more and more to dissociate themselves from the orthodoxy of the Church and the established Catholic parties. One might ask, then, why there is this impulse to abandon traditional politics even in countries where the Communist Parties still represent the only strong and organized opposition to the power structure? Why the interest in a new American style, just at the time when American prestige in Europe is at its lowest? A possible answer lies in the general crisis of European culture, which has proved incapable of coping effectively with the new problems of the advancing mass society. Emphasis here is always put on the so-called technological gap between Europe and the United States; not enough attention has been given so far to the cultural lag, in a time when the two societies are acquiring more and more the same features.

Some forty years ago, in the isolation of prison, where the Fascists tried to "stop his brain," the Italian Marxist Gramsci wrote some surprising notes on *Babbitt,* which still seem to throw light on the situation:

The existence of a literary current of realism in America which begins to be critical of its mores is a cultural fact of great importance: it means that a new American civilization is being born, conscious of its strengths and weaknesses. The European intellectuals have already lost this function to a large extent: they no longer represent cultural self-criticism, the self-criticism of the ruling class. They have either become direct agents of the ruling class or have separated into a little caste with no national roots. Babbitt is a philistine in a country in motion; the European petty bourgeoisie are philistines in conservative countries, rotting away in the swamps of a parochialism which preens itself on being a great culture.

Forty years later a new generation fully realizes, as Gramsci had suggested, that "the European Babbitt does not even fight against his philistinism; on the contrary he thrives on it." Therefore, this generation rejects its "great tradition" and sides with the dissenters born out of the culture of "self-criticism." In accepting the new American hero, however, today's European intellectual does not throw out the baby with the bath water; rather, he frequently reintegrates the Marxism in his outlook through, say, an American dimension of Marcuse's work. The latter's validity, then, must also be seen in perspective. The transcripts of a recent debate between the German-American philosopher and some Berlin students, published in *Das Ende der Utopie* (Berlin, 1967), show not only that Marcuse takes his lead from Marx but also that the students constantly try to bring him back to Marx. Many seem worried that the "end of utopia" might lead to another kind of utopia too far removed from contemporary reality. This is also strongly felt among many of the Italian students, whose documents suggest the need for a "linking of the student movement with the political forces of the workers' movement through parties and unions. . . ."

The failures of European Social Democracy and the inflexibility shown by the old party-line Marxism have often in the past provoked a reassessment of the ideological foundations of the revolutionary movements and led to positions independent of the traditional parties of the Left; but these were designed to bring pressure on them from the outside, rather than to by-pass them. In this context one might say that in France and Italy there has been on the whole no open split between the student movement and the old Left, but that a tension was created by a justifiable difference in outlook while the need for possible common action was emphasized. The fact that it was a student-worker First of May celebration which took place in Rome a few weeks ago emphasizes this point. Even Marcuse, answering a German student during his recent Berlin seminar, had to admit that "the tradition of the working class seems to be still very strong, at least in most European countries, while in America, where it previously existed, it is now extinguished." *(Das Ende der Utopie.)*

But it is striking that now for the first time the old European notion of the intellectual as the "conscience" of society has found for many its embodiment mainly on the other side of the ocean, and travels back to Europe in American dress. This adds to the responsibility of American intellectuals, who often appear unaware of the new burden that sits on their shoulders. Their victories and their failures will from now on affect us too.

If it is true that many young Europeans find inspiration in the moral upsurge of the American intelligentsia, they are not blind to the limitations exposed by J. P. Nettl in his recent *Nation* article ("Are Intellectuals Obsolete?" March 4), the attention he calls to a lack of "purpose and direction." The American "neo-intellectuals"—as Nettl calls them—might even find what was *creatively* borrowed from them by the European students (and used differently within the historical and social framework of each European nation) was a loan that could pay excellent interest if only they were willing to analyze what use was being made of it.

If the new American hero, who today replaces the old American clichés on the Continent, is content to be no more than a new "myth," his survival is problematic. This would be true also of those over here who might content themselves with accepting the new hero as a myth, instead of making him a living agent of change. The new hero would in such case become just another consumer product on the intellectual market. But if this discovery of the "other America" should develop into a two-way link between two new cultures, the achievement could very well be revolutionary. The anti-hero of dissent and rejection might then find his place among the purposeful agents of social change that C. Wright Mills so clearly identified in his later years. The new European generation has found in the American "dissenter" the missing link between the post-illuministic age and the post-technological era; but the problem now is to find an adequate setting for the new man yet to be born.

The European student movement should act as a warning to its American counterpart insofar as it shows the need to fill the ideological vacuum of the old Left with an organic construction of aims for the new "New Left." The revolutionary impact of American "dissent" on the European student movement needs to be emphasized, for its importance is great; on the other hand, it is also necessary to be clear about what distinguished the two. One need only refer to "Protest, Power and the Future of Politics" by Carey McWilliams

(*The Nation,* January 15), where it was very plainly stated that the task of American radicalism is more than ever "to concentrate for a change on the political problems." European students know this full well, even if some of them, like their American friends, may think it possible or profitable to avoid the task.

☐ INTEGRATION

The place of Negroes in American society has always been near the center of American protest movements. Over a century ago there was the Abolitionist movement, which produced, among other things, one of the classics of protest literature—Henry David Thoreau's essay on *Civil Disobedience,* in which he explained with devastating simplicity why he refused to pay taxes to a government which condoned slavery:

It is not a man's duty, as a matter of course, to devote himself to the eradication of any, even the most enormous wrong; he may still properly have other concerns to engage him; but it is his duty, at least, to wash his hands of it, and, if he gives it no thought longer, not to give it practically his support. If I devote myself to other pursuits and contemplations, I must see, at least, that I do not pursue them sitting upon another man's shoulders.

In the 1950s, incidents in the South signaled a quickening demand for change—an impatience that was to grow and spread throughout the country. Out of the new movement in the South came new organizations: the Southern Christian Leadership Conference and the Student Nonviolent Coordinating Committee; new heroes and martyrs: Martin Luther King, Jr. and James Meredith, Viola Liuzzo and Medgar Evers, Jr.; and opponents who would become the leaders of the counter-protest movement: Jim Clark and Bull Connor, Ross Barnett and Lester Maddox, and George Wallace.

The Reverend Martin Luther King was an obscure young minister in an Alabama church when he took part, in 1955, in a historic act of protest: the organized boycott by Negroes of the Montgomery bus system.

In August of 1963, the civil rights movement reached a climax of emotion and optimism when some 200,000 people went to Washington, gathered at the Washington Monument, and marched to the Lincoln Memorial. This was probably the largest peaceful protest in history, and neither its size nor its mood of hope for immediate transformation of society has since been equaled.

The Washington march proved the effectiveness of one kind of protest; the series of marches which took place in Selma, Alabama in 1965 proved the effectiveness of another kind. Millions of Americans watched their television sets, saw and were shocked by the violence of Sheriff James G. Clark and his men. The account of one portion of the Selma struggle by Warren Hinckle and David Welsh shows the divisions in both sides: moderates and radicals in the law-enforcement agencies, moderates and radicals among the protesters. Sheriff Clark's action in Selma was one of the most valuable public-relations triumphs of the civil rights movement. With the help of television, the polarization process was nationwide and instantaneous.

Montgomery, Washington, and Selma provided some of the more heroic moments of the civil rights movement. Peter de Lissovoy's article deals with some of the smaller scenes: a Negro shoeshine boy's venture into a white restaurant, a sojourn in a Georgia jail and a brief interracial exchange among pool hustlers.

THE MONTGOMERY BUS BOYCOTT

Martin Luther King, Jr.

One place where the peace had long been precarious was on the city-wide buses. Here the Negro was daily reminded of the indignities of segregation. There were no Negro drivers, and although some of the white men who drove the buses were courteous, all too many were abusive and vituperative. It was not uncommon to hear them referring to Negro passengers as "niggers," "black cows," and "black apes." Frequently Negroes paid their fares at the front door, and then were forced to get off and reboard the bus at the rear. Often the bus pulled off with the Negro's dime in the box before he had had time to reach the rear door.

An even more humiliating practice was the custom of forcing Negroes to stand over empty seats reserved for "whites only." Even if the bus had no white passengers, and Negroes were packed throughout, they were prohibited from sitting in the first four seats (which held ten persons). But the practice went further. If white passengers were already occupying all of their reserved seats and additional white people boarded the bus, Negroes sitting in the unreserved section immediately behind the whites were asked to stand so that the whites could be seated. If the Negroes refused to stand and move back, they were arrested. In most instances the Negroes submitted without protest. Occasionally, however, there were those, like Vernon Johns, who refused.

A few months after my arrival a fifteen-year-old high school girl, Claudette Colvin, was pulled off a bus, handcuffed, and taken to jail because she refused to give up her seat for a white passenger. This atrocity seemed to arouse the Negro community. There was talk of boycotting the buses in protest. A citizens committee was formed to talk with the manager of the bus company and the City Commission, demanding a statement of policy on seating and more courtesy from the drivers.

From pp. 40–45 in STRIDE TOWARD FREEDOM *(hardbound ed.) by Martin Luther King, Jr. Copyright © 1958 by Martin Luther King, Jr. Reprinted by permission of Harper & Row, Publishers.*

I was asked to serve on this committee. We met one afternoon in March 1955 in the office of J. E. Bagley, manager of the Montgomery City Lines. Dave Birmingham, the police commissioner at the time, represented the city commission. Both men were quite pleasant, and expressed deep concern over what had happened. Bagley went so far as to admit that the bus operator was wrong in having Miss Colvin arrested, and promised to reprimand him. Commissioner Birmingham agreed to have the city attorney give a definite statement on the seating policy of the city. We left the meeting hopeful; but nothing happened. The same old patterns of humiliation continued. The city attorney never clarified the law. Claudette Colvin was convicted with a suspended sentence.

But despite the fact that the city commission and the bus company did not act, something else had begun to happen. The long repressed feelings of resentment on the part of the Negroes had begun to stir. The fear and apathy which had for so long cast a shadow on the life of the Negro community were gradually fading before a new spirit of courage and self-respect. The inaction of the city and bus officials after the Colvin case would make it necessary for them in a few months to meet another committee, infinitely more determined. Next time they would face a committee supported by the longings and aspirations of nearly 50,000 people, tired people who had come to see that it is ultimately more honorable to walk the streets in dignity than to ride the buses in humiliation.

On December 1, 1955, an attractive Negro seamstress, Mrs. Rosa Parks, boarded the Cleveland Avenue Bus in downtown Montgomery. She was returning home after her regular day's work in the Montgomery Fair—a leading department store. Tired from long hours on her feet, Mrs. Parks sat down in the first seat behind the section reserved for whites. Not long after she took her seat, the bus operator ordered her, along with three other Negro passengers, to move back in order to accommodate boarding white passengers. By this time every seat in the bus was taken. This meant that if Mrs. Parks followed the driver's command she would have to stand while a white male passenger, who had just boarded the bus, would sit. The other three Negro passengers immediately complied with the driver's request. But Mrs. Parks quietly refused. The result was her arrest.

There was to be much speculation about why Mrs. Parks did not obey the driver. Many people in the white community argued that she had been "planted" by the NAACP in order to lay the ground-work for a test case, and at first glance that explanation seemed plausible, since she was a former secretary of the local branch of the NAACP. So persistent and persuasive was this argument that it convinced many reporters from all over the country. Later on, when I was having press conferences three times a week—in order to accommodate the reporters and journalists who came to Montgomery from all over the world—the invariable first question was: "Did the NAACP start the bus boycott?"

But the accusation was totally unwarranted, as the testimony of both Mrs. Parks and the officials of the NAACP revealed. Actually, no one can understand the action of Mrs. Parks unless he realizes that eventually the cup of endurance runs over, and the human personality cries out, "I can take it no longer." Mrs. Parks' refusal to move back was her intrepid affirmation that she had had enough. It was an individual expression of a timeless longing for human dignity and freedom. She was not "planted" there by the NAACP, or any other organization; she was planted there by her personal sense of dignity and self-respect. She was anchored to that seat by the accumulated indignities of days gone by and the boundless aspirations of generations yet unborn. She was a victim of both the forces of history and the forces of destiny. She had been tracked down by the *Zeitgeist*—the spirit of the time.

Fortunately, Mrs. Parks was ideal for the role assigned to her by history. She was a charming person with a radiant personality, soft spoken and calm in all situations. Her character was impeccable and her dedication deep-rooted. All of these traits together made her one of the most respected people in the Negro community.

Only E. D. Nixon—the signer of Mrs. Parks' bond—and one or two other persons were aware of the arrest when it occurred early Thursday evening. Later in the evening the word got around to a few influential women of the community, mostly members of the Women's Political Council. After a series of telephone calls back and forth they agreed that the Negroes should boycott the buses. They immediately suggested the idea to Nixon, and he readily concurred. In his usual courageous manner he agreed to spearhead the idea.

Early Friday morning, December 2, Nixon called me. He was so caught up in what he was about to say that he forgot to greet me with the usual "hello" but plunged immediately into the story of what had happened to Mrs. Parks the night before. I listened, deeply shocked, as he described the humiliating incident. "We have taken this type of thing too long already," Nixon concluded, his voice trembling. "I feel that the time has come to boycott the buses. Only through a boycott can we make it clear to the white folks that we will not accept this type of treatment any longer."

I agreed at once that some protest was necessary, and that the boycott method would be an effective one.

Just before calling me Nixon had discussed the idea with Rev. Ralph Abernathy, the young minister of Montgomery's First Baptist Church who was to become one of the central figures in the protest, and one of my closest associates. Abernathy also felt a bus boycott was our best course of action. So for thirty or forty minutes the three of us telephoned back and forth concerning plans and strategy. Nixon suggested that we call a meeting of all the ministers and civic leaders the same evening in order to get their thinking on the proposal, and I offered my church as the meeting place. The three of us got busy immediately. With the sanction of Rev. H. H. Hubbard— president of the Baptist Ministerial Alliance—Abernathy and I began calling all of the Baptist ministers. Since most of the Methodist ministers were attending a denominational meeting in one of the local churches that afternoon, it was possible for Abernathy to get the announcement to all of them simultaneously. Nixon reached Mrs. A. W. West—the widow of a prominent dentist—and enlisted her assistance in getting word to the civil leaders.

By early afternoon the arrest of Mrs. Parks was becoming public knowledge. Word of it spread around the community like uncontrolled fire. Telephones began to ring in almost rhythmic succession. By two o'clock an enthusiastic group had mimeographed leaflets concerning the arrest and the proposed boycott, and by evening these had been widely circulated.

As the hour for the evening meeting arrived, I approached the doors of the church with some apprehension, wondering how many of the leaders would respond to our call. Fortunately, it was one of those pleasant winter nights of unseasonable warmth, and to our relief, almost everybody who had been invited was on hand. More than forty people, from every segment of Negro life, were crowded into the large church meeting room. I saw physicians, schoolteachers, lawyers, businessmen, postal workers, union leaders, and clergymen. Virtually every organization of the Negro community was represented.

The largest number there was from the Christian ministry. Having left so many civic meetings in the past sadly disappointed by the dearth of ministers participating, I was filled with joy when I entered the church and found so many of them there; for then I knew that something unusual was about to happen.

Had E. D. Nixon been present, he would probably have been automatically selected to preside, but he had had to leave town earlier in the afternoon for his regular run on the railroad. In his absence, we concluded that Rev. L. Roy Bennet—as president of the Interdenominational Ministerial Alliance—was the logical person to take the chair. He agreed and was seated, his tall, erect figure dominating the room.

The meeting opened around seven-thirty with H. H. Hubbard leading a brief devotional period. Then Bennet moved into action, explaining the purpose of the gathering. With excited gestures he reported on Mrs. Parks' resistance and her arrest. He presented the proposal that the Negro citizens of Montgomery should boycott the buses on Monday in protest. "Now is the time to move," he concluded. "This is no time to talk; it is time to act."

So seriously did Bennet take his "no time to talk" admonition that for quite a while he refused to allow anyone to make a suggestion or even raise a question, insisting that we should move on and appoint committees to implement the proposal. This approach aroused the opposition of most of those present, and created a temporary uproar. For almost forty-five minutes the confusion persisted. Voices rose high, and many people threatened to leave if they could not raise questions and offer suggestions. It looked for a time as though the movement had come to an end before it began. But finally, in the face of this blistering protest, Bennet agreed to open the meeting to discussion.

Immediately questions began to spring up from the floor. Several people wanted further clarification of Mrs. Parks' actions and arrest. Then came the more practical questions. How long would the protest last? How would the idea be further disseminated throughout the community? How would the people be transported to and from their jobs?

As we listened to the lively discussion, we were heartened to notice that, despite the lack of coherence in the meeting, not once did anyone question the validity or desirability of the boycott itself. It seemed to be the unanimous sense of the group that the boycott should take place.

The ministers endorsed the plan with enthusiasm, and promised to go to their congregations on Sunday morning and drive home their approval of the projected one-day protest. Their cooperation was significant, since virtually all of the influential Negro ministers of the city were present. It was decided that we should hold a city-wide mass meeting on Monday night, December 5, to determine how long we would abstain from riding the buses. Rev. A. W. Wilson—minister of the Holt Street Baptist Church—offered his church, which was ideal as a meeting place because of its size and central location. The group agreed that additional leaflets should be distributed on Saturday, and the chairman appointed a committee, including myself, to prepare the statement.

Our committee went to work while the meeting was still in progress. The final message was shorter than the one that had appeared on the first leaflets, but the substance was the same. It read as follows:

Don't ride the bus to work, to town, to school, or any place Monday, December 5.

Another Negro woman has been arrested and put in jail because she refused to give up her bus seat.

Don't ride the buses to work, to town, to school, or anywhere on Monday. If you work, take a cab, or share a ride, or walk.

Come to a mass meeting, Monday at 7:00 P.M., at the Holt Street Baptist Church for further instruction.

After finishing the statement the committee began to mimeograph it on the church machine; but since it was late, I volunteered to have the job completed early Saturday morning.

The final question before the meeting concerned transportation. It was agreed that we should try to get the Negro taxi companies of the city—eighteen in number, with approximately 210 taxis—to transport the people for the same price that they were currently paying on the bus. A committee was appointed to make this contact, with Rev. W. J. Powell, minister of the Old Ship A.M.E. Zion Church, as chairman.

With these responsibilities before us the meeting closed. We left with our hearts caught up in a great idea. The hours were moving fast. The clock on the wall read almost midnight, but the clock in our souls revealed that it was daybreak.

I was so excited that I slept very little that night, and early the next morning I was on my way to the church to get the leaflets out. By nine o'clock the church secretary had finished mimeographing the 7000 leaflets and by eleven o'clock an army of women and young people had taken them off to distribute by hand.

Those on the committee that was to contact the taxi companies got to work early Saturday afternoon. They worked assiduously, and by evening they had reached practically all of the companies, and triumphantly reported that every one of them so far had agreed to cooperate with the proposed boycott by transporting the passengers to and from work for the regular ten-cent bus fare.

Meanwhile our efforts to get the word across to the Negro community were abetted in an unexpected way. A maid who could not read very well came into possession of one of the unsigned appeals that had been distributed Friday afternoon. Apparently not knowing what the leaflet said, she gave it to her employer. As soon as the white employer received the notice she turned it over to the local newspaper, and the *Montgomery Advertiser* made the contents of the leaflet a front-page story on Saturday morning. It appears that the *Advertiser* printed the story in order to let the white community know what the Negroes were up to; but the whole thing turned out to the Negroes' advantage, since it served to bring the information to hundreds who had not previously heard of the plan. By Sunday afternoon word had spread to practically every Negro citizen of Montgomery. Only a few people who lived in remote areas had not heard of it.

After a heavy day of work. I went home late Sunday afternoon and sat down to read the morning paper. There was a long article on the proposed boycott. Implicit throughout the article, I noticed, was the idea that the Negroes were preparing to use the same approach to their problem as the White Citizens Councils used. This suggested parallel had serious implications. The White Citizens Councils, which had had their birth in Mississippi a few months after the Supreme Court's school decision, had come into being to preserve segregation. The Councils had multiplied rapidly throughout the South, purporting to achieve their ends by the legal maneuvers of "interposition" and "nullification." Unfortunately, however, the actions of some of these Councils extended far beyond the bounds of the law. Their methods were the methods of open and covert terror, brutal intimidation, and threats of starvation to Negro men, women, and children. They took open economic reprisals against whites who dared to protest their defiance of the law, and the aim of their boycotts was not merely to impress their victims but to destroy them if possible.

Disturbed by the fact that our pending action was being equated with the boycott methods of the White Citizens Councils, I was forced for the first time to think seriously on the nature of the boy-cott. Up to this time I had uncritically accepted this method as our best course of action. Now certain doubts began to bother me. Were we following an ethical course of action? Is the boycott method basically unchristian? Isn't it a negative approach to the solution of a problem? Is it true that we would be following the course of some of the White Citizens Councils? Even if lasting practical results came from such a boycott, would immoral means justify moral ends? Each of these questions demanded honest answers.

I had to recognize that the boycott method could be used to unethi-cal and unchristian ends. I had to concede, further, that this was the method used so often by the White Citizens Councils to deprive many Negroes, as well as white persons of good will, of the basic necessi-ties of life. But certainly, I said to myself, our pending actions could not be interpreted in this light. Our purposes were altogether dif-ferent. We would use this method to give birth to justice and freedom, and also to urge men to comply with the law of the land; the White Citizens Councils used it to perpetuate the reign of injustice and human servitude, and urged men to defy the law of the land. I reasoned, therefore, that the word "boycott" was really a misnomer for our proposed action. A boycott suggests an economic squeeze, leaving one bogged down in a negative. But we were concerned with the positive. Our concern would not be to put the bus company out of business, but to put justice in business.

As I thought further I came to see that what we were really doing was withdrawing our cooperation from an evil system, rather than merely withdrawing our economic support from the bus company. The bus company, being an external expression of the system, would naturally suffer, but the basic aim was to refuse to cooperate with evil. At this point I began to think about Thoreau's *Essay on Civil Disobedience*. I remembered how, as a college student, I had been moved when I first read this work. I became convinced that what we were preparing to do in Montgomery was related to what Thoreau had expressed. We were simply saying to the white community, "We can no longer lend our cooperation to an evil system."

Something began to say to me, "He who passively accepts evil is as much involved in it as he who helps to perpetuate it. He who accepts evil without protesting against it is really cooperating with it." When oppressed people willingly accept their oppression they only serve to give the oppressor a convenient justification for his acts.

Often the oppressor goes along unaware of the evil involved in his oppression so long as the oppressed accept it. So in order to be true to one's conscience and true to God, a righteous man has no alternative but to refuse to cooperate with an evil system. This I felt was the nature of our action. From this moment on I conceived of our movement as an act of massive noncooperation. From then on I rarely used the word "boycott."

Wearied, but no longer doubtful about the morality of our proposed protest, I saw that the evening had arrived unnoticed. After several telephone calls I prepared to retire early. But soon after I was in bed our two-week-old daughter—Yolanda Denise—began crying; and shortly after that the telephone started ringing again. Clearly condemned to stay awake for some time longer, I used the time to think about other things. My wife and I discussed the possible success of the protest. Frankly, I still had doubts. Even though the word had gotten around amazingly well and the ministers had given the plan such crucial support, I still wondered whether the people had enough courage to follow through. I had seen so many admirable ventures fall through in Montgomery. Why should this be an exception? Coretta and I finally agreed that if we could get 60 per cent cooperation the protest would be a success.

Around midnight a call from one of the committee members informed me that every Negro taxi company in Montgomery had agreed to support the protest on Monday morning. Whatever our prospects of success, I was deeply encouraged by the untiring work that had been done by the ministers and civic leaders. This in itself was a unique accomplishment.

After the midnight call the phone stopped ringing. Just a few minutes earlier "Yoki" had stopped crying. Wearily, I said good night to Coretta, and with a strange mixture of hope and anxiety, I fell asleep.

My wife and I awoke earlier than usual on Monday morning. We were up and fully dressed by five-thirty. The day for the protest had arrived, and we were determined to see the first act of this unfolding drama. I was still saying that if we could get 60 per cent cooperation the venture would be a success.

Fortunately, a bus stop was just five feet from our house. This meant that we could observe the opening stages from our front window. The first bus was to pass around six o'clock. And so we waited through an interminable half hour. I was in the kitchen drinking my coffee when I heard Coretta cry, "Martin, Martin, come quickly!" I put down my cup and ran toward the living room. As I approached the front window Coretta pointed joyfully to a slowly moving bus: "Darling, it's empty!" I could hardly believe what I saw. I knew that the South Jackson line, which ran past our house, carried more Negro passengers than any other line in Montgomery, and that this first bus was usually filled with domestic workers going to their jobs. Would all of the other buses follow the pattern that had been set by the first? Eagerly we waited for the next bus. In fifteen minutes it rolled down the street, and like the first, it was empty. A third bus appeared, and it too was empty of all but two white passengers.

I jumped in my car and for almost an hour I cruised down every major street and examined every passing bus. During this hour, at the peak of the morning traffic, I saw no more than eight Negro passengers riding the buses. By this time I was jubilant. Instead of the 60 per cent cooperation we had hoped for, it was becoming apparent that we had reached almost 100 per cent. A miracle had taken place. The once dormant and quiescent Negro community was now fully awake.

All day long it continued. At the afternoon peak the buses were still as empty of Negro passengers as they had been in the morning. Students of Alabama State College, who usually kept the South Jackson bus crowded, were cheerfully walking or thumbing rides. Job holders had either found other means of transportation or made their way on foot. While some rode in cabs or private cars, others used less conventional means. Men were seen riding mules to work, and more than one horse-drawn buggy drove the streets of Montgomery that day.

During the rush hours the sidewalks were crowded with laborers and domestic workers, many of them well past middle age, trudging patiently to their jobs and home again, sometimes as much as twelve miles. They knew why they walked, and the knowledge was evident in the way they carried themselves. And as I watched them I knew that there is nothing more majestic than the determined courage of individuals willing to suffer and sacrifice for their freedom and dignity.

Many spectators had gathered at the bus stops to watch what was happening. At first they stood quietly, but as the day progressed they began to cheer the empty buses and laugh and make jokes. Noisy youngsters could be heard singing out, "No riders today."

Trailing each bus through the Negro section were two policemen on motorcycles, assigned by the city commissioners, who claimed that Negro "goon squads" had been organized to keep other Negroes from riding the buses. In the course of the day the police succeeded in making one arrest. A college student who was helping an elderly woman across the street was charged with "intimidating passengers." But the "goon squads" existed only in the commission's imagination. No one was threatened or intimidated for riding the buses; the only harassment anyone faced was that of his own conscience.

Around nine-thirty in the morning I tore myself from the action of the city streets and headed for the crowded police court. Here Mrs. Parks was being tried for disobeying the city segregation ordinance. Her attorney, Fred G. Gray—the brilliant young Negro who later became the chief counsel for the protest movement—was on hand to defend her. After the judge heard the arguments, he found Mrs. Parks guilty and fined her ten dollars and court costs (a total of fourteen dollars). She appealed the case. This was one of the first clear-cut instances in which a Negro had been convicted for disobeying the segregation law. In the past, either cases like this had been dismissed or the people involved had been charged with disorderly conduct. So in a real sense the arrest and conviction of Mrs. Parks had a twofold impact: it was a precipitating factor to arouse the Negroes to positive action; and it was a test of the validity of the segregation law itself. I am sure that supporters of such prosecutions would have acted otherwise if they had had the prescience to look beyond the moment.

THE MARCH ON WASHINGTON

Lerone Bennett, Jr.

It was the beginning of something, and the ending of something.

It came 100 years and 240 days after the signing of the Emancipation Proclamation.

It came like a force of nature.

Like a whirlwind, like a storm, like a flood, it overwhelmed and stunned by its massiveness and finality.

A quarter-million people were in it, and of it; and millions more watched on TV and huddled around radios.

A TV spectacular, a Sunday School picnic, a political convention, "an impressive demonstration of Negro unity," "a visible expression of interracial brotherhood," "an almost unprecedented exhibition of resolve," a display of religious solidarity, a new concept of lobbying, a living petition, a show of strength, a call to the national conscience: the mammoth March on Washington was everything they said it was, and more; and it moved men and women as they had never been moved before.

It threatened, at points, to become a meaningless gesture, an extravaganza, an outing, a prayer said to the wind. But the people, the old ladies and the young boys, the students and the dreamers, the young girls in bright babushkas and the old men in shiny blue suits: the people—they redeemed it, and made it something to remember.

They came, these people, from points all over America, and several overseas; they assembled in Washington on the grassy slopes of the Washington Monument and walked about a mile to the Lincoln Monument where they said with their bodies that the Negro had been waiting 100 years and 240 days and that he was still not free (the Emancipation Proclamation to the contrary notwithstanding) and that 100 years and 241 days were too long to wait. There, in balmy, 84-degree weather, in the shadow of Lincoln and the presence of God, they recalled (in Archibald MacLeish's phrase) "the holy

Lerone Bennett, Jr., "Biggest Protest March—Masses Were March Heroes," EBONY, *November 1963. Reprinted by permission.*

dream we were to be"—recalled the dream and made it flesh and blood and bone in their black and white togetherness.

This, then, was the March: a long and uncomfortable trip on trains and buses and planes, a short walk down Constitution and Independence Avenues, words said in the sun and, beneath it all, a quiet anger, a fierce hope and the wind and the fire of a dream.

Dreams brought the demonstrators to this particular place at this particular time—dreams and drastic demands within them. We are accustomed now to the dreams of the young, but there is a certain poetry in the fact that this march was the product of the dreams of a New Negro who was born in 1889. For Asa Philip Randolph, 74, founder-President of the Brotherhood of Sleeping Car Porters, and Vice President of the AFL-CIO, the March was the culmination of a half-century of agitation. He had threatened such a march in 1941 and wartime Washington panicked and gave him what he wanted: a Fair Employment Practices Order. Back in January, he suggested a March on Washington to dramatize the plight of unemployed Negroes; but nobody was listening and nobody seemed to care—except a few students and militants. Then came Birmingham; then came the thunder of Negroes in the streets; then came the Summer of Discontent; and men remembered the Old Man and what he had done in 1941 and what he wanted to do in 1963. In the end, the five major Negro organizations—NAACP, SCLC, SNCC, CORE and Urban League—closed ranks behind Randolph and his dream. A Jew, a Catholic, a Protestant and a labor leader completed the cast of leaders. They named Randolph director and the Old Man went back to his Harlem office, and the years fell from him. He chose as his deputy director Bayard Rustin, a brilliant but controversial mover and shaker in the Freedom Movement. Before Randolph and Rustin lay a formidable task: moving 100,000 or more people into Washington and out in one day, feeding, organizing, and to be blunt, restraining them for 24 hours. That this was done, and with such aplomb, tells much about the quality of Negro leadership.

Through the late summer, as the fires of discontent burned in the streets, Randolph and his aides prodded, pushed, organized. As they worked, ripples of fear spread across the nation. Washington, D. C., already more than one-half Negro, was hysterical; the general feeling, the Washington *Daily News* said, was that the Vandals were coming again to sack Rome. Powerful politicians and big men in labor and business urged the leaders to abandon the March; it was unwise, they said, imprudent, unnecessary and perhaps illegal. The press took up the cry, saying with increasing stridence that the March was social dynamite and that violence was almost unavoidable. Despite the furor or perhaps because of it, preparations continued. In a yellow building in Harlem and in another yellow building in Washington, MOW men wrestled with unprecedented logistical problems: over 1,500 organizations were contacted, regional directors were named, organizational manuals were issued.

March leaders went to extraordinary lengths to insure a peaceful demonstration. As originally conceived by some of the more venturesome leaders, the March was to be a rasp across an exposed nerve. One student leader announced early in the summer that he and his wife and baby planned to pitch a tent on the White House lawn. Others spoke of sit-ins in the offices of Senator James Eastland of Mississippi and other like-minded Senators. The leaders vetoed these plans; they banned inciting signs and forbade picketing at the White House and on Capitol Hill. An internal police system was set up to isolate and exclude troublemakers and Communists. The March, they said, was for Freedom and Jobs. The immediate aim was to prod Congress on the pending Civil Rights Bill.

As the big day drew near, excitement grew at March headquarters. In the beginning, it seemed that the March would be a flop. Newspapers across the nation reported hopefully a general lack of interest in the March; they said sponsors were having trouble filling chartered trains and buses. In this, as in other things about the March, the press was wrong. Toward the end of August, March headquarters was swamped with requests from organizations who wanted to get on the bandwagon. The feeling was growing—it was in the air—that this one was going to be big and, as always, men and organizations wanted to be with the winner.

Staff members were hard at work in New York, Martin Luther King, Jr. was in his Atlanta home, A. Philip Randolph was in his Harlem apartment when the wheels began to turn. Weeks before the March, Jay Hardo, an 82-year-old man left Dayton, Ohio, on a silver bicycle with a large American eagle on the handlebars. A week or so later, Ledger Smith, an NAACP member, left Chicago on roller skates. Four days before the March, David Parker, a Los Angeles pants presser, got into a battered old Ford with five friends and started the 3000-mile trip across the nation. Parker said he was going to Washington "because my people got troubles."

Monday came, August 26, and the feeling took shape and substance. They were leaving now from New Canaan, Connecticut and Barre, Vermont; they were leaving now from towns in Oregon and cities in California, from Las Vegas, Nevada, and Seattle, Washington, from Durham and Greensboro, from West Memphis and Selma, from Dallas and St. Paul and Miami and Gary.

Across the country, in Washington, D. C., the tempo picked up. The leaders arrived and set up command posts; the vanguard of the well heeled arrived and took up positions in the lobbies of the swank hotels. By Tuesday night, practically all of the ten leaders were domiciled in the Statler-Hilton where they worked late, tightening up and refining the plans.

As they worked, trains and planes began to move.

Wheels turned, engines throbbed and the great mass moved toward Washington in a massive orchestration of sound and movement and emotion. As they came, on buses and trains and in cars, they sang Spirituals, prayed and talked. In the air, over Nevada, a woman from California tried to explain to her white seatmate the meaning of Negroness. "You can never know what it's like to be a Negro. No matter how hard you try, you can't imagine going into a hamburger shop with your children and being told, 'We don't serve niggers here.' "

On they came, on wheels of every description, and Washington waited, tight with tension. The day, Wednesday, August 28, 1963, dawned clear and slightly cool, with the streets deserted and a large number of the white inhabitants in self-imposed exile in Virginia and Maryland enclaves. The Government and private businesses, fearing violence or traffic tie-ups or both, had urged employes to take the day off; bars and whisky stores had been closed. Washington, in the early morning, looked like a city under seige. Burly MPs, Negroes and whites, directed traffic and scurried about the city in jeeps and command cars.

The crowd gathered slowly. At 7 A.M., there were only 1000 people at the Washington Monument, where the crowd was to assemble. There was fear in some quarters and hope in others that the expected crowd wouldn't come.

But the crowd continued to increase, slowly at first and then with a rush. At 9:30, there were 40,000 people around the tall white pencil of the Washington Monument; an hour later, there were 50,000 and police reported that the Baltimore-Washington expressway was packed solidly with cars and buses moving "bumper-to-bumper." By

11 A.M. there were at least 90,000 people on the grassy slopes of the Monument and the Ellipse behind the White House.

There had never been such a crowd.

There were Negro society women in new hats and old women in Sunday go-to-church black; there were bright young men from the top level of the agencies, looking important and hurried, and lost; there were pretty girls and plain ones, priests, preachers, and rabbis, union members, seminarians, housewives, and teachers.

One remembers most the faces and the feet. There were feet of every imaginable description, some of them bare, some of them stylishly shod; the feet of old women who had stood long over white folks' stoves and the feet of old men who had stood long in mines and factories; feet used to the outdoors, flat, square, strong feet that ached easily and were favored gently as the people walked. These feet contrasted strongly with the feet of the young, feet fresh from college campuses and offices, feet modishly shod, free, it seemed, from the bunions and the calluses and the memories of the old. Of whatever description, however shod, the feet moved in protest, and affirmation. And above them, the faces shone with boundless pride.

The crowd was gay and sad, happy and angry. Correspondents went away and wrote long articles on the "remarkable sweetness" of the crowd, proving once again that they still do not understand Negroes or themselves. They had expected a wild mob and what they saw were students, organization-men and old women who could have been anybody's aunt. And so they were astounded, not realizing that things are seldom all one thing or another, that men can smile and cry inside, that they can bleed and sing to staunch the wound.

There was about this crowd the wonderful two-tongued ambivalence of the blues. It was neither all one thing nor all another. Many moods competed, but two dominated: a mood of quiet anger and buoyant exuberance. There was also a feeling of power and a certain surprise, as though the people had discovered suddenly who they were and what they had.

They had come from different places, in different ways, for different reasons. But, once there, they were welded into a whole and living thing. The magic of the crowd began to work on them and they moved, pulled along by the force of an idea.

The people stood for a long time in the assembly area, listening to speeches and songs from stage and screen celebrities. Then, spontaneously, they began to move. Little knots stepped into Constitution Avenue and began to march. The trickle became a flood and, at 11:20 A.M., 10 minutes ahead of schedule, the March began, with the followers leading.

The marchers moved in two great waves, shoulder to shoulder, down Constitution and Independence Avenues. On they came, a riot of sound and color, signs bobbling up above the sea of their heads, Spirituals coming from the well of their throats; on they came, feet pounding on the hot pavement of history; on they came, wave after wave beating against the sandy beach of American indifference.

At the Lincoln Monument, the marchers regrouped on both sides of the reflecting pool and deployed under the giant elms and oaks. They stretched almost a mile to the east and stood in scattered groups in a great semi-circle around the steps of the Monument where the speakers and honored guests were seated.

For almost three hours, the multitudes listened to speakers who demanded immediate passage of a Civil Rights Bill and immediate implementation of the basic guarantees of the Declaration of Independence, and the Thirteenth, Fourteenth, and Fifteenth Amendments.

Out of the blurred montage of words and symbols six clear pictures emerge: a picture of Asa Philip Randolph, the Father of the March, saying that this was the beginning and not the ending and that "wave after wave" would come back to Washington if immediate changes were not made in American life; of Carson Blake, head of the Presbyterian Church, indicting American Christians and saying repeatedly, "We come—late, late we come"; of Rabbi Joachim Prinz recalling the downfall of Germany and saying that the basic problem is not evil but silence and indifference; of Mahalia Jackson rolling one hundred years of wrong into one pregnant verse; of John Lewis calling for a real, a "serious revolution"; of Martin Luther King, Jr., etching the blueprints of a dream.

Let us consider Mahalia Jackson, Martin Luther King and John Lewis: they are the keys to that day.

There is a nerve that lies beneath the smoothest of exteriors, a nerve 400 years old and throbbing with hurt and indignation. Mahalia Jackson penetrated the facades and exposed the nerve to public view. She was singing *I've Been 'Buked and I've Been Scorned,* doing all the right things in the right way, and then, suddenly it happened.

> I'm gonna tell my Lord
> When I get home,
> I'm gonna tell my Lord
> When I get home,
> Just how long you've
> Been treating me wrong.

A spasm ran through the crowd.

The button-down men in front and the old women way back came to their feet, screaming and shouting. They had not known that this thing was in them and that they wanted it touched. From different places, in different ways, with different dreams, they had come and, now, hearing this sung, they were one.

John Lewis, the new chairman of the Student Non-Violent Coordinating Committee, came on, working in the major leagues for the first time. He had come armed with a prepared speech which said that politicians, all politicians, were low, despicable people—and that none of them meant the Negro any good. He had wanted to tell them youths were still being whipped for urging Negroes to vote, and that old men were in jail. He had wanted to tell them that if the March was only a gesture that it was obscene; that he and his kind, the children who made the revolution, had nothing but contempt for old men who dealt in gestures. He had wanted to say many things about marching through Dixie like Sherman—he had wanted to say many things but a white bishop objected and he had been forced to tone his speech down.

He came on, now, scowling, and he said pretty much what he had intended to say—only in polite language. And when he finished the older Negro leaders rushed to pump his hand.

A second man, now: Martin Luther King, Jr., coming to the lectern amid thunderous applause. He read for a time from a prepared speech and then he took off in a flight of pungent language, speaking of a dream big enough to include all men and all children, of little black boys and little black girls joining hands with little white boys and little white girls as sisters and brothers.

"I have a dream," he said, over and over, and each elaboration evoked hysterical cheers.

It was not so much the words, eloquent as they were, as the manner of their saying: the rhythms and the intonations and the halts and breaks. These called back all the old men and women who had had this dream and had died dishonored; called back rickety

Negro churches on dirt roads and the men and women who sat in them, called them back and found them not wanting, nor their hoping in vain. The rhythms and the intonation called back all the struggle and all the pain and all the agony, and held forth the possibility of triumph; they called back Emmett Till and Medgar Evers and all the others; called back ropes and chains and bombs and screams in the night; called back one-room walk-up flats and roaches and rats, called them back and said they would soon be over.

When it was all over, they screamed, cheered, cried. Then they sat down quietly, wondering at the thing that had happened to them.

Late in the afternoon, they went to the planes and trains and buses and disappeared into the anonymity from whence they had come. No one could say, really, whether they had made any measurable impact on Congress. Almost everyone agreed, however, that the March had impressed millions of whites in America and Europe.

More important, however, was the impact of the March on the participants. The participants knew that if the March changed no votes in Congress or no hearts in America that it had changed them. Those who thought, in the beginning, that it was too respectable, and those who thought it was too radical; the young people who didn't want to wait another minute, and the old ones who had waited, now, for 81 and 82 and 94 years; the smooth operators from New York and Chicago and the fieldhands from Mississippi; the church women from Atlanta and the gay crowd from Harlem: for a moment in time, they were one.

They would disagree later; there would be disappointments, bombings, outrages; there would be backsliders and it would be necessary perhaps to do it all over again; but for one moment, for one unforgettable moment, the militants and the moderates, the timid liberals and the fire-eating activists, the old church women and the barmaids: for one single, electrifying moment they were one. And they would remember. If the bridge held, and if it didn't rain, men and women would look back on this day and tell their children and grandchildren: "There was a March in the middle of the twentieth century, the biggest demonstration for civil rights in history—and I was there."

THE BATTLES OF SELMA

Warren Hinckle and David Welsh

The legal-size mimeographed forms were deadly complete—name, address, next-of-kin, authorization for representation by counsel. Everyone who marched had to fill one out in case of arrest, injury, or death. But there weren't enough forms to go around Sunday morning when the marchers came in from Boykin and Jones and Marion, from Atlanta, from Chicago, from New York. They came to Brown's Chapel—the red brick church towering over the red brick apartment buildings of the George Washington Carver Homes housing project in the Negro section of Selma.

Brown's Chapel was the assembly point for the planned march over U.S. Highway 80 through the swamps and hills and white racist strongholds of rural, black belt Alabama to the ornate colonial capitol at Montgomery, where the dual flags of the Conferedate States of America and the Sovereign State of Alabama hung together limply in the still air around the capitol dome.

The girl handing out the forms said she needed more. A Negro boy ran down unpaved Sylvan Street, which intersects the federal housing project, and turned right on Alabama Street toward the Student Non-Violent Co-ordinating Committee (SNCC) headquarters located three blocks uptown. He went to the top floor of a three-story, rickety Negro office building with unlighted hallways and atrophied doors set in warped door-jambs. From the Selma City Jail directly across the street, police watched the young Negro go into the dreary building and come out a few minutes later carrying a freshly printed pile of registration forms.

This historic Confederate city on the banks of the muddy Alabama river is a citadel of Southern resistance to integration. Only in the Trailways bus station do Negroes and whites mix. This is why SNCC, in 1963, selected Selma as a prime target for its organizing activities. The Confederate establishment immediately began to skirmish with the civil rights invaders, and when Dr. Martin Luther King and his

Condensed from Warren Hinckle and David Welsh, "The Five Battles of Selma," RAMPARTS, June, 1965. Reprinted by permission of the editors.

100

Southern Christian Leadership Conference (SCLC) joined forces with SNCC in Selma early this year, the Conferedate "police action" escalated into a conflict of military proportions not seen in the South since the Battle of Selma nominally ended the Civil War in April of 1865.

Like all wars, this one became deadly serious after the first casualty, Jimmy Lee Jackson, a 26-year-old Negro woodcutter, was gunned down by an Alabama state trooper during a racial demonstration in nearby Marion. When he died eight days later in Selma's Negro Good Samaritan Hospital, he was a war hero. The Montgomery march of Sunday, March 7, was called more to honor Jimmy Jackson than to seriously petition Governor George Wallace for the redress of racial inequities he has sworn to preserve.

As the young Negro left the SNCC offices with a fresh supply of registration forms, his progress was reported to the Confederate Command Post operating in Sheriff Jim Clark's Dallas County Court House offices in downtown Selma. "The nigger's leaving there now . . . he's goin' back down Alabama Street . . . carryin' papers . . . back to the church . . ." A middle-aged woman wearing rimless glasses, a Confederate flag pinned to her white blouse, sat on a stool, her legs crossed, writing everything down. A large sign near the doorway of the first floor suite read "Quiet Please, We are Trying to Monitor Three Radios."

One of the command post radios crackled: "There's three more cars of niggers crossing the bridge. Some white bastards riding with them. Heading for Brown's Chapel." The bridge was the Edmund Pettus Bridge, a stumpy concrete edifice stretching between the debris-lined bluffs of the sluggish Alabama River and linking Selma with Highway 80 (the Jefferson Davis Highway), the road to Montgomery. This was the bridge the marchers would have to cross.

It was early afternoon. The State Troopers were preparing to block off traffic on the heavily-traveled thoroughfare. They moved their patrol cars into position on both sides of the divided highway, facing north.

Sheriff Clark's good friend, Colonel Al Lingo, head of the Alabama State Troopers, sat in an unmarked car at the side of the highway, watching his men prepare for battle. Clark and Lingo had worked out battle plans that would not only scatter the Union forces but make their defeat an object lesson. The white citizens of Alabama had grown weary of "moderate" handling of the Selma voter registration demonstrations led by Dr. Martin Luther King. Selma's Public Safety Director, Wilson Baker, had insisted on mass arrests to control the demonstrators. Now the Confederate leadership wanted something more effective. "If the Negroes refuse to disperse, we shall not make mass arrests," Colonel Lingo said. He said it the way a general says his side will take no prisoners.

Filling out a marching form at Brown's Chapel was 16-year-old Viola Jackson of Selma (no relation to the late Jimmy Lee Jackson). *Have you ever been arrested?* NO. *Have you ever been beaten?* YES. *Do you have any ailments that should be checked before the march?* NO. She handed in the paper and went outside where the marchers were forming.

The march itself was planned in military style: participants were to line up two abreast, grouped into squads of 25 people, and then into companies of four squads each. The leaders of the march—John Lewis of SNCC and Hosea Williams of SCLC—had originally planned to organize the squads on paper. But the last minute influx of marchers made that impractical, so everyone was ordered outside to the playground behind Brown's Chapel and told to line up in pairs. Forty-five minutes later, six companies were ready to march.

The Union leadership had, in its own way, prepared for the expected confrontation with the Confederate forces: four ambulances were parked on Sylvan Street; ten doctors and nurses, mostly from New York, had flown to Montgomery and driven to Selma the night before. They were volunteers of the Medical Committee for Human Rights. When the march started, they followed in the file of ambulances at the end of the line.

Viola Jackson found herself in the second company, first squad. Standing in front of her was a young Negro wearing a sweatshirt. His marching companion was a tall white youth carrying a round knapsack on his back. They introduced themselves. The Negro was Charles Mauldin, an 18-year-old junior at the R. B. Hudson High School, Selma's Negro high, and President of the 1500-member Selma Youth Movement. The white was Jim Benston, an unsalaried member of the SCLC Selma staff.

The march began without heraldry. Viola Jackson and Charles Mauldin and Jim Benston walked close together as the three-block-long line moved slowly down Sylvan Street and up Water Avenue, through the Negro business district, to the bridge.

The view from the other side of the Pettus Bridge—looking toward

Selma—was less than inspiring. The old brick buildings that line the bluffs above the slow-flowing river were gradually falling away. The sloping bluffs were spotted with bricks, discarded building materials and decaying underbrush. Viola Jackson and Charles Mauldin and Jim Benston could look back at the river bluffs and the long line of marchers behind them on the bridge, but they couldn't tell what was happening ahead of them on the highway. All they could see were police cars, State Trooper cars, sheriff's cars—a silent, stationary armada filling all four lanes of the Jefferson Davis Highway. A large, surly crowd of Selma white citizens stood on the trunks of parked cars or jammed the frontage area of roadside businesses, seeking ring-side seats. Newsmen were herded together in front of the Lehman Pontiac building some distance from the marchers and assigned several troopers for "protection."

State Troopers, headed by Major John Cloud, lined the highway three deep. Colonel Lingo watched from his automobile parked near Lehman's Grocery. As the marchers approached, Major Cloud hailed them: "This is an unlawful assembly," he said. "You have two minutes to turn around and go back to your church." The leaders of the march were now within several feet of the phalanx of troopers who held their clubs at the ready. Major Cloud took out his watch and started counting. The silence was total. Exactly one minute and five seconds later Major Cloud ordered, "Troopers forward." The blue-clad troopers leaped ahead, clubs swinging, moving with a sudden force that bowled over line after line of marchers. The first groups of Negroes went to the ground screaming, their knapsacks and bags spilling onto the highway.

The marchers, pushed back by the billy club attack, grouped together on the grassy, gasoline-soiled dividing strip in the center of the highway. They knelt and began to pray. The troopers rushed in again, banging heads, and then retreated. Viola and the two boys knelt together. For two minutes a tense silence was broken only by the sound of the Confederate forces strapping on their gas masks and the buzz-buzz-buzz of the cattle prods.

As the troopers heaved the first tear gas bombs into the praying Negroes, the crowd of several hundred white onlookers broke into prolonged cheering. The first were feeler bombs; the marchers coughed and gagged, but didn't move. Then the troopers let loose with a heavy barrage of gas shells. Several bombs landed near Viola and the two boys, and then they couldn't see each other anymore.

For Charles Mauldin, it was like a quick visit to hell. "The gas was so thick that you could almost reach up and grab it. It seemed to lift me up and fill my lungs and I went down." Some of the marchers panicked and ran. They couldn't see where they were going and they ran into cars and buildings. Those who were too young or too old to move fast enough got hit the most. When they got to the Selma end of the bridge, the possemen and deputies who had been patiently waiting there attacked them anew with clubs and whips and chased them through the streets down toward the Negro quarter.

For Jim Benston, it was worse. After the first tear gas attack, he lay on the ground trying to breathe. He looked up and a trooper was standing in front of him, staring down through the big goggle-eyes of his gas mask. The trooper slowly lifted his tear gas gun and shot it off directly into Benston's face. "I was knocked out for maybe five minutes. When I woke up I was in a cloud. I couldn't breathe and I couldn't see. I was coughing and I was sick. It was like the world had gone away. I laid there on the grass for a few minutes and then I felt around me, trying to see if anybody else was still there. I couldn't feel anybody. They were all gone. I was the only one left." Benston staggered off to his right, through a used car lot, and collapsed in a small field. A dozen or so other marchers lay there, bleeding, coughing, trying to catch their breath. Then Benston heard horses, and shrill rebel battle yells. "They came charging through where we were laying on the grass and tried to hit us with the horses, but the horses had more sense. One posseman tried to get his horse to rear up and land on top of a man near me, but the horse wouldn't do it. Horses have more sense." The marchers got up and ran toward the bridge. The possemen rode in front of them and set off tear gas bombs in their path, forcing them through the new pockets of gas. On the bridge, Benston was clubbed at least 25 times. As he ran down the narrow pedestrian sidewalk, possemen would take turns, galloping by, clubbing him, laughing. He pulled his knapsack up to cover his head and neck. "That knapsack saved my life," he said.

For Viola Jackson, it didn't last long. She was knocked down on the dividing strip and dug her fingernails into the ground. The thick tear gas hung like heavy cigarette smoke between the blades of grass and curled around her fingers. She managed to get up and tried to run, but she couldn't go on. Her breath came shorter. Then she couldn't see, and she fell down onto the ground and didn't get up. More shells fell nearby, and the gas covered her fallen body like a blanket.

The police at first wouldn't let the waiting Union ambulances onto the bridge to pick up the wounded. When they did, finally, the volunteer drivers and doctors and nurses worked frantically, loading the injured and racing them to the Good Samaritan Hospital.

Sheriff Clark's possemen chased the Negroes down to the housing project, but were stopped by Selma Safety Director Baker. Baker said he had his city police surrounding the project area and saw no need for further force. The Selma *Times-Journal* quoted Clark as replying to Baker: "I've already waited a month too damn long about moving in."

After the Negroes in the project were forced indoors, Sheriff Clark's posse rode uptown, looking for more Negroes. They yelled at Negroes walking on the streets and beat with their night-sticks on the hoods of cars with Negro drivers. "Get the hell out of town. Go on. We mean it. We want all the niggers off the street."

By dusk, not one Negro could be found on the streets of Selma.

Wednesday afternoon, as the Confederate forces were lining up before the national television cameras for a massive show of force on Sylvan Street, the Sheriff was at his resplendent best. His boots were spit-polished, the crease on the pants of his dark business suit cutting-edge sharp, the alabaster purity of his crash helmet broken only by a painted Confederate flag. In his lapel was a round white button bearing the single word "NEVER." This is Clark's rejoinder to "We Shall Overcome," and it appeared "Never" would be the order of the day as the armed forces of the State of Alabama assumed battle formation a half block down from Brown's Chapel. State Troopers, sheriff's deputies, city policemen, Alabama Soil Conservation officers, even Alabama Beverage Control officers, lined up in two and three squad car rows on Sylvan Street, flanking in reserve to the right and left down Selma Avenue and filling yet another block of Sylvan Street beyond the boundaries of the Negro housing project. The Mayor of Selma had said the Union could not march today and the troops were here to see that they would not.

This huge assemblage of police cars and troopers was good tonic for Sheriff Clark. He moved in between his deputies' cars, playfully snapping the rawhide hanging from his billy club at the khaki-clad buttocks of his possemen. He didn't act at all like a soldier who had just been dressed down by his commander-in-chief.

Governor Wallace had summoned Clark to his capital offices the day before and told him to call off his posse and their whips and horses. Wallace, who seemed concerned about Alabama's image, upbraided Clark for the posse's Attila-the-Hun tactics on Sunday, before the lenses of television cameras. The Governor wasn't really mad about the whips, but he was mad as hell about the television cameras. When Clark left, red-faced and angry, he had instructions to keep his men out of the omniscient television eye. The Sheriff was also told that Wilson Baker would call the shots in Selma and he didn't like that, either.

Wilson Baker is the Director of Public Safety of Selma. For public safety director, read police chief. Mr. Baker is one of the few police officials in Alabama who does not make the title ludicrous by his actions. He thinks like a dedicated cop and not like a storm trooper. He would rather cajole or, at worst, arrest civil rights demonstrators than beat them. This moderate approach has alienated him from Sheriff Clark. "Those two have been at it all month long like two dogs in a pit," a Justice Department observer in Selma said. In the last two months of racial demonstration, Baker's tactics have kept the lid on this troubled and tense town. Massive violence came only once—Sunday at the bridge, when the Clark/Lingo coalition took over.

Baker has been criticized recently by Selma white townspeople—both racists and "moderates." They feel the demonstrations have gone too long and too far. But Baker is the kind of tough cop who does his job without regard to public opinion. This is not to say that Baker isn't a segregationist. He is. But he is a segregationist who seems to have some feeling for the Negro's struggle for human dignity. "If I was a nigger, I'd be doing just what they're doing," he once said.

The Union demonstrators boiled out of Brown's Chapel. They stood in the street, chatting casually, as if they had just come out of a regular Sunday service, then began to form ranks. There were some 500 of them, a good sixty per cent of them white and most of that number ministers and nuns. Baker strode forward to the front echelon of Selma police officers who were lined up across Sylvan Street. Beyond them, the Confederate forces stretched in a flow of color worthy of a Camelot set.

The marchers formed up four abreast and started down Sylvan Street toward the line of police a half block away. When they got within 12 feet, Baker stepped forward and raised his big left hand in a lazy arc, the cigar still between his fingers: "Reverend Anderson, you cannot march today." Standing beside Baker was Joseph

T. Smitherman, Selma's young and nervous Mayor. The Rev. L. L. Anderson, a Selma Negro leader who was heading the marchers, made his reply directly to the Mayor:

"We are asking your Honor to permit us to march to the Courthouse. We are not registered voters but we want to be; it is our God-given constitutional right. We shall move like the children of Israel, moving toward the promised land."

The Mayor blinked. The streets were jammed with spectators. People stood on nearby rooftops. The omni-present television cameras were trained directly on him. Newsmen shoved microphones under his nose. He was the Mayor: 35 years old, a former appliance dealer, a close political ally of Governor Wallace. It was his decision to ban any further demonstrations or marches outside of the Brown's Chapel area. He cleared his throat, twice, and folded his slender arms in front of the dark business suit which looked like it belonged on someone a size larger. "You have had opportunity after opportunity to register your people to vote," he said. (The Dallas County Courthouse is open two days a month to register new voters.) "We have enforced the laws impartially . . . we expect to see our orders obeyed."

The Mayor stepped back to the sanctuary of the squad cars. The newsmen crowded in around Baker and the Rev. Anderson. "I would like to introduce some people of good will, who have some statements to make," said Anderson. "You can make all the statements you want, but you are not going to march," replied Baker.

The nuns, ministers, priests, rabbis, lay church leaders and the Negro leaders who made up the majority of the marchers, spoke to the press for the next ninety minutes while the youngsters in the housing project played and giggled on the sidewalks.

As the speakers talked on, damning Selma with all the moral fervor at their command, it became evident that only their fellow marchers and the newsmen were listening. The spectators walked idly about on the sidewalk; children chased each other in between the rows of brick apartment buildings; the troops broke ranks, stood in small groups chatting, sipping cokes, slipping their riot helmets back to let the sun on their foreheads. Mayor Smitherman picked up one of the sandwiches and fiddled with the wax paper wrappings for a moment before he opened it. He looked unhappily at the crowd of demonstrators. "I don't understand it," he said. "Martin Luther King can walk into the White House any time he wants for conferences with the President, but the Mayor of Selma can't even get an appointment. I sent the President a telegram asking for a meeting, but some sort of fifth assistant answered it."

"King? Where is King?" a man asked. "He's in town," said the Mayor. "I don't know why he isn't here."

Martin Luther King wasn't there because he was in trouble in his own movement. His absence explained the absence, also, of the usual throngs of Selma teenagers who gave life and spirit and rhythm to every mass Negro meeting in Selma, and of the tough, militant SNCC workers who had been in Selma for two years now. King wasn't there because he was afraid he would be publicly booed by his own people.

Dr. King was at the home of a Selma Negro dentist, Dr. Sullivan Jackson. It was there, early Tuesday morning, that the pajama-clad Nobel Prize winner met with former Florida Governor LeRoy Collins, now head of the Federal Community Relations Service and President Johnson's unofficial Ambassador to the Union forces. Collins had been sent by special jet from Washington to work out a compromise that would avoid repetition of Sunday's bloodshed on Tuesday afternoon, when another attempt at the march to Montgomery (this one led by Dr. King) was scheduled to cross the Edmund Pettus Bridge. A federal judge had issued a temporary restraining order against the march and Dr. King was in a quandary. His organization prided itself on never violating the law—or a court order; yet, he had pledged to lead this march (King was absent Sunday), and civil rights workers and ministers from all over the South were gathering at Brown's Chapel. They all wanted to march. Collins offered a typically Johnson compromise: He had conferred with Colonel Lingo and obtained a pledge that the marchers would be unharmed if they turned back a small distance down Highway 80. Lingo had even drawn a rough map, showing where the Union forces must halt. Collins handed the Confederate map to King: this way, he said, both sides would save face—and King would have a dramatic moment. King hesitated, then took the map. He sent a message to the crowd at Brown's Chapel: "I have decided it is better to die on the highway than to make a butchery of my conscience."

There was, of course, no danger of butchery. The plan worked. The marchers were halted, knelt, said a prayer and turned back. The deal became obvious to SNCC people when, Colonel Lingo, in a mild Southern doublecross, pulled his troopers back, leaving the highway to Montgomery open as King rose to lead his followers in retreat to Selma. The move was meant to embarrass King and it did. King later called the second march "the greatest confrontation for freedom" in the South. King was accused of "betraying" the movement and collaborating with the enemy.

King's fall from favor was only momentary. The diverse elements in the Union expeditionary force were united later that week by the death of the Rev. James J. Reeb, a white Unitarian minister from Boston, who died of wounds from a night-time beating at the hands of some Selma white citizens as he left a restaurant in the Negro district. But though momentary, King's disgrace was significant because it illustrated in dramatic fashion a long-standing split in the Union leadership.

It was the same split that divided the Abolitionists in the 1850's and the 1860's over whether to support Lincoln and work within the Republican party for their goals or to continue to take outside, radical social action. It is the old polarity between action and negotiation, between politics and revolution. It is the struggle between those who would work within the Establishment and those who reject the Establishment policies of compromise and consensus, and agitate for more direct solutions. This division is evident in the methodology of the civil rights movement, from the NAACP on the right to SNCC and then the black nationalist groups on the left.

MOMENTS IN A SOUTHERN TOWN

Peter de Lissovoy

Two hours after the President put his name to the civil rights bill last July, Nathaniel "Spray-man" Beech pulled open the wood-and-glass front door of the Holiday Inn restaurant in Albany, Ga., and dashed, like musical chairs, to the very first table he saw. In a near corner, a plump, brown-suited woman popped a white hand to her full mouth, but let escape: "Oh my soul and body!" To the right, a child pointed, and its mother slapped the tiny hand and whispered

Peter de Lissovoy, "Moments in a Southern Town," THE NATION, *December 21, 1964. Reprinted by permission.*

urgently. Spray-man tucked a shirt wrinkle into his black, high-pegged trousers, removed his shades, studied a water glass.

In the split moment that the door stood open, Phyllis Martin, a SNCC field worker from New York, had slipped in before him. Her skin is soft mahogany, her hair natural, a silver-black bowl about her head. She stood, dark-eyed, staring around the dining room, and I came up, after Spray-man, and stood next to her. When the wax-smiling head waitress approached, Phyllis raised her eyes a little and pointed sternly, and the waitress obediently led the way to a central table. After a moment Spray-man summoned up his long limbs, rose, breathing deep and joined us; and by the time we had ordered he was holding down a nervous grin.

But when his steak arrived, Spray-man could hardly eat it. "Jus' ain' hungry," he apologized, more to the meat than anything else. He mopped his forehead with a handkerchief, and leaned over to explain: "What it is, I was expectin' everything but this. I was expectin' this waitress to say, 'Would y'all min' fallin' back out that door you jus' come in at?' The niceness got my appetite, I guess."

At this time, Spray-man was operating a shoeshine stand—among other things, for to "spray" is to hustle—in the entrance way of the Beehive Bar in Albany's Harlem. In his few years, he has seen a great deal of this country and taken his meals from many tables; yet here was one at which he had never expected to sit—nor ever wanted to. The white man could walk as he pleased on *his* side of town, but let him watch his step in Harlem: that was the geography of Spray-man's pride. And yet, improvised from a harsh reality though his was, pride hates all boundaries, and I was hardly surprised when he told me he wanted to come along when we tried out the new law. If he was supposed to have a right, he would enjoy it—once anyway. In the car, he was full of cracks; and then, in front of the restaurant, I felt him grow tense. A sense of Southern realities deeper than his pride told him he would have to fight, go to jail perhaps, and he was ready.

But the waitress was icily gracious all during the meal. Such was the strength of the President's signature. Nobody sat at the tables directly adjacent to ours, but nobody got up and left. Everybody stared or took pains to avoid staring. Nearest to us, a family of five giggled and glanced as if galloping through some marvelous adventure.

"Reminds me of up North," said Phyllis.

"What—the stares?" I suggested.

"Yeah . . . and the music." From some hidden orifice, the tensionless, sexless music that you hear in airplanes before take-off was falling like gray rain. We decided that the next thing would be to integrate the *sounds* of places.

Spray-man gave up on his steak about halfway through. When Phyllis finished, the waitress descended upon her plates like a cheery vulture, hurrying us. Abruptly, we were weary. "You 'bout ready?" Phyllis asked. I scraped up a little more and we rose. Spray-man left the waitress an exorbitant tip.

All heads turned to watch us leave. Several white men followed us from the foyer into the parking lot. I started the motor and we rolled out into the street. Spray-man looked out the window. "Well . . ." he started; and then again, "Well . . ." Phyllis turned to him. "What's the matter? Doesn't progress make you happy?"

At about two in the morning, Sunday, July 12, Bo Riggins, manager and part-owner of the Cabin in the Pines, tapped me on the shoulder and nodded toward the door. The "Pines" is a bar and dance hall, a key club, a motel, and a restaurant all strung out beneath some scraggly Georgia pine on a lonely road just south of the Albany city limits. With some white money behind it and Bo Riggins fully at the mercy of the Dougherty County police, who are a good deal more rabid than the very rabid city cops, the night-spot had formerly been "black only." When the civil rights bill became law, I took a certain pleasure in seeing it integrated.

But, following me outside this night, Riggins was a frightened man. Sure, he conceded to me, though I had said nothing, there was the new law; but since when had *law* meant anything around here? Somebody might not know who I was. I might get cut, or shot, and where would he be then? He didn't have anything against me personally— nor my color—but he had to think of his business. Couldn't I understand? He paused; but before I could respond, he blurted, "Ah! Here the police now."

Sure enough, a county patrol car had rolled up, and two uniformed men were sauntering over.

"This boy causin' any disturbance?"

"No suh, but I'm scared they be some trouble. It's late . . ."

"You want him off yo premises?"

"He ain't did nothin', but ita be bes' I think. I don' want him aroun'. . . ."

My mouth full of the irony of it all, I was packed off quickly to the county jail, charged with trespassing and drunk-and-disorderly— the latter a simple frame and the former a matter of law. The chief deputy told me that he didn't know what the country was coming to, and he grew red in the face. He introduced me at the "tank" door ("Comin' up, another nigguh-lovuh . . ."), and I was pitched, biting my lips, into the company of a check-artist, an escapee, a dognapper, two mattress thieves, a wife-beater, a safe-cracker and assorted winos—all very white and proud of it.

The next day, in Harlem, a collection was started for my bond money; but that was going to take time. A friend of mine, a Baptist deacon and old schoolmate of Bo Riggins, paid the man a call to bawl him out and ask him to drop charges: "Now the whites startin' to do right, we can't one of us keep the wrong alive." This was simplifying matters somewhat, because it was white pressure of course that made Riggins do what he had done; but he was obstinate. Indignation spread in the black community, and was frustrated.

But the reaction among Negroes might have been anticipated. The sentiments of the white men with whom I had to live for a week in jail were a bit more complicated. Had I been arrested while participating in the standard sort of demonstration or sit-in, their response would have been straightforward: open hostility and perhaps the convening of a kangaroo court, with a beating or jail fine as sentence. But as it was, the two initial reactions were a sneering, almost moral disapproval, as if I had been arrested for public indecency, and a simple, stark astonishment that I could have been so stupid, so lacking in imagination, as to think that I could get away with "mixin' " in south Georgia.

Jail is a place for talking, like a barbershop. In a south Georgia jail, all are friends, if not kin, and the jailbirds pass their time reminiscing, berating mutual acquaintances, and reassuring one another of their deeper innocence. There were three real talkers in the cell with me: The escapee, who had sawed through the bars with a file smuggled to him in a bag of crushed ice, only to trip over a sleeping dog a few feet from the jail; one of the mattress thieves, who claimed to have stolen all manner of valuables in his career, only to suffer the irony of being framed as a $5 mattress-pincher; and the fat, hairy safe-cracker, who spent the time he wasn't talking trying to seduce the dognapper, a rosy-cheeked 18-year-old, who threw shoes and tobacco cans at him. Inevitably, my presence injected "race" into every day's bull session. I remember one fragment. The safe-cracker was off chasing his indignant prey; the unsuccessful escapee, the mattress thief and I were leaning on an improvised sofa at one end of the cell:

UE: *The new law . . .*

MT: *What new law?*

UE: *The nigguh law. Jesus! The civil rights law. It's gonna change some things, but mos' alla life down heah gonna go on jes' the same. . . .*

MT: *It ain' gonna change me. It ain' nothin' but anothuh civil wah gonna change me an' then they hafta shoot me 'fo I sit down t' able with one a them.*

UE: (turning to me): *You see how it is down heah?* (He reached over and pinched the thief's cheek.) *This heah a Southern white man. But overlook it. S'posin' it works an' we all mixed up in the hotels an' restaur'ants. So what? After a while, somebody gonna get tired a the bad feelin'—nigguhs or the white folk one—an' they'll stop comin'. This law ain't gonna mean shit along the whole run a life.*

I had to agree; after all, I was in jail because of my little bit of confidence in the new law. I didn't tell him that I wished the act had some teeth in it; I didn't tell him that I wanted federal armies to make it work, that I wanted stronger, wider legislation in the future. As a matter of fact, there were a whole lot of banners I wasn't waiving. I was doing what in a black man would be called "Tomming"—and I was glad I knew how. I wasn't going to get my head broken trying to reform men that nobody—from Jesus to Johnson—could have swayed.

Later in the week, a tall, solid fellow with snakes inked up and down his arms was led in to "sober up." He never got the chance—or perhaps it was a ruse from the start. One of the deputies took a good look at his face and build and promised him a pint of whiskey if he would knock me down a few times. But the others were not much for it; they had gotten used to me and, if they weren't about to lay hands on him in my defense, they weren't going to encourage him either. Most of the fun for him would have been in the applause, so I got off with buying him a pint. Liquor can always be had for a price on the Dougherty County Jail black market, though you can't be too sure of your brand. It came in a large, waxed dixie cup. He got properly loaded then, and it was necessary to lose heavily at blackjack to keep him peaceful.

In the end, most of the jailbirds came to pity me. "Boy, that ol' judge gonna hang yo' ass. This south *Georgia,* boy, you can't get away with things like maybe in New York. . . ." And when it came to the pinch, it was the law that was the enemy. They kidded me almost warmly when I was called out for the commitment hearing that Attorney C. B. King had arranged. " 'Lessen that nigguh lawyer a yours do some mighty fine talkin', we gonna see you back 'fo long. Save you a place in the game."

The judge dismissed both charges. Bo Riggins couldn't remember anyone who had seen me "drunk and disorderly" and I had several witnesses to swear that I was neither. The judge did not seem to have heard of the civil rights law—or at least considered it irrelevant and inapplicable to the trespassing charge; but he had to dismiss it when Riggins admitted that he never actually asked me to leave, but rather just complied with the apparent wishes of the police in the matter.

It seemed to have gone amazingly smoothly. Outside, Attorney King explained why: An election was imminent. My case was virtually unknown in the white community; the newspapers had made nothing out of it. So the judge could gain nothing by sending me back to jail, and he just might catch a few black votes if he did the "nigguh lawyer" a favor. I wondered if the jailbirds would figure it out. A little later I sent them some ice cream. I was going back to the "Pines" and I didn't know but that I would be seeing them again.

Early on a Saturday afternoon some days later, a dark, gawky boy in jeans and sport shirt was rigging a microphone and amplifier in the barren front yard of an unpainted clapboard house in Harlem. He placed two boxes before the mike, sat upon one, lowered the silver head of the device to the level of his mouth, and then produced a guitar which he picked idly until a great, black woman in pink flowing robes and blue-cloth crown poured suddenly from the house porch and heaved down beside him. She took the guitar and commenced tuning it, hummed and tuned, hummed and tuned, until a crowd had started. And then she sang.

Her voice was weary but warm, thick but expressive, a blues voice. She sang religious songs and old ballads and songs made popular by the Movement. Her favorite, the one she repeated most often during the day and evening, was a talking blues that roved around the chorus: "Oh, there was a death in Dallas that day. . . ." It was not so much ominous or foreboding as just terribly regretful, a sighing, head-shaking exclamation of loss. Like each of her songs, the Kennedy-blues worked into a sermon, the substance of which was invariably "trust in the Lord, who giveth and taketh away, for they ain't nothin' else trustworthy" (with a few minor forays into such areas as the evil inherent in woman). Then she passed the hat.

The crowd of listeners was always large. I was in Harlem that day and stayed until nearly midnight, listening to her. At about eight in the evening, the size of her audience reached its peak, spilling over a curbstone in one direction, backing into a gas station in another. There were sharecroppers, factory workers, housewives; dancing, scurrying children; the celebrated and gently lunatic old woman who checks the doors and windows of all the business establishments in Harlem shortly after midnight every night and reports to the cop on the beat any unusual discoveries, happy tonight, shouting, grinning; and the occasional hipster, sheepish at being in this crowd, at wanting to be there, an eye cocked for the running mate who would most surely call sarcastically, "Hey baby, got 'ligion? Go on now—get happy!" About 8:30, a late-model Chevrolet rolled to a halt at the edge of the gathering, and three young white men got out, slamming doors, and moved into the singing crowd.

One of them immediately engaged a Negro youth in nervous, eyes-flicking conversation. The second, a tall and rake-thin fellow, with long, narrow sideburns, began, modestly, to enjoy himself, clapping and singing in perfect rhythm, his face glowing slightly. The third was drunk. For minutes, he seemed uncertain about what was happening or where he was; then, when things began to clear, he started singing and clapping too—or rather shouting hoarsely and beating his hands together at arbitrary and irregular intervals. At this display, his tall friend was shocked to the point of fright. He tried to get the drunk to the car, gave it up when he grew red and loud and stiffly resistant, and then simply moved away, attempting to dissociate himself.

For a long time, the drunken white boy was merely a tiny shallows in a great, fast river, really offensive only to the thinning few around him. Then, suddenly, as if responding to some vision or internal force, he strode violently forward and demanded the microphone from the ironically—and tolerantly—smiling lady preacher, to ask: "What y'all starin' at us fo'? We white—sho. But that ain' no reason to stare. The bill a rights done been pass'! We got a right. We gonna stay, an I'm gonna as' this kin' lady to sing *This lil' light a mine* fo' the white people a Albany, G-A, who need it, God knows. . . ."

The drunk's two friends were visibly mortified. Not at what he had said, but at his having drawn unnecessary and additional attention to their presence. The first intensified his dialogue with the Negro youth as if to shut out the awful reality of what had just happened. In a moment, the taller, side-burned white man had seized his swaying buddy around the shoulders and bundled him, yelling and protesting, off to their car. The talker trotted to catch up. The car roared and the tall white waved an apologetic and helpless goodby from the driver's wheel. The drunk slumped in the seat, whooping: "Hooray fo' the nigguhs! Hoo-hoo-hooray fo' the nigguhs!"

But already the singer had taken up where she had left off. Nobody much bothered to hear the drunk's rantings; it was a matter of discipline, a very old discipline.

I was shooting nine-ball in a Harlem poolroom. It was dinner time, family time, on a Friday night in America, and the room was filled with people who had no better place to go. I powdered my hands and sank the winning ball in a combination with the two—and looked up to see five white hustlers appear in the doorway like apparitions out of the foggy night, combing their hair, wiping the water from their foreheads.

"Who wants to shoot?" drawled the skinniest. His voice cracked at the end, and so he repeated the question with force. It sounded belligerent, so he smiled, stupidly.

Eyes blinked. Bodies stirred. Butterball, who had been napping in the corner, rose up and stretched his bulk. He settled his red baseball cap over his eyes. "You got any money, Whitey?" When the white boy flashed a roll, I stepped back from my table. Butter' picked up a stick and called for the houseman to rack.

"What's your name, Whitey?"

For a moment, the white fellow wondered how to answer this question most forcefully, and then he simply let it out, a short nasal squeak. Butter' looked down the row of tables: "Hey, Rut! You hear that? Go on look up his daddy in the phone book, fin' out how much coin he got. I'm gonna take all Whitey's money tonight!" He leaned back on the heels of his tennis shoes and laughed with all his weight.

"No you ain't!" Rut, just as heavy as Butter' and infinitely meaner in the eyes, was heaving down the aisle. "Whitey got way more money'n you can have by y'self, big as you *is*." He stood before the rest of the white team. "Which one a you boys gonna put a ten down on this first game?"

On a Friday night, the poolroom is always crowded by eight. Tonight, when word got around what was happening, old men and young poured in until the house had to close its doors, so that the players might have space to shoot. It looked like the Olympic games; and, in a sense, it was.

Butter' and Whitey were a good match. They played past midnight, and, as it turned out, Butter' lost a little. On other tables, "Schoolboy" Terry and Peter "Rabbit" Harris skinned a blond-headed boy whose nickname really *was* "Whitey," and a laconic, bespectacled, middle-aged hustler with a beautiful if inaccurate stroke. Side bets went round and round. On the whole, the whites lost money, but not nearly as much as would be claimed the next day. When it was all over, Butter', gentleman that he is, took the crew around the corner for drinks. "How 'bout it Whitey?" he asked. "We gonna shoot a little over your side tomorrow?"

"Sure."

"Won't be no shit?"

"Not if you bring your money."

For weeks, the game ran on—the white hustlers appearing in Harlem, black hustlers visiting the white poolrooms. "It's the new law," said Butter'. "Integration always starts over sport."

But not every small-town hustler can shoot nine-ball for $5 and $10 a game. Most make their little money disillusioning country boys, in from the dim lights and hacked tables of south Georgia's tinier hamlets, or the Albany workingmen, tanked up and sure that they are the greatest. "Integrated pool" was only for the best, who could win, or lose big money at big matches. The best soon knew one another and were wary; the novelty wore off and the poolrooms, white and black, returned to their normal, and tedious, business.

It is November. The man who signed a bill and integrated the poolrooms is retained in power. I wonder if Butter' voted. Or Sprayman, taking time off from shining shoes.

That first night, after the Holiday Inn, he had been confused; the experience had not had any immediate meanings. But a few hours later, outside a Negro bar in south Albany, called the Playhouse, he had nodded at the crowded doorway: "Lookit all them Negroes, don't know nothin' bout what's happened yet."

A few minutes and a few beers later, he was checking the hand of a girl who was about to drop a dime in the juke box. He carried a chair to the center of the floor, climbed atop it, shouted the crowd silent and the dancing to a halt, and related, in a loud, laughing voice, the events over on the white side. A few applauded. Most listened politely for a minute or two, but soon conversation started again, and Spray-man was struggling against an indifferent current. He looked over at me, apologetically I felt. I waved with great emotion for him to forget it, but he had his hackles up and went on.

A young man with ironic eyes nudged me. "It's fine," he said. "Fine, if you got plenty money to eat at the Holiday Inn. Me, all I got's this one little quarter, an' I ain't expectin' nothin' soon. Tell y' frien' I'm sorry, but I gotta put it in the piccolo. I'm gonna have me 25¢ worth a soun', an' no history. . . ."

When the music started, Spray-man glanced around angrily. But, when it was clear he was overcome; drowned in sound, he grinned reluctantly, then wide. He shrugged, stepped across the floor to replace the chair and, in a moment was dancing.

☐ BLACK POWER

At about the same time—early 1965—that Martin Luther King, Jr. was leading marches in Selma, Alabama, Malcolm X was shot to death as he addressed a black nationalist meeting in New York.

Malcolm X represented a different view of the American racial problem, one that emphasized the reasons why blacks should reject American society, not aspire toward integration into it; one that— and this distinction is essential—addressed its arguments primarily to blacks rather than to whites.

Where once the term that described the aspirations of Negroes in America had been integration or civil rights, the new phrase gaining increased currency—and increasingly ominous connotations—was black power. It was ominous partly because it was ambiguous. While to a member of the older generation of Negro leadership it could mean organization for political effectiveness, to a young militant it could mean arming against subjugation by a white society.

One of the persons most closely associated with the concept of black power is Stokely Carmichael, formerly president of the Student Nonviolent Coordinating Committee (SNCC), who, in the essay *What We Want,* expresses the demand of Negroes for control of their movement.

What We Want is an essay, a discussion of the meaning of black power. Eldridge Cleaver's *Letter from Jail* is another kind of essay, this one describing a black man's first encounter with armed militants of his own race. The scene which he recounts, the confrontation outside of the *Ramparts* office in San Francisco, freezes an image of one moment in the age of protest, as resistance skirts closest to rebellion and armed black men face armed white policemen in the streets of an American city.

THE PILGRIMAGE OF MALCOLM X

I. F. Stone

Malcolm X was born into Black Nationalism. His father was a follower of Marcus Garvey, the West Indian who launched a "Back to Africa" movement in the Twenties. Malcolm's first clash with white men took place when his mother was pregnant with him; a mob of Klansmen in Omaha, Nebraska, waving shotguns and rifles, warned her one night to move out of town because her husband was spreading trouble among the "good" Negroes with Garvey's teachings. One of his earliest memories was of seeing their home burned down in Lansing, Michigan, in 1929, because the Black Legion, a white Fascist organization, considered his father an "uppity" Negro. The body of his father, a tall, powerful black man from Georgia, soon afterwards was found literally cut to pieces in one of those mysterious accidents that often veil a racial killing.

His mother was a West Indian who looked like a white woman. Her unknown father was white. She slowly went to pieces mentally under the burden of raising eight children. When the family was broken up, Malcolm was sent to a detention home, from which he attended a white school. He must have been a bright and attractive lad, for he was at the top of his class and was elected class president in the seventh grade. Many years later, in a speech on the Black Revolution which is included in the collection, *Malcolm X Speaks,* he was able to boast bitterly, "I grew up with white people. I was integrated before they even invented the word." The reason for the bitterness was an incident that changed his life. His English teacher told him he ought to begin thinking about his career. Malcolm said he would like to be a lawyer. His teacher suggested carpentry instead. "We all here like you, you know that," the teacher said, "but you've got to be realistic about being a nigger."

Malcolm X left Lansing deeply alienated and in the slums of Boston and New York he became a "hustler," selling numbers, women, and dope. "All of us," he says in his *Autobiography* of his friends in the human jungle, "who might have probed space or cured cancer or built industries, were instead black victims of the white man's American social system." Insofar as he was concerned, this was no exaggeration. He was an extraordinary man. Had he been wholly white, instead of irretrievably "Negro" by American standards, he might easily have become a leader of the bar. In the underworld he went from marijuana to cocaine. To meet the cost he took up burglary. He was arrested with a white mistress who had become his look-out woman. In February, 1946, not quite twenty-one, he was sentenced to ten years in prison in Massachusetts. The heavy sentence reflected the revulsion created in the judge by the discovery that Malcolm had made a white woman his "love slave." In prison, he went on nutmeg, reefers, Nembutal, and benzedrine in a desperate effort to replace the drugs. He was a vicious prisoner, often in solitary. The other prisoners nicknamed him "Satan." But the prison had an unusually well stocked library to which he was introduced by a fellow prisoner, an old-time burglar named Bimbi. Through him, Malcolm first encountered Thoreau. Prison became his university; there also he was converted to the Nation of Islam, the sect the press calls Black Muslims.

The important word here is conversion. To understand Malcolm's experience, one must go to the literature of conversion. "Were we writing the history of the mind from the purely natural history point of view," William James concluded in his *Varieties of Religious Experience,* "we would still have to write down man's liability to sudden and complete conversion as one of his most curious peculiarities." The convert's sense of being born anew, the sudden change from despair to elation, bears an obvious resemblance to the manic-depressive cycle, except that the change in the personality is often permanent. But those who experience it must first—to borrow Gospel language—be brought low. James quotes the theological maxim, "Man's extremity is God's opportunity." It is only out of the depths that men on occasion experience this phenomenon of renewal. The success of the Black Muslims in converting and rehabilitating criminals and dope addicts like Malcolm X recalls the mighty phrases James quotes from Luther. "God," he preached, "is the God . . . of those that are brought even to nothing . . . and his nature is . . . to save the very desperate and damned." Malcolm had been brought to nothing, he was one of those very desperate and damned when he was "saved" by Elijah Muhammad, the self-proclaimed Messenger of Allah to the lost Black Nation of that imaginary Islam he preaches.

The tendency is to dismiss Elijah Muhammad's weird doctrine as another example of the superstitions, old and new, that thrive in the Negro ghetto. It is not really any more absurd than the Virgin Birth or the Sacrifice of Isaac. The rational absurdity does not detract from the psychic therapy. Indeed the therapy may lie in the absurdity. Converts to any creed talk of the joy in complete surrender; a rape of the mind occurs. *"Credo quia absurdum,"* Tertullian, the first really cultivated apologist for Christianity, is said to have exulted, "I believe because it *is* absurd." Tertullian was himself a convert. Black Nationalists may even claim him as an African, for his home was Carthage.

There is a special reason for the efficacy of the Black Muslims in reaching the Negro damned. The sickness of the Negro in America is that he has been made to feel a nigger; the genocide is psychic. The Negro must rid himself of this feeling if he is to stand erect again. He can do so in two ways. He can change the outer world of white supremacy, or he can change his inner world by "conversion." The teachings of the Black Muslims may be fantastic but they are superbly suited to the task of shaking off the feeling of nigger-ness. Elijah Muhammad teaches that the original man was black, that Caucasians are "white devils" created almost 6,000 years ago by a black genius named Yakub. He bleached a number of blacks by a process of mutation into pale-faced blue-eyed devils in order to test the mettle of the Black Nation. This inferior breed has ruled by deviltry but their time will soon be up, at the end of the sixth millennium, which may be by 1970 or thereabouts. To explain the white man as a devil is, as Malcolm X says in the *Autobiography,* to strike "a nerve center in the American black man" for "when he thinks about his own life, he is going to see where, to him personally, the white man sure has acted like a devil." To see the white man this way is, in Gospel imagery, to cast out the devil. With him go his values, as he has impressed them on the Black Man, above all the inner feeling of being a nigger. To lose that feeling is to be fully emancipated. For the poor Negro no drug could be a stronger opiate than this black religion.

With rejection of the white man's values goes rejection of the white man's God. "We're worshipping a Jesus," Malcolm protested in one of his sermons after he became a Black Muslim Minister, "who doesn't even *look* like us." The white man, he declared, "has brainwashed us black people to fasten our gaze upon a blond-haired, blue-eyed Jesus." This Black Muslim doctrine may seem a blasphemous joke until one makes the effort to imagine how whites would feel if taught to worship a black God with thick African lips. Men prefer to create a God in their own image. "The Ethiopians," one of the pre-Socratic Greek philosophers observed a half millennium before Christ, "assert that their gods are snub-nosed and black" while the "Nordic" Thracians said theirs were "blue-eyed and red-haired." When Marcus Garvey, the first apostle of Pan-Africanism, toured Africa, urging expulsion of the white man, he called for a Negro religion with a Negro Christ. Just as Malcolm Little, in accordance with Black Muslim practice, rejected his "slave name" and became Malcolm X, so Malcolm X, son of a Baptist preacher, rejected Christianity as a slave religion. His teacher, Elijah Muhammad, did not have to read Nietzsche to discover that Christianity was admirably suited to make Rome's slaves submissive. In our ante-bellum South the value of Christian teaching in making slaves tractable was widely recognized even by slaveholders themselves agnostic. The Negro converted to Christianity was cut off from the disturbing memory of his own gods and of his lost freedom, and reconciled to his lot in the white man's chains. Here again the primitivistic fantasies of the Black Muslims unerringly focus on a crucial point. It is in the Christian mission that what Malcolm X called the "brainwashing" of the blacks began.

Racism and nationalism are poisons. Sometimes a poison may be prescribed as a medicine, and Negroes have found in racism a way to restore their self-respect. But black racism is still racism, with all its primitive irrationality and danger. There are passages in the *Autobiography* in which Malcolm, recounting some of his Black Muslim sermons, sounds like a Southern white supremacist in reverse, vibrating with anger and sexual obsession over the horrors of race pollution. There is the same preoccupation with rape, the same revulsion about mixed breeds. "Why," he cried out, "the white man's raping of the black race's woman began right on those slave ships!" A psychoanalyst might see in his fury the feeling of rejection by the race of his white grandfather. A biologist might see in the achievements of this tall sandy-complexioned Negro—his friends called him "Red"—an example of the possibilities of successful racial mixture. But Malcolm's feelings on the subject were as outraged as those of a Daughter of the Confederacy. He returned revulsion for revulsion and hate for hate. He named his first child, a daughter,

Attilah, and explained that he named her for the Hun who sacked Rome.

But hidden under the surface of the Black Nationalist creed to which he was won there lay a peculiar anti-Negroism. The true nationalist loves his people and their peculiarities; he wants to preserve them; he is filled with filial piety. But there is in Elijah Muhammad's Black Muslim creed none of the love for the Negro one finds in W.E.B. du Bois; or of that yearning for the ancestral Africa which obsessed Garvey. Elijah Muhammad—who himself looks more Chinese than Negro—teaches his people that they are Asians, not Africans; that their original tongue is Arabic. He turns his people into middle-class Americans. Their clothes are conservative, almost Ivy League. Their religious services eschew that rich antiphony between preacher and congregation which one finds in Negro churches. The Nigerian, E. U. Essien-Udom, whose *Black Nationalism* is the best book on the Black Muslims, was struck by their middle-class attitudes and coldness to Africa and African ways. In Black Muslim homes, when jazz was played, he writes that he was "often tempted to tap his feet to the tune of jazz" but was inhibited because his Black Muslim hosts "listened to it without ostensible response to the rhythm." In their own way the Black Muslims are as much in flight from Negritude as was Booker T. Washington. Indeed Elijah Muhammad's stress on Negro private business and his hostility to trade unionism in his own dealings with Negroes are very much in the Booker T. Washington pattern. The virtues of bourgeois America are what Elijah·Muhammad seeks to recreate in his separate Black Nation. This is the banal reality which lies behind all his hocus-pocus about the Koran, and here lie the roots of his split with Malcolm X.

For Elijah Muhammad practices separation not only from American life but from the American Negro community, and from its concrete struggles for racial justice. Malcolm X was drawn more and more to engagement in that struggle. In the midst of describing in the *Autobiography* his happy and successful years as a Black Muslim organizer, Malcolm X says:

If I harbored any personal disappointment, whatsoever, it was that privately I was convinced that our Nation of Islam could be an even greater force in the American black man's overall struggle—if we engaged in more *action*. By that I mean I thought privately that we should have amended or relaxed, our general non-engagement policy. I felt that, wherever black people committed themselves, in the Little Rocks and Birminghams and other places, militantly disciplined Muslims should also be there—for all the world to see, and respect and discuss. It could be heard increasingly in the Negro communities: "Those Muslims *talk* tough, but they never *do* anything, unless somebody bothers Muslims." (Italics in original.)

This alone was bound to divide the prophet and disciple. But there were also personal factors. Elijah Muhammad won Malcolm's devotion by his kindness in corresponding with the young convict when Malcolm was still in prison. But Malcolm's intellectual horizons were already far wider than those of the rather narrow, ill-educated, and suspicious Messenger of Allah. In the prison library Malcolm X was finding substantiation for the Black Muslim creed in *Paradise Lost* and in Herodotus; this passionate curiosity and voracious reading were bound to make him outgrow Elijah's dream-book theology. On the one side envy and on the other disillusion were to drive the two men apart. The crowds drawn by Malcolm and his very organizing success made Elijah Muhammad and his family jealous. On the other hand, Malcolm, who had kept the sect's vows of chastity, was shocked when former secretaries of Elijah Muhammad filed paternity suits against the prophet. Malcolm had nothing but a small salary and the house the sect had provided for him. Elijah Muhammad's cars (two Cadillacs and a Lincoln Continental), his $200 pin-striped banker-style suits, his elegantly furnished 18-room house in one of the better sections of Chicago's Hyde Park, began to make a sour impression on Malcolm. The hierarchy lives well in practically all religions, and their worldly affluence fosters schism. Malcolm was too big, too smart, too able, to fit into the confines of this little sect and remain submissive to its family oligarchy. He began to open up a larger world, and this endangered Elijah Muhammad's hold on the little band of unsophisticated faithful he had recruited.

Muhammad Speaks, the weekly organ of the Black Muslims, had begun to play down Malcolm's activities. The break came over Malcolm's comment on Kennedy's assassination. Within hours after the President's killing, Elijah Muhammad sent out a directive ordering the cult's ministers to make no comment on the murder. Malcolm, speaking at Manhattan Center a few days afterward, was asked in the question period what he thought of the assassination. He answered that it was a case of "the chickens coming home to roost." Malcolm explains in the *Autobiography,* "I said that the hate in white men had not stopped with the killing of defenseless black people but . . .

finally had struck down the President." He complains that "some of the world's most important personages were saying in various ways, and in far stronger ways than I did, that America's climate of hate had been responsible for the President's death. But when Malcolm X said the same thing it was ominous." Elijah Muhammad called him in. "That was a very bad statement," he said. "The country loved this man." He ordered Malcolm silenced for ninety days so that the Black Muslims could be "disassociated from the blunder." Malcolm agreed and submitted. But three days later he heard that a Mosque official was suggesting his own assassination. Soon after, another Black Muslim told him of a plan to wire his car so that it would explode when he turned the ignition key. Malcolm decided to build a Muslim Mosque of his own, and open its doors to black men of all faiths for common action. To prepare himself he decided to make the pilgrimage to Mecca.

This visit to Mecca was a turning-point for Malcolm. His warm reception in the Arabic world, the sight of white men in equal fraternity with black and brown, marked a second conversion in his life. "For the past week," Malcolm wrote home, "I have been utterly speechless and spellbound by the graciousness I see displayed all around me by people *of all colors.*" The italics were his. The man who made the seven circuits around the Ka'ba and drank the waters of Zem-Zem emerged from his pligrimage no longer a racist or a Black Muslim. He took the title of El Hajj earned by his visit to Mecca and called himself henceforth El-Hajj Malik El-Shabazz. He turned Muslim in the true sense of the word. How indelibly he also remained an American go-getter is deliciously reflected in a passage of the *Autobiography* where he says that while in Mecca:

I saw that Islam's conversions around the world could double and triple if the colorfulness and the true spiritualness of the Hajj pilgrimage were properly advertised and communicated to the outside world. I saw that the Arabs are poor at understanding the psychology of non-Arabs and the importance of public relations. The Arabs said "Inshah Allah" (God willing)—then they waited for converts, but I knew that with improved public relations methods the new converts turning to Allah could be turned into millions.

He had become a Hajj, but remained in some ways a Babbitt, the salesman, archetype of our American society. A creed was something to *sell*. Allah, the Merciful, needed better merchandising.

Malcolm returned from abroad May 21, 1964. Several attempts

were made on his life. On February 21, 1965, he was killed by gunmen when he got up to speak at a meeting in New York's Audubon Ballroom. He was not quite forty when he died. The most revealing tribute paid him was the complaint by Elijah Muhammad after Malcolm was killed. "He came back preaching that we should not hate the enemy . . . He was a star who went astray." What nobler way to go astray? In Africa and in America there was almost unanimous recognition that the Negro race had lost a gifted son; only the then head of the U. S. Information Agency, Carl Rowan, immortalized himself with a monumental Uncle Tomism. "All this about an ex-convict, ex-dope peddler who became a racial fanatic," was Rowan's obtuse and ugly comment; it ranks with his discovery, as USIA Director, of what he called the public's "right *not* to know."

From tape-recorded conversations, a Negro writer, Alex Haley, put together the *Autobiography;* he did his job with sensitivity and with devotion. Here one may read, in the agony of this brilliant Negro's self-creation, the agony of an entire people in their search for identity. But more fully to understand this remarkable man, one must turn to *Malcolm X Speaks,* which supplements the *Autobiography.* All but one of the speeches were made in those last eight tumultuous months of his life after his break with the Black Muslims when he was seeking a new path. In their pages one can begin to understand his power as a speaker and to see, more clearly than in the *Autobiography,* the political legacy he left his people in its struggle for full emancipation.

Over and over again in simple imagery, savagely uncompromising, he drove home the real truth about the Negro's position in America. It may not be pleasant but it must be faced. "Those Hunkies that just got off the boat," he said in one of his favorite comparisons, "they're already Americans. Polacks are already Americans; the Italian refugees are already Americans. Everything that comes out of Europe, every blue-eyed thing, is already an American. And as long as you and I have been over here, we aren't Americans yet. They don't have to pass civil rights legislation to make a Polack an American." In a favorite metaphor, he said, "I'm not going to sit at your table and watch you eat, with nothing on my plate, and call myself a diner. Sitting at the table doesn't make you a diner, unless you eat some of what's on the plate. Being here in America doesn't make you an American. Being born here in America doesn't make you an American." He often said, "Don't be shocked when I say that I was in prison. You're still in prison. That's what America means—prison." Who can deny that this is true for the black man? No matter how high he rises, he never loses consciousness of the invisible bars which hem him in. "We didn't land on Plymouth Rock," Malcolm was fond of saying. "It landed on us."

He counselled violence but he defended this as an answer to white violence. "If they make the Klan non-violent," he said over and over again, "I'll be non-violent." In another speech he said, "If violence is wrong in America, violence is wrong abroad. If it is wrong to be violent defending black women and black children and babies and black men, then it is wrong for America to draft us and make us violent abroad in defense of her." He taunted his people in the same speech that "As long as the white man sent you to Korea, you bled . . . You bleed for white people, but when it comes to seeing your own churches being bombed and little black girls murdered, you haven't any blood." In a speech he made about the brutal beating of Fannie Lou Hamer of Mississippi, he said of the white man, "If he only understands the language of a rifle, get a rifle. If he only understands the language of a rope, get a rope. But don't waste time talking the wrong language to a man if you really want to communicate with him." In preaching Pan-Africanism, he reached down into the aching roots of Negro self-hatred as few men have ever done. "You can't hate Africa and not hate yourself," he said in one speech. "This is what the white man knows. So they make you and me hate our African identity . . . We hated our heads, we hated the shape of our nose, we wanted one of those long dove-like noses, you know; we hated the color of our skin, hated the blood of Africa that was in our veins. And in hating our features and our skin and our blood, we had to end up hating ourselves." No man has better expressed his people's trapped anguish.

Malcolm's most important message to his people is muted in the *Autobiography,* perhaps because Alex Haley, its writer, is politically conventional, but it comes out sharply in *Malcolm X Speaks* which was edited and published by a group of Trotskyists. This was the idea that while the Negro is a minority in this country, he is part of a majority if he thinks of common action with the rest of the world's colored peoples. "The first thing the American power structure doesn't want any Negroes to start," he says in the *Autobiography,* "is thinking internationally." In a speech at Ibadan University in Nigeria, he relates in the *Autobiography,* he urged the Africans to bring the

American Negro's plight before the United Nations: "I said that just as the American Jew is in political, cultural, and economic harmony with world Jewry, I was convinced that it was time for all Afro-Americans to join the world's Pan-Africanists." Malcolm persuaded the Organization of African Unity at its Cairo conference to pass a resolution saying that discrimination against Negroes in the United States was "a matter of deep concern" to the Africans, and *The New York Times* in August 1964 reported that the State and Justice Departments had begun "to take an interest in Malcolm's campaign because it might create 'a touchy problem' for the U.S. if raised at the UN." In the UN debate over U.S. intervention to save white lives in the Congo, African delegates at the UN for the first time accused the U.S. of being indifferent to similar atrocities against blacks in Mississippi. This is what Malcolm wanted when he spoke of putting the Negro struggle in a world context.

An Italian writer, Vittorio Lanternari, published a remarkable book five years ago, which appeared here in 1963 as *The Religions of the Oppressed: A Study of Modern Messianic Cults*. It suggests that wherever white men have driven out or subdued colored men, whether in the case of the American Indians, or in Africa, or with the Maoris in New Zealand, as with the Tai-Pings in China and the Cao Dai in Vietnam or among the uprooted blacks and harried Indians in the Caribbean and Latin America, Messianic cults have arisen, rejecting white men's values and seeking the restoration of shattered cultural identities as the first step toward political freedom. He did not include in his survey the cults which thrive in our Negro ghettoes though they are of the same character. One striking common bond among all these sects of the oppressed has been their effort to free their people from drinking the white man's "firewater" or (in China) smoking his opium. To see the Black Muslims and Malcolm's life in this perspective is to begin to understand the psychic havoc wrought around the world by white imperialism in the centuries since America was discovered and Afro-Asia opened up to white penetration. There are few places on earth where whites have not grown rich robbing the colored races. It was Malcolm's great contribution to help make us all aware of this.

His assassination was a loss to the country as well as to his race. These two books will have a permanent place in the literature of the Afro-American struggle. It is tantalizing to speculate on what he might have become had he lived. What makes his life so moving a story was his capacity to learn and grow. New disillusions, and a richer view of the human condition, lay ahead for the man who could say, as he did in one of his last speeches, when discussing the first Bandung conference, "once they excluded the white man, they found they could get together." Since then India and Pakistan, Singapore and Malaysia, the rebellion against the Arabs in Zanzibar and the splits in Black Africa itself have demonstrated that fratricide does not end with the eviction of the white devil. Various Left sects, Maoist and Trotskyist and Communist, sought to recruit him, but he was trying to build a movement of his own. He was shopping around for new political ideas. He was also becoming active in the South instead of merely talking about a Dixie Mau-Mau from the relative safety of Harlem. I believe there was in him a readiness painfully to find and face new truths which might have made him one of the great Negroes, and Americans, of our time.

WHAT WE WANT

Stokely Carmichael

One of the tragedies of the struggle against racism is that up to now there has been no national organization which could speak to the growing militancy of young black people in the urban ghetto. There has been only a civil rights movement, whose tone of voice was adapted to an audience of liberal whites. It served as a sort of buffer zone between them and angry young blacks. None of its so-called leaders could go into a rioting community and be listened to. In a sense, I blame ourselves—together with the mass media—for what has happened in Watts, Harlem, Chicago, Cleveland, Omaha. Each time the people in those cities saw Martin Luther King get slapped, they became angry; when they saw four little black girls bombed to death, they were angrier; and when nothing happened, they were steaming. We had nothing to offer that they could see, except to go out and be beaten again. We helped to build their frustration.

Reprinted with permission of the Student Nonviolent Coordinating Committee. Published in THE NEW YORK REVIEW OF BOOKS, *September 22, 1966.*

For too many years, black Americans marched and had their heads broken and got shot. They were saying to the country, "Look, you guys are supposed to be nice guys and we are only going to do what we are supposed to do—why do you beat us up, why don't you straighten yourselves out?" After years of this, we are at almost the same point—because we demonstrated from a position of weakness. We cannot be expected any longer to march and have our heads broken in order to say to whites: come on, you're nice guys. For you are not nice guys. We have found you out.

An organization which claims to speak for the needs of a community—as does the Student Nonviolent Coordinating Committee— must speak in the tone of that community, not as somebody else's buffer zone. This is the significance of black power as a slogan. For once, black people are going to use the words they want to use— not just the words whites want to hear. And they will do this no matter how often the press tries to stop the use of the slogan by equating it with racism or separatism.

An organization which claims to be working for the needs of a community—as SNCC does—must work to provide that community with a position of strength from which to make its voice heard. This is the significance of black power beyond the slogan.

Black power can be clearly defined for those who do not attach the fears of white America to their questions about it. We should begin with the basic fact that black Americans have two problems: they are poor and they are black. All other problems arise from this two-sided reality: lack of education, the so-called apathy of black men. Any program to end racism must address itself to that double reality.

Almost from its beginning, SNCC sought to address itself to both conditions with a program aimed at winning political power for impoverished Southern blacks. We had to begin with politics because black Americans are a propertyless people in a country where property is valued above all. We had to work for power, because this country does not function by morality, love, and nonviolence, but by power. Thus we determined to win political power, with the idea of moving on from there into activity that would have economic effects. With power, the masses could *make or participate in making* the decisions which govern their destinies, and thus create basic change in their day-to-day lives.

But if political power seemed to be the key to self-determination, it was also obvious that the key had been thrown down a deep well many years earlier. Disenfranchisement, maintained by racist terror, makes it impossible to talk about organizing for political power in 1960. The right to vote had to be won, and SNCC workers devoted their energies to this from 1961 to 1965. They set up voter registration drives in the Deep South. They created pressure for the vote by holding mock elections in Mississippi in 1963 and by helping to establish the Mississippi Freedom Democratic Party (MFDP) in 1964. That struggle was eased, though not won, with the passage of the 1965 Voting Rights Act. SNCC workers could then address themselves to the question: "Who can we vote for, to have our needs met—how do we make our vote meaningful?"

SNCC had already gone to Atlantic City for recognition of the Mississippi Freedom Democratic Party by the Democratic convention and been rejected; it had gone with the MFDP to Washington for recognition by Congress and been rejected. In Arkansas, SNCC helped thirty Negroes to run for School Board elections; all but one were defeated, and there was evidence of fraud and intimidation sufficient to cause their defeat. In Atlanta, Julian Bond ran for the state legislature and was elected—twice—and unseated—twice. In several states, black farmers ran in elections for agricultural committees which make crucial decisions concerning land use, loans, etc. Although they won places on a number of committees, they never gained the majorities needed to control them.

All of the efforts were attempts to win black power. Then, in Alabama, the opportunity came to see how blacks could be organized on an independent party basis. An unusual Alabama law provides that any group of citizens can nominate candidates for county office and, if they win 20 per cent of the vote, may be recognized as a county political party. The same then applies on a state level. SNCC went to organize in several counties such as Lowndes, where black people—who form 80 per cent of the population and have an average annual income of $943—felt they could accomplish nothing within the framework of the Alabama Democratic Party because the qualifying fee for this year's elections was raised from $50 to $500 in order to prevent most Negroes from becoming candidates. On May 3, five new county "freedom organizations" convened and nominated candidates for the offices of sheriff, tax assessor, members of the school boards. These men and women are up for election in November—if they live until then. Their ballot symbol is the black panther: a bold, beautiful animal, representing the strength and dignity of black demands today. A man needs a black panther on his side when he and his family must endure—as hundreds of Alabamians have endured —loss of job, eviction, starvation, and sometimes death, for political activity. He may also need a gun and SNCC reaffirms the right of black men everywhere to defend themselves when threatened or attacked. As for initiating the use of violence, we hope that such programs as ours will make that unnecessary; but it is not for us to tell black communities whether they can or cannot use any particular form of action to resolve their problems. Responsibility for the use of violence by black men, whether in self-defense or initiated by them, lies with the white community.

This is the specific historical experience from which SNCC's call for "black power" emerged on the Mississippi march last July. But the concept of "black power" is not a recent or isolated phenomenon: It has grown out of the ferment of agitation and activity by different people and organizations in many black communities over the years. Our last year of work in Alabama added a new concrete possibility. In Lowndes County, for example, black power will mean that if a Negro is elected sheriff, he can end police brutality. If a black man is elected tax assessor, he can collect and channel funds for the building of better roads and schools serving black people—thus advancing the move from political power into the economic arena. In such areas as Lowndes, where black men have a majority, they will attempt to use it to exercise control. Where Negroes lack a majority, black power means proper representation and sharing of control. It means the creation of power bases from which black people can work to change statewide or nationwide patterns of oppression through pressure from strength—instead of weakness. Politically, black power means what it has always meant to SNCC: the coming-together of black people to elect representatives and *to force those representatives to speak to their needs*. It does not mean merely putting black faces into office. A man or woman who is black and from the slums cannot be automatically expected to speak to the needs of black people. Most of the black politicians we see around the country today are not what SNCC means by black power. The power must be that of a community, and emanate from there.

SNCC today is working in both North and South on programs of voter registration and independent political organizing. In some places, such as Alabama, Los Angeles, New York, Philadelphia, and New Jersey, independent organizing under the black panther symbol is in progress. The creation of a national "black panther party" must come about; it will take time to build, and it is much too early to predict its success. We have no infallible master plan and we make no claim to exclusive knowledge of how to end racism; different groups will work in their own different ways. SNCC cannot spell out the full logistics of self-determination but it can address itself to the problem by helping black communities define their needs, realize their strength, and go into action along a variety of lines which they must choose for themselves. Without knowing all the answers, it can address itself to the basic problem of poverty; to the fact that in Lowndes County, 86 white families own 90 per cent of the land. What are black people in that county going to do for jobs, where are they going to get money? There must be re-allocation of land, of money.

Ultimately, the economic foundations of this country must be shaken if black people are to control their lives. The colonies of the United States—and this includes the black ghettoes within its borders, north and south—must be liberated. For a century, this nation has been like an octopus of exploitation, its tentacles stretching from Mississippi and Harlem to South America, the Middle East, southern Africa, and Viet-Nam; the form of exploitation varies from area to area but the essential result has been the same—a powerful few have been maintained and enriched at the expense of the poor and voiceless colored masses. This pattern must be broken. As its grip loosens here and there around the world, the hopes of black Americans become more realistic. For racism to die, a totally different America must be born.

This is what the white society does not wish to face; this is why that society prefers to talk about integration. But integration speaks not at all to the problem of poverty, only to the problem of blackness. Integration today means the man who "makes it," leaving his black brothers behind in the ghetto as fast as his new sports car will take him. It has no relevance to the Harlem wino or to the cottonpicker making three dollars a day. As a lady I know in Alabama once said, "the food that Ralph Bunche eats doesn't fill my stomach."

Integration, moreover, speaks to the problem of blackness in a despicable way. As a goal, it has been based on complete acceptance of the fact that *in order to have* a decent house or education, blacks must move into a white neighborhood or send their children to a white school. This reinforces, among both black and white, the idea

that "white" is automatically better and "black" is by definition inferior. This is why integration is a subterfuge for the maintenance
of white supremacy. It allows the nation to focus on a handful of
Southern children who get into white schools, at great price, and to
ignore the 94 per cent who are left behind in unimproved all-black
schools. Such situations will not change until black people have
power—to control their own school boards, in this case. Then Negroes
become equal in a way that means something, and integration ceases
to be a one-way street. Then integration doesn't mean draining skills
and energies from the ghetto into white neighborhoods; then it can
mean white people moving from Beverly Hills into Watts, white
people joining the Lowndes County Freedom Organization. Then
integration becomes relevant.

Last April, before the furor over black power, Christopher Jencks
wrote in a *New Republic* article on white Mississippi's manipulation
of the anti-poverty program:

The war on poverty has been predicated on the notion that there is such
a thing as *a community* which can be defined geographically and mobilized
for a collective effort to help the poor. This theory has no relationship to
reality in the Deep South. In every Mississippi county there are *two* communities. Despite all the pious platitudes of the moderates on both sides,
these two communities habitually see their interests in terms of conflict
rather than cooperation. Only when the Negro community can muster
enough political, economic and professional strength to compete on somewhat equal terms, will Negroes believe in the possibility of true cooperation and whites accept its necessity. En route to integration, the Negro
community needs to develop greater independence—a chance to run its
own affairs and not cave in whenever "the man" barks . . . Or so it
seems to me, and to most people with whom I talked in Mississippi. To
OEO, this judgement may sound like black nationalism . . .

Mr. Jencks, a white reporter, perceived the reason why America's
anti-poverty program has been a sick farce in both North and South.
In the South, it is clearly racism which prevents the poor from
running their own programs; in the North, it more often seems to
be politicking and bureaucracy. But the results are not so different:
In the North, non-whites make up 42 per cent of all families in
metropolitan "poverty areas" and only six per cent of families in areas
classified as not poor. SNCC has been working with local residents
in Arkansas, Alabama, and Mississippi to achieve control by the poor
of the program and its funds; it has also been working with groups
in the North, and the struggle is no less difficult. Behind it all is a

federal government which cares far more about winning the war on the Vietnamese than the war on poverty; which has put the poverty program in the hands of self-serving politicians and bureaucrats rather than the poor themselves; which is unwilling to curb the misuse of white power but quick to condemn black power.

To most whites, black power seems to mean that the Mau Mau are coming to the suburbs at night. The Mau Mau are coming, and whites must stop them. Articles appear about plots to "get Whitey," creating an atmosphere in which "law and order must be maintained." Once again, responsibility is shifted from the oppressor to the oppressed. Other whites chide, "Don't forget—you're only ten per cent of the population; if you get too smart, we'll wipe you out." If they are liberals, they complain, "What about me?—don't you want my help anymore?" These are people supposedly concerned about black Americans, but today they think first of themselves, of their feelings of rejection. Or they admonish, "You can't get anywhere without coalitions," when there is in fact no group at present with whom to form a coalition in which blacks will not be absorbed and betrayed. Or they accuse us of "polarizing the races" by our calls for black unity, when the true responsibility for polarization lies with whites who will not accept their responsibility as the majority power for making the democratic process work.

White America will not face the problem of color, the reality of it. The well-intended say: "We're all human, everybody is really decent, we must forget color." But color cannot be "forgotten" until its weight is recognized and dealt with. White America will not acknowledge that the ways in which this country sees itself are contradicted by being black—and always have been. Whereas most of the people who settled this country came here for freedom or for economic opportunity, blacks were brought here to be slaves. When the Lowndes County Freedom Organization chose the black panther as its symbol, it was christened by the press "the Black Panther Party"—but the Alabama Democratic Party, whose symbol is a rooster, has never been called the White Cock Party. No one ever talked about "white power" because power in this country *is* white. All this adds up to more than merely identifying a group phenomenon by some catchy name or adjective. The furor over that black panther reveals the problems that white America has with color and sex; the furor over "black power" reveals how deep racism runs and the great fear which is attached to it.

Whites will not see that I, for example, as a person oppressed because of my blackness, have common cause with other blacks who are oppressed because of blackness. This is not to say that there are no white people who see things as I do, but that it is black people I must speak to first. It must be the oppressed to whom SNCC addresses itself primarily, not to friends from the oppressing group.

From birth, black people are told a set of lies about themselves. We are told that we are lazy—yet I drive through the Delta area of Mississippi and watch black people picking cotton in the hot sun for fourteen hours. We are told, "If you work hard, you'll succeed"—but if that were true, black people would own this country. We are oppressed because we are black—not because we are ignorant, not because we are lazy, not because we're stupid (and got good rhythm), but because we're black.

I remember that when I was a boy, I used to go to see Tarzan movies on Saturday. White Tarzan used to beat up the black natives. I would sit there yelling, "Kill the beasts, kill the savages, kill 'em!" I was saying: Kill *me*. It was as if a Jewish boy watched Nazis taking Jews off to concentration camps and cheered them on. Today, I want the chief to beat hell out of Tarzan and send him back to Europe. But it takes time to become free of the lies and their shaming effect on black minds. It takes time to reject the most important lie: that black people inherently can't do the same things white people can do, unless white people help them.

The need for psychological equality is the reason why SNCC today believes that blacks must organize in the black community. Only black people can convey the revolutionary idea that black people are able to do things themselves. Only they can help create in the community an aroused and continuing black consciousness that will provide the basis for political strength. In the past, white allies have furthered white supremacy without the whites involved realizing it— or wanting it, I think. Black people must do things for themselves; they must get poverty money they will control and spend themselves, they must conduct tutorial programs themselves so that black children can identify with black people. This is one reason Africa has such importance: The reality of black men ruling their own natives gives blacks elsewhere a sense of possibility, of power, which they do not now have.

This does not mean we don't welcome help, or friends. But we want the right to decide whether anyone is, in fact, our friend. In the past, black Americans have been almost the only people whom everybody and his momma could jump up and call their friends. We have been tokens, symbols, objects—as I was in high school to many young whites, who liked having "a Negro friend." We want to decide who is our friend, and we will not accept someone who comes to us and says: "If you do X, Y, and Z, then I'll help you." We will not be told whom we should choose as allies. We will not be isolated from any group or nation except by our own choice. We cannot have the oppressors telling the oppressed how to rid themselves of the oppressor.

I have said that most liberal whites react to "black power" with the question, What about me?, rather than saying: Tell me what you want me to do and I'll see if I can do it. There are answers to the right question. One of the most disturbing things about almost all white supporters of the movement has been that they are afraid to go into their own communities—which is where the racism exists— and work to get rid of it. They want to run from Berkeley to tell us what to do in Mississippi; let them look instead at Berkeley. They admonish blacks to be nonviolent; let them preach nonviolence in the white community. They come to teach me Negro history; let them go to the suburbs and open up freedom schools for whites. Let them work to stop America's racist foreign policy; let them press this government to cease supporting the economy of South Africa.

There is a vital job to be done among poor whites. We hope to see, eventually, a coalition between poor blacks and poor whites. That is the only coalition which seems acceptable to us, and we see such a coalition as the major internal instrument of change in American society. SNCC has tried several times to organize poor whites; we are trying again now, with an initial training program in Tennessee. It is purely academic today to talk about bringing poor blacks and whites together, but the job of creating a poor-white power bloc must be attempted. The main responsibility for it falls upon whites. Black and white can work together in the white community where possible; it is not possible, however, to go into a poor Southern town and talk about integration. Poor whites everywhere are becoming more hostile—not less—partly because they see the nation's attention focused on black poverty and nobody coming to them. Too many young middle-class Americans, like some sort of Pepsi generation, have wanted to come alive through the black community; they've wanted to be where the action is—and the action has been in the black community.

Black people do not want to "take over" this country. They don't want to "get whitey"; they just want to get him off their backs, as the saying goes. It was for example the exploitation by Jewish landlords and merchants which first created black resentment toward Jews —not Judaism. The white man is irrelevant to blacks, except as an oppressive force. Blacks want to be in his place, yes, but not in order to terrorize and lynch and starve him. They want to be in his place because that is where a decent life can be had.

But our vision is not merely of a society in which all black men have enough to buy the good things of life. When we urge that black money go into black pockets, we mean the communal pocket. We want to see the cooperative concept applied in business and banking. We want to see black ghetto residents demand that an exploiting storekeeper sell them, at minimal cost, a building or a shop that they will own and improve cooperatively: they can back their demand with a rent strike, or a boycott, and a community so unified behind them that no one else will move into the building or buy at the store. The society we seek to build among black people, then, is not a capitalist one. It is a society in which the spirit of community and humanistic love prevail. The word love is suspect; black expectations of what it might produce have been betrayed too often. But those were expectations of a response from the white community, which failed us. The love we seek to encourage is within the black community, the only American community where men call each other "brother" when they meet. We can build a community of love only where we have the ability and power to do so: among blacks.

As for white America, perhaps it can stop crying out against "black supremacy," "black nationalism," "racism in reverse," and begin facing reality. The reality is that this nation, from top to bottom, is racist; that racism is not primarily a problem of "human relations" but of an exploitation maintained—either actively or through silence—by the society as a whole. Camus and Sartre have asked, can a man condemn himself? Can whites, particularly liberal whites, condemn themselves? Can they stop blaming us, and blame their own system? Are they capable of the shame which might become a revolutionary emotion?

We have found that they usually cannot condemn themselves, and so we have done it. But the rebuilding of this society, if at all possible, is basically the responsibility of whites—not blacks. We won't fight to save the present society, in Vietnam or anywhere else. We are just going to work, in the way *we* see fit, and on goals *we* define, not for civil rights but for all our human rights.

A LETTER FROM JAIL

Eldridge Cleaver

I fell in love with the Black Panther Party for Self-Defense immediately upon my first encounter with it; it was literally love at first sight. It happened one night at a meeting in a dingy little storefront on Scott Street in the Fillmore district, the heart of San Francisco's black ghetto. It was February 1967. The meeting was the latest in a series of weekly meetings held by a loose coalition functioning under the name of the Bay Area Grassroots Organizations Planning Committee. The purpose of the coalition was to coordinate three days of activities with the worthy ambition of involving the total black community in mass action commemorating the fourth anniversary of the assassination of Malcolm X. The highlight and culmination of the memorial was to be the appearance of Sister Betty Shabazz, Malcolm X's widow, who was to deliver the keynote speech at a mass meeting at the Bayview Community Center in Hunters Point.

Among the topics on the agenda for this fortuitous meeting was the question of providing security for Sister Betty during the 24 hours she was to be our guest in the Bay Area. There was a paranoia around—which I did not share—that assassins by the dozens were lurking everywhere for the chance to shoot Sister Betty down. This fear, real or imagined, was a fact and it kept everybody uptight.

I had arrived at the meeting late, changing at the last minute a previous decision not to attend at all. I was pissed off at everyone in the room. Taking a seat with my back to the door I sat there with, I'm sure, a scornful frown of disdain upon my face. Roy Ballard

Eldridge Cleaver, "A Letter from Jail," RAMPARTS, *June 15, 1968. Reprinted by permission of the editors.*

(if the normal brain had three cylinders his would have one) sat opposite me, across the circle formed by the placement of the chairs. He, above all, understood the expression on my face, for he had done the most to put it there; this accounted, I thought, for the idiot grin on his own.

On Roy's left sat Ken Freeman, chairman of the now defunct Black Panther Party of Northern California, who always looked to me like Dagwood, with his huge round bifocals and the bald spot in the front of his natural. On Roy's right sat a frightened-looking little mulatto who seemed to live by the adage, "It's better to remain silent and be thought a fool than to open one's mouth and remove all doubt." He probably adopted that rule from observing his big fat yellow wife, who was seated on his right and who had said when I walked in, just loud enough for me to hear, "Shit! I thought we agreed after last week's meeting that *he* wouldn't be allowed to attend any more meetings!"

Next to her sat Jack Trueblood, a handsome, earnest youth in a black Russian cap who represented San Francisco State College's Black Students Union and who always accepted whatever tasks were piled upon him, insuring that he would leave each weekly meeting with a heavy load. On his right sat a girl named Lucky. I could never tell why they called her that—not, I'm sure, because she happened to be Roy Ballard's old lady; maybe because she had such a beautiful smile.

Between Lucky and myself sat Marvin Jackmon who was known as a poet, because after Watts went up in flames he had composed a catchy ditty entitled "Burn, Baby, Burn!" and a play entitled "Flowers for the Trashman." (It is hard for me to write objectively about Marvin. My association with him, dating from the third week of December 1966, ended in mutual bitterness with the closing of the Black House. After getting out of prison that month, he was the first person I hooked up with. Along with Ed Bullins, a young playwright who now has a few things going for himself off-Broadway, and Willie Dale, who had been in San Quentin with me and was trying to make it as a singer, we had founded the Black House in January 1967. Within the next two months the Black House, located in San Francisco, became the center of non-Establishment black culture throughout the Bay Area.)

On my right sat Bill Sherman, an ex-member of the Communist Party and at that time a member of the Central Committee of the

Black Panther Party of Northern California. Next to Bill was Victoria Durant, who dressed with what the black bourgeoisie would call "style" or, better yet, "class." She seemed so out of place at those meetings. We were supposed to be representing the common people —grassroots—and here was Victoria ready to write out a $50 check at the drop of a hat. She represented, as everyone knew, the local clique of black Democrats who wanted inside info on everything even hinting of "organizing" in their stomping grounds—even if the price of such info was a steady flow of $50 checks.

Then there was a Marianne Waddy, who kept everybody guessing because no one was ever sure of where or what she really was. One day she'd be dressed in flowing African gowns with her hair wrapped up in a pretty *skashok,* the perfect picture of the young Afro-American lady who had established a certain identity and relationship to traditional African culture. The next day she would be dressed like a man and acting like a man who would cut the first throat that got in his way.

Next to Marianne sat a sneaky-looking fellow called Nasser Shabazz. Sitting between Nasser and Ken Freeman, completing the circle, was Vincent Lynch, as smooth and black as the ebony statues he had brought back from his trip to Nigeria and the only member of the Black Panther Party of Northern California I ever liked or thought was sincere. Somewhere in the room, too, was Ann Lynch, Vincent's wife, with their bright-eyed son, Patrice Lumumba Lynch. Ann was the head of Black Care, the women's auxiliary to this Panther Party. These sisters spent all of their time talking about the impending violent stage of the black revolution, which was inevitable, and how they, the women, must be prepared to care for the men who would be wounded in battle.

I had come out of prison with plans to revive the Organization of Afro-American Unity, the vehicle finally settled upon by Malcolm X to spearhead the black revolution. The OAAU had never really gotten off the ground, for it was cut short by the assassins' bullets that felled Malcolm on the stage of the Audubon Ballroom in New York City. I was amazed that no one else had moved to continue Malcolm's work in the name of the organization he had chosen, which seemed perfect to me and also logically necessary in terms of historical continuity. The three-day memorial, which was but part of the overall plan to revive the OAAU, was to be used as a forum for launching the revival. In January, I had put the plan on paper and circulated it throughout the Bay Area, then issued a general call for a meeting to establish a temporary steering committee that would see after things until the start of the memorial. At this time we would have a convention, found the Bay Area branch of the Organization of Afro-American Unity and elect officers whom Sister Betty Shabazz would install, giving the whole effort her blessings in a keynote address on the final day of the memorial.

By February the plan had been torn to shreds. If the plan was a pearl, then I had certainly cast it before swine, and the biggest swine of all, Roy Ballard, had hijacked the plan and turned it into a circus. It soon became clear that if the OAAU was to be reborn, it would not be with the help of this crew, because all they could see was the pageantry of the memorial. Beyond that, their eyes blotted out all vision. Far from wanting to see an organization develop that would put an end to the archipelago of one-man showcase groups that plagued the black community with division, they had each made it their sacred cause to insure the survival of their own splinter group.

From the beginning, when the plan was first put before them, they took up each separate aspect and chewed it until they were sure it was either maimed for life or dead. Often after an idea had gone around the circle, if it still showed signs of life they would pounce upon it and rend it some more. When they finished, all that was left of the original plan was a pilgrimage to the site where a sixteen-year-old black youth, Matthew Johnson, had been murdered by a white cop, putting some pictures of Malcolm X on the walls of the Bayview Community Center, a hysterical speech by Ken Freeman and 24 hours of Sister Betty Shabazz's time.

In all fairness, however, I must confess that the whole plan was impossible to achieve, mostly because it did not take into account certain negative aspects of the black man's psychological heritage from 400 years of oppression here in Babylon. Then, too, I was an outsider. Having gone to prison from Los Angeles, I had been paroled to San Francisco. I was an interloper unfolding a program to organize *their* community. Fatal. It didn't matter to them that we were dealing with the concept of the Black Nation, of colonized Afro-America, and that all the boundaries separating our people were the stupid impositions of the white oppressors and had to be obliterated. Well, no matter; I had failed. Proof of my failure was Roy Ballard, sitting there before me like a gaunt buzzard, presiding over the carcass of a dream.

Suddenly the room fell silent. The crackling undercurrent that for weeks had made it impossible to get one's point across when one had the floor was gone; there was only the sound of the lock clicking as the front door opened, and then the soft shuffle of feet moving quietly toward the circle. Shadows danced on the walls. From the tension showing on the faces of the people before me, I thought the cops were invading the meeting, but there was a deep female gleam leaping out of one of the women's eyes that no cop who ever lived could elicit. I recognized that gleam out of the recesses of my soul, even though I had never seen it before in my life: the total admiration of a black woman for a black man. I spun round in my seat and saw the most beautiful sight I had ever seen: four black men wearing black berets, powder blue shirts, black leather jackets, black trousers, shiny black shoes—and each with a gun! In front was Huey P. Newton with a riot pump shotgun in his right hand, barrel pointed down to the floor. Beside him was Bobby Seale, the handle of a .45 caliber automatic showing from its holster on his right hip, just below the hem of his jacket. A few steps behind Seale was Bobby Hutton, the barrel of his shotgun at his feet. Next to him was Sherwin Forte, an M1 carbine with a banana clip cradled in his arms.

Roy Ballard jumped to his feet. Licking his lips, he said, "For those of you who've never met the brothers, these are the Oakland Panthers."

"You're wrong," said Huey P. Newton. "We're not the Oakland Panthers. We happen to live in Oakland. Our name is the Black Panther Party for Self-Defense."

With that the Panthers seated themselves in chairs along the wall, outside the circle. Every eye in the room was riveted upon them. What amazed me was that Roy Ballard did not utter one word in contradiction, nor was there any other yakkitty-yak around the room. There was absolute silence. Even little Patrice Lumumba Lynch seemed to sit up and take notice.

Where was my mind at? Blown! Racing through time, racing through the fog of a perspective that had just been shattered into a thousand fragments. Who are these cats? I wondered at them, checking them out carefully. They were so cool and it seemed to me not unconscious of the electrifying effect they were having on everybody in the room. Then I recalled a chance remark that Marvin Jackmon had once made. We were discussing the need for security at the Black House because the crowds were getting larger and larger and we had had to bodily throw out a cat who was high and acting like he owned the place. I said that Marvin, Ed, Dale and I had better each get ourself a gun. As I elaborated on the necessity as I saw it, Marvin said: "You need to forget about the Black House and go across the bay and get with Bobby Seale." And then he laughed.

"Who is Bobby Seale?" I asked him.

At first he gave no answer, he seemed to be carefully considering what to say. Finally he said, "He's arming some brothers across the bay." Though I pressed him, he refused to go into it any further, and at the time it didn't seem important to me, so I forgot about it. Now, sitting there looking at those Panthers, I recalled the incident with Marvin. I looked at him. He seemed to have retreated inside himself, sitting there looking like a skinny black Buddha with something distasteful and menacing on his mind.

"Do you brothers want to make a speech at the memorial?" Roy Ballard asked the Panthers.

"Yes," Bobby Seale said.

"O.K.," said Ballard. "We have the program broken down into subjects: Politics, Economics, Self-Defense and Black Culture. Now which section do you brothers want to speak under?" This was the sort of question which in my experience had always signaled the beginning of a two-hour debate with this group.

"It doesn't matter what section we speak under," Huey said. "Our message is one and the same. We're going to talk about black people arming themselves in a political fashion to exert organized force in the political arena to see to it that their desires and needs are met. Otherwise there will be a political consequence. And the only culture worth talking about is a revolutionary culture. So it doesn't matter what heading you put on it, we're going to talk about political power growing out of the barrel of a gun."

"O.K.," Roy Ballard said. He paused, then added, "Let's put it under Politics." Then he went on to start the specific discussion of security for Sister Betty, who would pick her up at the airport, etc. Bobby Seale was jotting down notes in a little black book. The other Panthers sat quietly, watchfully.

Three days before the start of the memorial, I received a phone call from Los Angeles. The man on the other end identified himself as Mr. Hakim Jamal, Malcolm X's cousin by marriage. He would be arriving with Sister Betty, he said, and both of them wanted to talk with me. They had liked, it turned out, an article on Malcolm that I had written and that was published in *Ramparts*. We agreed that when they got in from the airport I would meet them at the *Ramparts* office in San Francisco.

On the day that Sister Betty and Hakim Jamal were to arrive in San Francisco, I was sitting in my office tinkering with some notes for an article. One of the secretaries burst through the door. Her face was white with fear and she was shouting, "We're being invaded! We're being invaded!"

I couldn't tell just who her "we" referred to. Were the Chinese coming? Had the CIA finally decided to do *Ramparts* in? Then she said, "There are about 20 men outside with guns!"

I knew that Hakim Jamal and Sister Betty had arrived with their escort of armed Black Panthers.

"Don't worry," I said, "they're friends."

"Friends?" she gasped. I left her there with her eyes bugging out of her head and rushed to the front of the building.

I waded through *Ramparts'* staff jammed into the narrow hallway, fending off the frightened inquiries by repeating, "It's all right, it's all right." The lobby resembled certain photographs coming out of Cuba the day Castro took Havana. There were guns everywhere, pointed towards the ceiling like metallic blades of grass growing up out of the sea of black faces beneath the black berets of the Panthers. I found Hakim Jamal and Sister Betty surrounded by a knot of Panthers, who looked calm and self-possessed in sharp contrast to the chaotic reactions their appearance had set off. Outside where Broadway ran in four lanes to feed the freeway off-ramp, a massive traffic jam was developing and sirens could be heard screaming in the distance as cops sped our way.

I took Jamal and Sister Betty to an office down the hall. We talked for about 15 minutes about Malcolm. Sister Betty, her eyes concealed behind dark glasses, said nothing after we were introduced. She looked cool enough on the surface, but it was clear that she felt hard-pressed. Huey P. Newton was standing at the window, shotgun in hand, looking down into the up-turned faces of a horde of police. I left the room to get Sister Betty a glass of water, squeezing past Bobby Seale and what seemed like a battalion of Panthers in the hall guarding the door. Seale's face was a chiseled mask of determination.

A few yards down the hall, Warren Hinckle III, editor of *Ramparts,* was talking to a police lieutenant.

"What's the trouble?" the lieutenant asked, pointing at the Black Panthers with their guns.

"No trouble," Hinckle said. "Everything is under control."

The policeman seemed infuriated by this answer. He stared at Bobby Seale for a moment and then stalked outside. While I was in the lobby a TV cameraman, camera on his shoulder, forced his way through the front door and started taking pictures. Two white boys who worked at *Ramparts* stopped the TV man and informed him that he was trespassing on private property. When he refused to leave they picked him up and threw him out the door, camera and all.

When it was agreed that it was time to leave, Huey Newton took control. Mincing no words, he sent five of his men out first to clear a path through the throng of spectators clustered outside the door, most of whom were cops. He dispatched a phalanx of ten Panthers fast on their heels, with Hakim Jamal and Sister Betty concealed in their midst. Newton himself, along with Bobby Seale and three other Panthers, brought up the rear.

I went outside and stood on the steps of *Ramparts* to observe the departure. When Huey left the building, the TV cameraman who had gotten tossed out was grinding away with his camera. Huey took an envelope from his pocket and held it up in front of the camera, blocking the lens.

"Get out of the way!" the TV man shouted. When Huey continued to hold the envelope in front of the lens, the TV man started cursing, and reached out and knocked Huey's hand away with his fist. Huey coolly turned to one of the score of cops watching and said:

"Officer, I want you to arrest this man for assault."

An incredulous look came into the cop's face, then he blurted out: "If I arrest anybody it'll be you!"

Huey turned on the cameraman, again placing the envelope in front of the lens. Again the cameraman reached out and knocked Huey's hand away. Huey reached out, snatched the cameraman by the collar and slammed him up against the wall, sending him spinning and staggering down the sidewalk, trying to catch his breath and balance the camera on his shoulder at the same time.

Bobby Seale tugged at Huey's sleeve. "C'mon, Huey, let's get out of here."

Huey and Bobby started up the sidewalk toward their car. The cops stood there on the point, poised as though ready to start shooting at a given signal.

"Don't turn your backs on these back-shooting dogs!" Huey called out to Bobby and the other three Panthers. By this time the other Panthers with Sister Betty and Jamal had gotten into cars and melted into the traffic jam. Only these five were still at the scene.

At that moment a big, beefy cop stepped forward. He undid the little strap holding his pistol in his holster and started shouting at Huey, "Don't point that gun at me! Stop pointing that gun at me!" He kept making gestures as though he was going for his gun.

This was the most tense of moments. Huey stopped in his tracks and stared at the cop.

"Let's split, Huey! Let's split!" Bobby Seale was saying.

Ignoring him, Huey walked to within a few feet of the cop and said, "What's the matter, you got an itchy finger?"

The cop made no reply.

"You want to draw your gun?" Huey asked him.

The other cops were calling out for this cop to cool it, to take it easy, but he didn't seem to be able to hear them. He was staring into Huey's eyes, measuring him.

"O.K.," Huey said. "You big fat racist pig, draw your gun!"

The cop made no move.

"Draw it, you cowardly dog!" Huey pumped a round into the chamber of the shotgun. "I'm waiting," he said, and stood there waiting for the cop to draw.

All the other cops moved back out of the line of fire. I moved back, too, onto the top step of *Ramparts*. I was thinking, staring at Huey surrounded by all those cops and daring one of them to draw, "Goddam, that nigger is c-r-a-z-y!"

Then the cop facing Huey gave it up. He heaved a heavy sigh and lowered his head. Huey literally laughed in his face and then went off up the street at a jaunty pace, disappearing in a blaze of dazzling sunlight.

"Work out soul-brother," I was shouting to myself. "You're the baddest motherfucker I've ever seen!" I went into *Ramparts* and we all stood around chattering excitedly, discussing what we had witnessed with disbelief.

"Who was that?" asked Vampira, Warren Hinckle's little sister.

"That was Huey P. Newton," I said, "Minister of Defense of the Black Panther Party for Self-Defense."

"Boy, is he gutsy!" she said dreamily.

"Yeah," I agreed. "He's out of sight!"

The quality in Huey P. Newton's character which I had seen that morning in front of *Ramparts* and which I was to see demonstrated over and over again after I joined the Black Panther Party for Self-Defense was *courage*. I had called it "crazy," as people often do to explain away things they do not understand. I don't mean the courage "to stand up and be counted," or even the courage it takes to face certain death. I speak of that revolutionary courage it takes to pick up a gun with which to oppose the oppressor of one's people. That's a different kind of courage.

Oppressed people, Fanon points out, kill each other all the time. A glance through any black newspaper will prove that black people in America kill each other with regularity. This is the internalized violence of oppressed people. Angered by the misery of their lives but cowed by the overt superior might of the oppressor, the oppressed people shrink from striking out at the true objects of their hostility and strike instead at their more defenseless brothers and sisters near at hand. Somehow this seems safer, less fraught with dire consequences, as though one is less dead when shot down by one's brother than when shot down by the oppressor. It is merely criminal to take up arms against one's brother, but to step outside the vicious circle of the internalized violence of the oppressed and take up arms against the oppressor is to step outside of life itself, to step outside of the structure of this world, to enter, almost alone, the no-man's-land of revolution.

Huey P. Newton took that step. For the motto of the Black Panther Party he chose a quotation from Mao Tse-tung's Little Red Book: "We are advocates of the abolition of war; we do not want war; but war can only be abolished through war; and in order to get rid of the gun it is necessary to pick up the gun."

When I decided to join the Black Panther Party the only hang-up I had was with its name. I was still clinging to my conviction that we owed it to Malcolm to pick up where he left off. To me, this meant building the organization that he had started. Picking up where Malcolm left off, however, had different meanings for different people. For cats like Marvin Jackmon, for instance, it meant returning to the ranks of Elijah Muhammads's Nation of Islam, denouncing Malcolm as a heretic and pledging loyalty to Elijah, all in Malcolm's name. For Huey, it meant implementing the program that Malcolm advocated. When that became clear to me, I knew what Huey P. Newton was all about.

For the revolutionary black youth of today, time starts moving with the coming of Malcolm X. Before Malcolm, time stands still, going down in frozen steps into the depths of the stagnation of slavery. Malcolm talked shit, and talking shit is the iron in a young nigger's blood. Malcolm mastered language and used it as a sword to slash his way through the veil of lies that for 400 years gave the white man the power of the word. Through the breach in the veil, Malcolm saw all the way to national liberation, and he showed us the rainbow and the golden pot at its end. Inside the golden pot, Malcolm told us, was the tool of liberation. Huey P. Newton, one of the millions of black people who listened to Malcolm, lifted the golden lid off the pot and blindly, trusting Malcolm, stuck his hand inside and grasped the tool. When he withdrew his hand and looked to see what he held, he saw the gun, cold in its metal and implacable in its message: Death-Life, Liberty or Death, mastered by a black hand at last! Huey P. Newton is the ideological descendent, heir and successor of Malcolm X. Malcolm prophesied the coming of the gun to the black liberation struggle. Huey P. Newton picked up the gun and pulled the trigger, freeing the genie of black revolutionary violence in Babylon.

The genie of black revolutionary violence is here, and it says that the oppressor has no rights which the oppressed are bound to respect. The genie also has a question for white Americans: which side do you choose? Do you side with the oppressor or with the oppressed? The time for decision is upon you. The cities of America have tested the first flames of revolution. But a hotter fire rages in the hearts of black people today: total liberty for black people or total destruction for America.

The prospects, I confess, do not look promising. Besides being a dumb nation, America is mad with white racism. Whom the gods would destroy, they first make mad. Perhaps America has been mad far too long to make any talk of sanity relevant now. But there is a choice and it will be made, by decision or indecision, by action or inaction, by commission or omission. Black people have made their choice; a revolutionary generation that has the temerity to say to America that Huey P. Newton must be set free, also invested with the courage to kill, pins its hopes on the revolutionary's faith and says, with Che:

Wherever death may surprise us, it will be welcome, provided that this, our battlecry, reach some receptive ear, that another hand reach out to pick up weapons, and that other fighting men come forward to intone our funeral dirge with the staccato of machine guns and new cries of battle and victory.

☐ THE WAR

Opposition to the American military action in Vietnam has produced a wide variety of acts of protest: teach-ins, campus demonstrations, innumerable peace marches, draft-card burnings, refusal to pay income taxes, even several cases of self-immolation. It has also produced some profound arguments about what form protest *should* take in a democratic society, where the right of the individual to speak out or to act according to personal, moral, or religious conviction, becomes destructive to the society. The legal precedents claimed by the protesters have been the constitutional guarantees of freedom of speech, and the "Nuremberg doctrine," which holds all individuals accountable for the acts of their country.

Two of the following articles deal with individuals whose acts of protest brought them into direct confrontation with the law. The first, Captain Howard Levy, was sentenced to three years in Fort Leavenworth for refusal to train combat medics. The second, Dr. Benjamin Spock, was convicted in 1968 of conspiring to interfere with the Selective Service Act.

Perhaps the bitterest and most momentous of confrontations between protesters and authorities was the series of demonstrations in Chicago during the Democratic National Convention of 1968. As in Birmingham in 1963 or Selma in 1965 or Los Angeles' Century City in 1967, there was the familiar chain of demonstration, leading to police over-reaction, leading in turn to a polarization which increased the number and intensity of the demonstrators. But there was something else that gave Chicago a special significance—the convention. Inside a barricaded hall, an assembly of the leaders of the Democratic Party proceeded inexorably toward the nomination of Hubert Humphrey over the peace candidate, Eugene McCarthy. To many, this seemed overwhelming evidence that the official machinery of democracy moves according to needs of its own, unresponsive to those who vote in the primaries or to those who now marched through the streets of Chicago. It is too early to gauge the consequences of Chicago, but it is clear that it will become necessary for all political parties, particularly a party that aspires to liberal leadership, to find new forms, and styles, and leaders, in order to survive in an age of protest.

THE TRIAL OF CAPTAIN LEVY

Andrew Kopkind

At eleven in the morning of a drizzly day in June, Captain Howard Brett Levy, M.D., was seized and manacled, hurried from a barracks courtroom, and carried off in a staff car to the stockade at Fort Jackson, So. Carolina. He stayed the night in a small bare cell behind a crude wood-and-wire door, and the next day was inexplicably moved to an empty ward at the post hospital where he had served for nearly two years. There he is confined, under constant watch by an M.P., as he begins a sentence of three years at hard labor for crimes of conscience and belief. In a sense, Levy concurred in the findings of the court martial. He did what they said he did, and he is not sorry. He killed no guard, threw no bomb, raped no white woman, stole no secrets, packed no pumpkin. Nobody framed him; he is the wanted man. What is in contention is not the fact of his actions, but their meaning. Levy refuses to be complicit in a war he abhors; the Army calls that disobedient. He accepts responsibility for the consequences of his acts; that is unbecoming conduct, and it promotes, disloyalty. Levy did not seek to change the Army, but to ignore it, and he wanted not martyrdom but expression. The Army, in the way it often does, gave him just what he did not want.

Levy's progress from Brooklyn, where he was born thirty years ago, to the Fort Jackson stockade is lined with milestones familiar to his generation. He was the only child of conventionally nice Jewish parents. Toward the end of high school, he became vaguely aware of politics: "If I had been old enough I would have voted for Eisenhower." At N.Y.U. he studied hard ("I had to, I wasn't brilliant"), assembled a respectable record, and became the president of a fraternity which he helped found. "It was designed to do everything that fraternities don't do," he said. In that case, it was a useful way of avoiding the conformism of the era without actually opting out.

"The most radical thing I did in the Fifties," Levy said in the course of a long conversation one afternoon in the middle of the court martial, "was to go to folk music concerts, or read the Elektra Records catalogue." He went to Downstate Medical Center in 1958; in 1962 he interned at Maimonides Hospital in Brooklyn. "I was interested in the money part of medicine," he said. "But then a real change happened. I took part of my residency at Bellevue, and I was working with people who were destitute and down-trodden and completely cynical about the system. I began to identify with their problems in a real way."

There were others in America who were turning off "the system" in those years, but the effect of the new "generational" mood was indirect at best. "There was absolutely nobody to talk to. I tried to talk all the time. Everyone I knew disagreed. You know, if you hang around with old socialists all the time you begin to think that everyone's a socialist; it just ain't true. If you hang around with liberals, you think that everyone's a liberal. That just ain't true. But the people I hung around with were racists, and most people are racists. Period."

Levy read Paul Goodman and C. Wright Mills and went to lectures by Negro radicals. He listened to WBAI, the audience-supported radio station, and when its license was in jeopardy, he wrote a letter to the FCC. The license was renewed, and Levy was encouraged to write to President Johnson and the New York senators—"all those irrelevant people" on weightier matters. But now the letters did not do much good. The first "really activist thing" he did was join a welfare workers' picket line in 1965 in New York. "I was uncomfortable as hell," he remembered. "It was freezing and raining and a terrible day. But most of it was just the fear of having my friends see me."

At about that time, Levy's marriage began to disintegrate. He had married right after medical school, before his ideas of himself and his world began to change. "I said screw all the materialism; I don't want to be poor, but I'm not interested in the money part." Like many of his contemporaries whom he had never met and who were also changing. Levy began to believe that he might spend a part of his life in jail. There was nothing romantic about it. "Individual martyrdom is irrelevant in this society," he thought, "but sometimes you get yourself into situations. At Bellevue I saw people lined up in the morning defecating without even screens between them. That's just degrading. The *aim* is degradation. I feel more strongly about that than about Vietnam."

In medical school, Levy had signed up with the Army's Berry

Plan, which allows doctors to finish their training before accepting the inevitable draft call. There is no "selective" service for doctors; it is an across-the-board sweep, with no deferments for family status, few for physical impairments, and eligibility until the age of thirty-six. Levy was to report to the Army in July, 1965. Because of the crush of new commissions at the end of the academic year, there was no room for him in the orientation course given most Army doctors at Fort Sam Houston, Texas. He was expected at Fort Jackson, and for weeks beforehand he was anxious and depressed. He drank a lot and came home sick. His marriage was about over, and it was hard for him to separate the two traumas of change.

"It wasn't the regimentation of the Army that bothered me," Levy said, "although I didn't like it. It was Vietnam; it bothered me a lot then, and it bothers me a lot more now." He was two days late for duty at Fort Jackson (car trouble). He checked into the B.O.Q. the first night, discovered there was no hot water in the shower, and moved to an off-post apartment the next day. The second rebellion came soon afterward when he found a twelve-dollar bill for officers' club dues on his desk. He never paid it—or the bills which followed. He was not terribly popular with his superiors.

Fort Jackson is a basic-training center with a large transient population and not much connection with the neighboring city of Columbia. "Fort Jackson is barren of intellect, barren of life: the people aren't really alive in any sense of the term," Levy said. He felt isolated. One Saturday morning in a Columbia coffee shop he noticed an item in the paper about a Negro voter registration drive in a town called Newberry, So. Carolina. Levy had no idea where it was. But he quickly paid his check and started out to find the action. Somehow, he made his way to the county courthouse, where a demonstration was in progress. He found the local organizer, a young white Army veteran named Bill Treanor, and volunteered his services.

"It was very simple then, very romantic. The next afternoon we registered an old man in his nineties," Levy recalled. "He was all bent over, a sharecropper all his life, and he was so proud with his yellow registration slip. It made us feel so good. I don't think I'd feel the same way today."

Levy went to Newberry every weekend that summer, and in the fall joined in civil rights work in Columbia. Later, he staged a fund-raising rhythm-and-blues show ("it was monumentally unsuccessful financially but extremely successful artistically"), and last year began to publish an eight-page biweekly newspaper for the movement called *Contrast*. But civil rights organizing is not a usual pastime for a white Army officer in South Carolina, and Levy soon piqued the interest of the Counter-Intelligence Corps. Investigators got to him shortly after the summer project was over and questioned him closely about his politics, his reading matter, and his organizational affiliations. They were worried about the sponsorship of the Negro radicals' lectures (Trotskyist), and were not calmed by Levy's assurances that he only went to listen. They asked him to take a lie-detector test, and he refused. Finally, they asked whether he would follow an order of a superior officer under any circumstances, and Levy said, of course he would not.

All along, there had been minor run-ins with authority. Levy never could manage to wear his uniform correctly, nor keep his shoes shined, nor remember to have his hair cut. His manner is abrupt and defensive at times, but he can easily be warm and eager with those for whom he feels some companionship. More than anything, he is Brooklynesque, with none of the assimilated "shoe-ness" of the med-student style. That suits Levy and his friends, but it is not always successful with the types at Fort Jackson. One day he had an argument with an M.P. officer: something about a parking ticket. "I was short with him," Levy admitted. In his report, the M.P. gave more details:

When told to come to attention and salute, subject smirked, came to attention on one leg and half heartedly put his hand near his head with his fingers in a crumpled position, then threw his hand in the direction of the wall. His left hand remained in his pocket. Throughout the conversation, Captain Levy was insubordinate by facial expression, body movement and vocal inflection. Subject needed a haircut and his branch and US insignia were in reverse manner.

On post, Levy spent his time running a small dermatology clinic for soldiers (V.D.), dependents (acne), and retired personnel (psoriasis). He was well thought of professionally. Col. Chester H. Davis, the hospital's executive officer, had no complaints about the way Levy treated him for a dry spot on the buttocks ("Don't wash so much"). Then Fort Jackson initiated a training program for Special Forces medical aidmen—the part-combat, part-medic complement of the Green Berets—and Levy was assigned to give each of them five days of instruction in dermatology.

He trained them for three or four months—"with some reservations"—and found them the most interesting people on the base. There was a striking similarity between the backgrounds of the Green Berets and white civil rights workers: the alienation from middleclass families, the feeling of being trapped by the society, the urge to have some effect of one's own.

I talked to them about the war and about themselves, but after a while I realized that it wasn't doing any good. For a time, I pulled the kind of crap that some of the other doctors did—they just let the aidmen hang around and never really trained them. Then, last June, I just kicked them out.

It wasn't intellectualized in the beginning, but I had two reasons. First, I don't think you can possibly train guys for five days in dermatology to a point where they'll do more good than harm. And second, I don't think medicine should be used for political purposes. You can't separate it from the war. It's part and parcel of the same thing.

Levy's earlier commander heard that the aidmen had been refused training, but he let the matter slide after an inconclusive interview with the Captain. But Col. Henry Franklin Fancy, who took command of the hospital in mid-summer of 1966, was not quite so complaisant. He had noticed the "flag" on Levy's personnel file, denoting a security risk; "communistic," Colonel Fancy thought to himself (as he testified later). Then Fancy began hearing reports that Levy was telling aidmen and patients that the war in Vietnam was wrong, that he would not serve in Vietnam if ordered, and that if he were a Negro soldier he would come home to fight for civil rights. As for the Green Berets: They were "liars and thieves and killers of peasants and murderers of women and children." Worst of all, Levy had been talking like that to *enlisted* men, in violation of the responsibilities of rank.

Colonel Fancy was wondering just what to do when an intelligence agent told him the little secrets of Levy's "G-2" dossier. The full richness of its 180 pages has not yet been revealed even to Levy's civilian lawyers, but it contained such spicy information as this interview with a sergeant:

Levy expressed very leftist ideas and viewpoints. He spoke favorably about those persons who burned their draft cards, feeling that this was their right, and they should not be prosecuted for this. Source does not consider subject a loyal American because of his statements condemning US policies. . . . Levy was quite pro-Negro, to the side of the Negroes when discussing civil rights matters, and appeared to think more of the Negroid race than of the White race.

Colonel Fancy told his executive officer, Colonel Davis, that Levy was a "pinko." Then, after consultations with Army lawyers, Fancy issued a formal order to Levy to train the Special Forces aidmen. Levy did not comply. Colonel Fancy was ready to take non-judicial disciplinary action when, after another close look at the G-2 dossier, he and Heaven knows who else decided to escalate the proceedings. Fancy charged Levy with willful disobedience of an order (a capital offense in wartime), and with promoting disloyalty and disaffection among the troops. A general court martial was convened.

Levy is convinced that the ante was raised because of his politics, or Colonel Fancy's reading of them. There is nothing to suggest that the commandant was in any way flexible on the subject of pinkness. In a preliminary hearing, Colonel Fancy testified that the communist line, as he understands it, includes "the requirement for world domination . . . and the lack of what we consider God and their requirement not to believe in God. The requirement to agitate and propagandize in such a way that noncommunist people's minds are maintained in a state of chronic anxiety in the hope that this will not impair their will to resist the communist domination." The civil rights movement, he said, might well create such anxiety, and the anti-war protest was communist-based. That seemed to take care of Captain Levy. Colonel Fancy felt it necessary to warn a class of aidmen, in a graduation speech, to disregard the blandishments of left-wingers who might have infiltrated his hospital. Still, there was a touch of sentiment in the old bureaucrat. One day after the preliminary hearing had been concluded and the court martial was about to begin, Howard Levy received a birthday card in the mail: "Look to this day for it is life," the message read. "For yesterday is already a dream and tomorrow is only a vision. But today makes every yesterday a dream of happiness and every tomorrow a vision of hope. Hope your birthday is happy and the year ahead is full of all that means the most to you." It was signed "Bud and Cooksie Fancy."

Exactly why the Army permitted the Levy trial to blow up out of all rational proportions is still unclear. But the proceedings seemed to take on a life of their own. The actors were swept along by a play they never wrote. Last fall, Levy told his girl-friend, an art student at the University of South Carolina named Trina Sahli, that he believed no final action would be taken before he left the Army in July, 1967. Levy's lawyer gave the authorities any number of escapes—including an application for conscientious-objector status, which was promptly refused. But the charges kept increasing. In February, a third count was added, for "conduct unbecoming an officer and a gentleman," on the basis of the conversations with enlisted men. A few days later, two more came. They stemmed from a letter Levy wrote to Sgt. Geoffrey Hancock in Vietnam, at the suggestion of Bill Treanor, the civil rights worker in Newberry. Treanor had been stationed in Hawaii with Hancock. The two regularly corresponded, and Hancock (a white man married to a Negro girl) expressed some concern about the Vietnam protest movement at home. Treanor thought Levy could tell Hancock how it was:

I am one of those people back in the states who actively opposes our efforts there and would refuse to serve there if I were so assigned (Levy wrote). . . . I do not believe that you can realistically judge the Vietnam war as an isolated incident. It must be viewed in the context of the recent history of our foreign policy—at least from the start of the cold war. . . . Geoffrey, who are you fighting for? Do you know? . . . Your real battle is back here in the US, but why must I fight it for you? The same people who suppress Negroes and poor whites here are doing it all over again all over the world and you're helping them. Why? You . . . know about the terror the whites have inflicted upon Negroes in our country. Aren't you guilty of the same thing with regard to the Vietnamese? A dead woman is a dead woman in Alabama and in Vietnam. To destroy a child's life in Vietnam equals a destroyed life in Harlem.

The letter went on for eight pages, with a great deal of explanation and obvious passion. It ended with an invitation for reply (the two had never met), but Hancock did not answer. He kept the letter for fourteen months in a pile of trash, and when he saw a television news broadcast about the Levy affair on Okinawa, turned it over to his superiors.

At some point, the Army began to worry about the effects of the trial. Its tactics began to seem a little more cool. Col. Earl V. Brown, the service's chief law officer, was sent down from Washington to be the "judge." The Fort Jackson commanding general appointed a court martial composed of ten men of rank higher than Levy's, all career line officers, four of them combat veterans of Vietnam, and all but one Southerners. The line-up was out of a Frank Capra war movie: one quiet Negro, one inscrutable Nisei (both quite junior), and a major whose eye had been lost in a (friendly) mine explosion in Vietnam. There were no Jews, or doctors, or captains, or enlisted men, or women, or non-career officers. For the prosecution, the Army found a young Jewish lawyer in a camp in Georgia and brought him to Fort Jackson. Someone in the Pentagon had been reading Zola.

Capt. Richard M. Shusterman presents only one of the countless ironies of the Levy affair. Amiable, ambitious, square, deferential, liberal, and crew-cut, Shusterman is everything that Levy is not. He believes in military necessity and good order, the proper balance between the rights of men and the demands of institutions, the mutability of moral standards. He asserts that the world is too complex to be understood, and he makes a positive value of that uncomprehension. It gets him off the hook. If he had any doubts at the beginning, he had convinced himself of the moral rightness of his side by the time the court martial began. He even seemed to have allayed some of the difficulties he may once have had in supporting US policy in Vietnam.

Shusterman is Levy before Bellevue. He is the part of the generation of the late Fifties—by far the larger piece—which is continuous with its past, unmindful of its future. He votes for liberal Democrats and moderate Republicans, his favorite magazine is *The New Republic,* and he wishes that New Left students would shave their beards and dress neatly. It would help them sell their ideas in the marketplace. Phi Beta Kappa at Lafayette, a full scholarship to Penn Law, and a job, perhaps, with a tony firm in Philadelphia that now and then takes a few well turned-out Jews. He doesn't mind the officers' club at all, but would defend to the death anyone's right not to like it. Except, of course, when he is the chief prosecutor.

The trial began on May 10, in a small low-ceilinged hut on a sandy knoll at Fort Jackson. The court assembled each morning at 0900 hours, as everyone was fond of saying, in the way tourists on their first trip abroad enjoy the simplest Berlitz phrase. Newsmen and spectators drove to the court through fields of recruits doing calisthenics, romping over the "confidence course" (formerly, the obstacle course), or charging aimlessly with fixed bayonets. Women remarked sadly on the youthfulness of the soldiers marching down the roads.

Shusterman had an easy job. He had to prove that the facts of the case were as everyone agreed they were, that Colonel Fancy's order was lawful, and that Levy had said and written words ascribed to him. Colonel Brown, the law officer, ruled that the truth of the statements was immaterial, as was evidence of their effect. As a matter of fact, Howard Levy was not much of a subversive. No one became disaffected or disloyal. Shusterman did, however, have to prove Levy's intent to commit his crimes, but the court was permitted to draw its conclusions on that matter from the cirucumstances of the case, and from the pattern of Levy's political behavior.

Colonel Fancy was first on the stand, reciting softly and with no feeling the tribulations of life in the hospital with a trouble-making pinko. During much of his long testimony, he stared at the thin red carpet beneath him. The men on the court seemed sympathetic; no officer likes to be disobeyed. Levy's civilian counsel, Charles Morgan, Jr., tried to establish from the succession of aidmen who followed that they were essentially combat soldiers, not medics. Some carried Red Cross insignia on their I.D. cards, and some did not. The point was never established.

The first indication that Levy was not alone in his concern about complicity and responsibility at the Fort Jackson hospital came in the testimony of another Brooklyn Jewish doctor named Ivan Mauer. Levy had once told him: "You're no better than the rest. You're in sympathy with me, but you want to walk the tightrope." At last, Captain Mauer got off the tightrope. He was not teaching aidmen at present, he said, and he would not participate in the program if he were assigned. There seemed to be a small "doctors' revolt" brewing. A Negro ophthalmologist (who in the thousandth irony of the case was treating the wounded one-eyed major on the court) testified for Levy that he had serious doubts about training aidmen. He compromised with his scruples by merely letting the students look over his shoulder as he worked, with no formal instruction. He told the law officer he was afraid to say even that much, for fear of prosecution.

Morgan had begun the defense's case with a battery of character witnesses—Levy's father, Negro civil rights workers—and was admittedly creating "an aura of Nuremberg" when the law officer interrupted. If Morgan wanted seriously to invoke the Nuremberg defense—that soldiers have a duty not to obey orders to commit war crimes—then he had to prove that the US was following "a general policy or a pattern or practice" of war crimes in Vietnam. Morgan was stunned. "Give me an extra day," he asked Colonel Brown, half seriously.

Morgan actually had five days, but the task was hopeless from the start. For tactical and political reasons (for example, dissension within the American Civil Liberties Union, for which Morgan is Southern Regional Director), he decided to limit his testimony to criminal actions by the small Special Forces contingent in Vietnam.

That eliminated evidence of saturation bombing, napalming, and geonocide. A platoon of ACLU lawyers and staff assistants flew into Columbia from New York, accompanied by scores of new reporters. There were rumors of famous witnesses on the way—Sartre, Bertrand Russell, leaders of the NLF. At the end, there were only three: Robin Moore, the author of *The Green Berets;* Donald Duncan, the *Ramparts* editor who had served in the Special Forces himself and had told all in a magazine article; and Peter Bourne, a British-born US Army psychiatrist just back from a study tour in a Special Forces camp in Vietnam.

Moore was never actually a Green Beret. He was a Sheraton Hotels public relations man who went through Special Forces training to write his book (3½ million copies sold), and has not yet gone back to the P.R. business. He was embarrassingly chummy on the stand ("no sweat," he told the judge, and he called the Montagnards "Yards"—which indeed was kinder than a prosecution witness who called the Viet Cong "Luke the Gook"). But, like Duncan after him, he did provide some grisly tales of the tactics of Special Forces when they are done winning the hearts and minds of the natives. No one seemed particularly moved. Moore, Shusterman, and Colonel Brown kept chatting about the cheapness of life in the Orient, the superstitions of the Vietnamese, and the exigencies of war.

Peter Bourne provided the most convincing testimony about the way in which the Special Forces turn over prisoners to the South Vietnamese, to torture them as they please. The US maintains no prisoner-of-war camps, and "military necessity" demands the transfer to the South Vietnamese. Under the rules of war, military units that take prisoners are responsible for their well-being, but none of the testimony satisfied the law officer. He ruled the next day that a case for war crimes as a policy had not been made, and he did not allow the testimony of "isolated incidents" to go before the full court.

Nuremberg Day was followed by Ethics Day. The defense went back to its original line, that Colonel Fancy's order to Levy need not have been obeyed if it was contrary to the principles of medical ethics—that is, the rules against teaching medicine to those who will not practice it ethically. Three physicians (Victor Sidel of Harvard, Louis Lasagna of Johns Hopkins, and Benjamin Spock of everywhere) and a non-physician faculty member at Harvard, Jean Mayer, testified lucidly about the role of ethics in a physician's life. Shusterman tried to get them to admit that whatever good the Special

Forces aidmen might do in Vietnam justifies their military role, or at least is distinct from it. But they would not buy his cheerful pluralism. The aidmen's role is inextricable from the war policy. The aidmen and the pacification teams and the winners of peasants' hearts and minds do not make war any better; they merely make it (possibly) more complete, more effective, more legitimate.

Shusterman produced a physician from Duke Medical School to refute the defense's experts. Doctors may train "paramedical personnel," the witness said, but they need take no responsibility for what the paramedics do with their training. But the most frightening witness of all was Major Craig Llewellyn, a thirty-year-old Special Forces physician, who ran the program in Vietnam for a year-and-a-half and now directs training at the John F. Kennedy Special Warfare Center at Fort Bragg, No. Carolina. Llewellyn arrived in paratroop boots and an open shirt, his head shaved almost bald and his manner something like a karate instructor's. With cold passion, he argued that the Special Forces are the best thing that ever happened to Vietnam, or any other counter-insurgency situation, for that matter. The aidmen bring modern medicine to areas that know only "Chinese doctors"—"neither Chinese nor doctors." Llewellyn's case was as strong as any Calvinist missionary could ever have made, and with precisely the same logic. He proclaimed the new doctrine of participatory imperialism—let the people decide to accept American intervention. The court was impressed, and Shusterman rested the prosecution's rebuttal.

No one could reasonably believe that the court martial would not convict Levy. Aside from the disadvantages of military procedure and the rather disorganized if often brilliant defense, there was simply too much at stake for the Army. Levy was a symbol of anarchy and willfulness.

But at the motel in Columbia where the defense lawyers, Levy and his family, and most of the press hung out, there was a disturbing kind of euphoria. The out-of-towners were isolated and distracted by the strangeness of the small southern capital and the other-worldliness of the army base. More than that, they had developed a sympathy— for many a commitment—to Levy for which there were no appropriate forms of expression. In civil rights marches and peace demonstrations, the committed can shout and stomp and wave banners. If they like, they can make faces or fists at hostile segregationists or pro-war hecklers. But there was no visible enemy to be angry at in Columbia. The substitute was a bizarre, compulsive hilarity. There were gags and songs and cocktails late into the night. Levy joined in as thoroughly as anyone; his parents looked somewhat baffled, but did not leave the scene. No one really could leave. The motel was like some moored ship carrying a cargo of doomed but laughing passengers.

The party began to wear thin in the last few days. Sgt. Charles Sanders, a quite southern Army lawyer, serving as Levy's military counsel, was wrenched out of shape. He had started the case as a routine assignment. By the time it was over, he had to question his values, his background, his deepest sense of himself. Levy's act seemed to touch Sanders directly, at the same personal level on which it was made. Morgan had been working hard on the case for six months, and he was utterly involved and completely worn, but he managed to pull the pieces of the case together for a moving and masterly summation. Where it touched the law was not entirely apparent. But it was so painfully personal and so profoundly felt that even the court may have been moved to mercy.

"Events occur in the life of the world that are irrational, and the reason that they occur is that good men don't stop them," Morgan said. He is a great whale of a man, rumpled and sweaty at the slightest exertion, and he ranged around the small courtroom, talking without a script. "This case shouldn't be here. Dr. Levy shouldn't even be in the Army. Some place down the line, there was a place for this to stop, but it didn't. Now it's your responsibility to stop this thing as it monumentally cascades on to some crazy wild conclusion."

Morgan knew how things get out of hand. He had been a lawyer in Birmingham, Alabama, in 1963 when he spoke—tentatively at first—against white racism. He was forced to leave the state. "Men are constantly being fitted into structures and sometimes they conform and sometimes they don't. Sometimes men become martyrs by inadvertence, and around them swirl great movements. I don't want a martyr. I want acquittal and we're entitled to it and the Army will not fall if Levy goes free.

"More lives have been taken for heresy and witchcraft than for all the crimes in human history. More people have been tried for crimes that do not exist than for those which exist. Men are constantly put on trial for their minds and words. Your whole lives are involved in the context of freedom; true patriotism involves a man's right to dream and believe and think and speak and act. This trial has to do with free men and responsibility. I truly do not want a martyr. I want a free man."

The court did not oblige. Levy was found guilty on the three major charges, and of a slightly less serious offense on the two counts arising from the letter to Hancock. Shusterman seemed to be having some last-minute doubts about his severity; he asked for a dismissal of those two charges, and Colonel Brown agreed. The next morning Levy was sentenced. As the court rose, Col. Chester Davis—the hospital executive officer now cured of the dry spot on his buttocks— took Levy by the arm and pushed him into a chair. Flushed and trembling, Davis pulled a pair of silver handcuffs from his pocket, fumbled awkwardly, and clasped them around Levy's wrist. The lawyers shouted, Trina Sahli cried, and Levy started moving through the door. He had a most peculiar smile on his face, which was captured in all the news photos—something between sorrow and contempt, but for whom it was not possible to tell.

WHAT MAKES DR. SPOCK MARCH?

Gereon Zimmermann

Dr. Benjamin Spock took his first long stride as a peace marcher in Cleveland, Ohio, on Easter Saturday, 1962. This is the way it went: "I felt acutely self-conscious and ridiculous. I would have been delighted to have sunk into the pavement. As we went into the public square, a woman who had been marching for peace for decades pointed out two suave men in camel's hair coats and said, 'That's the police subversive squad.' They were writing down names and taking pictures. And I thought, *My God, is this the United States of America?*"

Recently, Dr. Spock took a longer stride. There was a button missing on his Brooks Brothers, dark-gray-worsted jacket as he scurried about his modest Manhattan apartment getting ready to go

Reprinted by permission of the editors. From the February 20, 1968 issue of LOOK MAGAZINE. *Copyright 1968 by Cowles Communications, Inc.*

to New York's City Hall to protest alleged police brutality visited upon Stop the Draft Week marchers. He is meticulous. So, this 64-year-old world pediatrician, who is always collar-clasped, watch-chained, vested, French-cuffed, braced and gartered, changed his suit. Moments later, he flung his 6'4" lankiness into a cab and rattled over the East River Drive to lead the parley with a mayor's aide. After the meeting, Dr. Spock pushed through a mob and told inter-viewers that the Vietnam war was "insane." Two days before, he had been arrested (on his fourth try) and jailed after symbolically violating a police line near the Whitehall Army induction center.

More mothers tore up his *Baby and Child Care,* the book that has sold 20.5 million copies and brought the Spock version of Dr. Sigmund Freud to the bassinet. Dr. Spock's main message was reas-surance, *not* permissiveness, and he became a Dutch uncle to the post-World War II American generation. Because of his prestige, he perforce leads objectors to the Vietnam war and nuclear-weapons testing. This man who served as a Navy lieutenant commander in World War II (as a psychiatrist) and backed UN intervention in Korea has, it seems to many, turned himself inside out. It is Mother-hood attacking Old Glory when he counsels draft-law violators. He is now under Federal indictment for those actions. A conviction could bring maximum penalties of five years in jail and $10,000 in fines.

His obstinacy might not have been necessary. In 1965 and 1966, he asked Sen. Robert F. Kennedy to directly confront Administration war policies: "Kennedy was the only one in the country with the recognition and the popularity to oppose President Johnson. He had all the strengths and the confidence of the American people. . . . Kennedy could not be called a wild man. I thought that millions of people would rally to him. Obviously, he didn't see it this way. The weakness of the peace movement is that we do not have such a national leader."

Also surprising is the head-knocking that Dr. Spock seeks with President Lyndon B. Johnson. He demands confrontation in rather angry language; but dialogue with dissenters is something the Com-mander in Chief is not having. In truth, national debates are mostly elusive; there is, for example, a publicly icy relationship between Secretary of State Dean Rusk and Chairman of the Senate Foreign Relations Committee J. William Fulbright, and no public standoff between the two. It might be said that the Administration plays a zone defense against its Southeast Asia-policy critics.

Years ago, I audited a lecture Dr. Spock gave to medical students at Western Reserve University. He explained in his warm, clear way that parental behavior—such as spanking a child—can be sadistic and can flood the parent with satisfaction. One student disagreed. He could not comprehend that slapping a kid around could give anyone a perverted joy. Patiently, Dr. Spock took the class over the traces of such an aberration, but the one student was shaking his head when the class ended. So, too, was Dr. Spock, because he felt that he had failed in presenting his thesis. Spock is like that as a teacher. Solicitous, engaged and not without humor.

We meet an angry man when it comes to the war and Lyndon Johnson. "Johnson," he says, "betrayed us. My own feeling is that he has kept escalating the war, and we who are trying to oppose him have got to keep escalating our efforts and our frankness. Very delicately, a year ago, we were talking about the 'credibility gap,' which really means Johnson has been lying; but I think we're afraid to say that for fear there are relatively few people ready to believe it. We would only discredit ourselves, rather than him.

"George Herman asked me on *Face the Nation* if I believed President Johnson is 'the enemy of the American people.' I said, 'I believe so, absolutely. . . . I feel particularly bitter in a personal kind of a way. . . . He not only betrayed the American people, he betrayed me and the other people who supported him publicly.' Every week, he escalates a little bit further, getting us closer to war with China and . . . the Soviet Union. And if we get that far, then certainly there's the terrible risk of nuclear war starting. Johnson is reported to have said, 'I refuse to be the first President in the history of the United States to lose a war.' This is the egotistical view. He did not say, 'Is this war just?' or 'Is it, this war, in any interest of the United States?' In other words, I would translate this to mean 'This war is to save Lyndon Johnson's face.' I think there's lots that's admirable about Johnson. But I'm ashamed to say I campaigned for him in 1964. His aspirations for the domestic economy and civil rights were sincere.

"One of the things that has discouraged me most is to realize that the closest advisers of the President in regard to Southeast Asia and the war are intellectuals. And closest of all has been Rusk, who is a person of education and fair distinction. He seems to me cold-blooded and obsessed with anticommunism. Then you have the two Bundys—McGeorge and William—and the two Rostows—Walt and

Eugene—who *really* have had academic careers. They have gone along with Johnson; they have not been restraining influences. This points out to me the dangerousness of relying on academic or intellectual brilliance unless one sees that it is balanced by strong humanitarian feelings. I'm not saying these people are not humanitarian when they are at home, with their families. But if you read their books, their speeches, they're always talking about *power*. They never talk about the good people of Southeast Asia. They're thinking cold-bloodedly when it comes to international affairs. Plato was entirely wrong when he suggested that countries ought to be ruled by a specially educated elite.

"I would end up by saying if you had to choose between the brilliant person who may not have had to show humanitarian concern and a stupid person who is good-hearted, I would rather have the latter person, the humanitarian, in charge of the government.

"We should remember the influence of Pope John: As far as I know, he wasn't particularly brilliant, he didn't produce poetry and so on. He had to offer simply a *human kindness*. He was obviously a *loving* person, and he didn't talk harshly of *barbarians* or *Protestants*. It is extraordinary to me how anti-Catholic prejudice in this country, and around the world, melted because of Pope John. Anybody in any job has to be thinking in terms of people and decency toward people, and this is particularly important with the leaders of the nations of the world."

Dr. Spock believes that America has become obsessed with anti-communism to the point of "sickness," and that the chief architect of this policy, the late John Foster Dulles, was an evangelist gone wrong. And, as the doctor sees it, Americans have moved from hating Russian communism to hating Chinese communism. For him, holocaust may lie ahead if the escalation of the Vietnam war continues: "There is a 25 per cent chance we will be at war with Red China before the elections in November."

As an early supporter of John F. Kennedy's candidacy, the life-long Republican moved from the contemplative to manipulative forms of politics. In 1962, he joined the National Committee for a Sane Nuclear policy, later became its co-chairman. He says his SANE activities freed him from the denial of reality—the reality being the possibility of nuclear disaster. Rumors began floating about his possible Ohio candidacy for the U.S. Senate, and even a spot on a

Presidential ticket with Dr. Martin Luther King. All of this leaked away.

Then, Dr. Spock went to Chicago last August for the convention of the National Conference for New Politics (he is now its co-chairman). That gathering was something else in American politics. Instead of delegates in $100 shiny suits and white shirts, and women in ridiculous hats—a normal coloration of such solemn bodies—there were, among the 3,000, many young people with beards, sandals, long hair and shades. The NCNP was almost fragmented by Black Power demands for *overrepresentation:* the blacks were entitled to about 5,000 votes, but wanted 28,498 votes—which was what the whites had. The blacks won their way. Dr. Spock, who deplores the anti-Zionist or anti-Semitic statements by some at the convention, sees no problem in the Negro coup. He believes the peace movement must embrace a total spectrum of political belief if it is to triumph.

The fracases of the New Left at the Chicago meeting polarized opinion about Dr. Spock. A New York liberal says, "Dr. Spock is like Henry Wallace. He has not wigged it, but he is often foolish. Anyway, we have our man now—Sen. Eugene McCarthy." And at least one of the doctor's former colleagues finds his political views "naïve." He may not know that on two occasions, Dr. Spock was invited to appear at Lord Russell's International War Crimes Tribunal and declined because he felt that the sessions were patently propagandistic.

Because of many marches, Dr. Spock says he is "thick-skinned about people yelling coward or Communist at me," but he puzzles about the impression that he is the cradle guru of the hippies and flower children because of his "permissive" writings.

"I'm not responsible for all those brats," he laughed in an address to a Brooklyn church group. He expounds: "When I wrote *Baby and Child Care* (in 1946), I was very much influenced by my time . . . by progressive education, and Freudian concepts. I was certainly pushing the pendulum along. But later, I kept emphasizing again and again, you can love a child, you can be flexible, but children still need parents to know *what's* flexible. In the second edition, there was heavy emphasis on babies' and children's need for guidance from parents.

"The bewilderment of a certain proportion of youth is related to the fact that parents are very uncertain about what to tell their kids. Not only what man's all about but whether there's God or there isn't God. Young people are designed by nature, in late adolescence and early adulthood, to try to gain some intellectual, spiritual and ideational freedom by rebelling against their parents. This is how man has made scientific and cultural advances. Otherwise, each generation would be a slavish replica of the previous generation. . . . We would make no progress.

"One of the biggest innovations in the human race is the American parents who are unsure of themselves. I think this is a new phenomenon: and my hunch is that it's easier, more comfortable for young people to rebel if they know exactly what their parents stand for.

"American parents are adrift because a number of factors are at work, beginning with the discovery of evolution. There has been a delayed impact on people's confidence in religion—the evidence that man is not so special to God and not that different. This has been a shattering blow to mankind. It has not been so shattering to the French because they have the tradition of the French family . . . in Great Britain, the tradition of service to the Empire. In the United States, parents have been less able to withstand the undermining effects of the loss of religious traditions because they didn't have other convictions too. I'm not saying this is disastrous. New convictions eventually come along. It's only painful in the transition period. We are now in transition up to our necks."

Dr. Spock, who does peace work at his own expense, retired from teaching at Western Reserve University last summer and is now writing three books. One is *Facts of Life for Teen-Agers*. He still uses the $8.50 pine drafting table he used some 20 years ago when he wrote, in longhand, *Baby and Child Care*. He and his wife Jane looked forward to an uncomplicated retirement of writing and sailing. They have a new, 35-foot auxiliary sloop, *Carapace,* and cruised the Caribbean early this winter.

"But on the way to retirement," he says, "I picked up this hobby—peace. By God, I certainly bit off more than I can chew."

That's just it, doctor, and all those middle-aged, Peter Pan-collared mothers who bought your book wonder about you. . . .

"I'm determined to win some authority for speaking for peace without having to be a senator to do it. I'm glad that I'm gradually being acknowledged somewhat grudgingly as a peace spokesman. I'm not a senile babe in the woods being used by SANE or the National Conference for New Politics. My eyes are wide open. Maybe three-fourths of my friends think I'm crazy, but I've been pioneering all my life, and I've been proved right, in pediatrics and in psychiatry. Maybe I'm a damned old fool, but I am obstinate. Until someone proves that I am wrong, especially about the Vietnam war, I have confidence."

Dr. Spock gets almost three beats out of one syllable of the Yankee English he speaks. It is the expert teacher's device. We had just finished luncheon when he told of more plans for his future.

"I think the most *unpopular* thing I could do is advocate the teaching of *morality* in the schools. I was christened an Episcopalian, but since we've been married, the only times Jane and I go to church is for weddings and funerals. My concept of what *God* is is certainly nowhere near what the people who translated the Bible originally intended. But I *believe* in spiritual *values* and idealism. Not just for myself. I believe this is the *nature* of man, that man cannot *exist* without ideals. He gets *sick* inside, he does not know how to comport himself. I want to help man find out in the last half of the twentieth century what *spiritual* aspirations have *validity*. And I would say that one of them is to get rid of *war,* which from most religious points of view is an abomination. And we should go out and feed the hungry. First in our own country, and then around the world.

"Parents' lack of direction is compounded by faculty people. I'm not assuming everyone will teach the same moral values. The good faculty person will say that others take opposite views. But young people need to be *reminded* that *morality* cannot be *dispensed* with. Man becomes not only nothing better than an *animal* but *worse* than any animal because of the *viciousness* he can let loose when he is operating without morality."

THE COPS AND THE KIDS

James Ridgeway

The clashes between police and demonstrators began as calculated maneuvers by The National Mobilization Committee to End the War in Vietnam, and the Youth International Party. The strategy was to confront the Chicago police, and thereby demonstrate that America was a police state. It ended as a full-blown insurrection of middle-class people against that state.

For the people who took part in this, the Democratic Convention was irrelevant; for them, politics is in the street. They either will be in the streets in increasing numbers from now on, or they will be returning to live the underground existence of the 1950's over again, leaving politics to the police.

The Chicago police department, not Mayor Daley, was the clear winner in the street fights. And the officers knew it. After they beat up the demonstrators Wednesday night, they were exultant. Where the youngsters had once made fun of the police, the officers now took to openly taunting the citizens—any citizen. Out of the debacle in Chicago, the police have emerged as an important political force. No candidate in America can run from now on without coming to terms with the police.

The city refused to give either the mobilization (mobs) or the yippies (yips) permits for their gathering. Instead they tried to run them out of town.

Plainclothesmen were assigned to tail both Rennie Davis and Tom Hayden, the two mob leaders. Others followed Paul Krassner and Jerry Rubin of the yips. This was good humored for a time; Krassner had a tail advise him where the best food was. Then on Sunday evening in Lincoln Park, near the lake in northern Chicago, where the yips were headquartered, Hayden and Davis tried to slip the dicks by running off into the darkness. By mistake, Hayden ran across the two officers, who threw him up against the side of a police car.

James Ridgeway, "The Cops and the Kids," THE NEW REPUBLIC, Sept. 7, 1968, © Harrison-Blaine of New Jersey, Inc. Reprinted by permission.

Hayden yelled for help and a small crowd gathered. "We're going to get you, you son-of-a-bitch," the dicks told Hayden, then they freed him.

Monday afternoon, the yips again gathered in Lincoln Park and Hayden and Krassner discussed plans for the Miss Yippie contest and the Yippie Olympics which Krassner was especially keen to begin. Hayden was talking to a group of people when he noticed the two dicks who had nabbed him the evening before approaching with a small convoy of paddy wagons and officers on motorcycles. They came right up, collared him and threw him into the paddy wagon and drove off before anybody could make a move.

On the way to the stationhouse, one of the officers turned to Hayden and pleasantly said to him, "We're going to get rid of you, you son-of-a-bitch." At the police station he was taken to a room, and while awaiting processing with others, was told to sit on the floor. As he waited a number of officers stopped off to pass the time of day. "If you guys want to kick the shit out of the cops," one of them said, "we'll kill every one of you."

"We'll spray you fuckers with submachine guns," said another.

"Phew," said a third, holding his nose. "God, do you stink."

(The police were especially angered by the radicals' slovenly dress and body odors. "Animals," they said in disgust. "Pigs," replied the yips. "Oink, oink.")

Shortly after Hayden was taken, the yips gathered, and after hoisting Red and Viet Cong flags, marched downtown to the police station. They were led by a sporty looking fellow with a plaid jacket and a peace-dove button pinned on it. He walked along with a black man dressed in green pants and sporting a McCarthy button. Both these characters were dicks.

At first the police were badly outnumbered and flustered as they ran along to catch up with the march. But they soon recovered their verve and dashed into the marchers and hauled out a lad. Pinning his arms behind his back, they threw him into a paddy wagon. A mild-looking man wearing glasses rushed up to protest. A policeman knocked off his glasses and sprayed some mace in his face. As they marched into the city, an air of insurgency swept through the crowd. Gail Carter of Berkeley, wearing a black beret, was hoisted onto a boy's shoulders, where she chanted, "Ho, Ho, Ho Chi Minh," and "Dump the Hump."

The marchers finally reached the police station, which was guarded by what looked to be several hundred officers; then they went over to Grant Park, which is opposite the Hilton Hotel, the convention headquarters. There they clustered around the statue of General Logan, a Civil War hero. A couple of boys climbed up on the statue and decked it with the Viet Cong flag. This angered the police, and several hundred of them formed a skirmish line. The officers charged at the statue, laying their billies to any youngster in the way. The youngsters rushed off from the statue in another direction yelling, "Here come de pig. Oink. Oink. Pig. Pig. Oink. Oink."

Meanwhile, Miss Carter approached the line of police, and going up to each man in the manner of an inspecting officer she paused, looked him hard in the eye, and said, "And you. What about you? I care for you. You know what I am saying. What do you feel in your heart? Or are you afraid to say what's in your heart?" A group of plainclothesmen took her picture with a Polaroid camera. But the films wouldn't develop properly and they fell to quarreling among themselves on that score and quite lost track of Miss Carter, who wandered off elsewhere.

Later that evening, the police charged into Lincoln Park, spraying tear gas into the yippies and others who had barricaded themselves in. The officers beat up the reporters and anyone else they could lay their hands on. Meanwhile, Hayden was charged with disorderly conduct for sitting on the grass and was bailed out. About midnight, he was about to enter the Hilton Hotel when a house dick recognized him and ordered him away. Coming away from the hotel, Hayden spotted two tails coming down the street. Seeking to avoid them, he walked across the intersection. At that moment, another plainclothesman, standing up the block, recognized Hayden and yelled out to the officer directing traffic, "Get him. Stop him." A dick grabbed Hayden from behind and threw him to the pavement. More police converged. Hayden yelled, "What have I done? I haven't done anything." But he was hustled off to the police station. An attorney who managed to see him there said the police wanted to charge Hayden with aggravated assault, but this was later dropped and he was charged with simple assault for spitting on a police officer. Bail was set at $1,000.

Hayden was released from custody about 3:30 that morning. On leaving the stationhouse with a handful of reporters and friends, he quickly ran into another car carrying plainclothesmen. At an intersection both dicks jumped out and said, "Hello, we're police officers, can we help you fellows?" After examining a White House press pass, they retreated. About an hour later, Hayden decided to go underground.

Tuesday evening, the yips, mobs, McCarthy youths and a lot of other people gathered to celebrate LBJ's birthday at the Colosseum which is a few blocks down Lake Michigan from the Hilton. There they listened to Jean Genet and William Burroughs berate the police. Draft cards were burned. Rock bands played. David Dellinger gave out the usual stuff about the movement. Paul Krassner gave LBJ the finger. Then the crowd joined in singing Happy Birthday LBJ, and "Fuck you, Lyndon Johnson."

At the end of the evening's entertainment, Rennie Davis said the plan was to disperse in small groups, then gather in full view of the television cameras at Grant Park. There they could greet the returning delegates.

It was midnight. The police were lined up on both sides of the street in front of the Hilton. A small band of people from Lincoln Park had already arrived and were waiting for the others from the Colosseum to march up. Scattered among them were the usual lot of plainclothesmen, doing their best to look like hippies but, as usual, chattering about the unwashed smell of the slobs they were sent to observe. Standing among them was a man with a porkpie hat and with a neat mustache. He chatted amiably with another fellow who appeared to be listening to the convention on a small transistor radio. Both looked rather like the artificially got-up detectives. But they weren't. The man in the hat was Hayden and his companion wasn't listening to the convention; he was tuned to the police radio bands, following the cops' movements. Here among the police was the mobs' field communications headquarters.

As the throng from the Colosseum flitted into the dark of the park, an air of expectancy grew. The police brought in buses full of fresh men and lined them up two deep. People began to chant, "Peace now, peace now," and then to burn draft cards before the television cameras. They yelled "Fuck you, LBJ," "Fuck you, Daley." More police were marched up. Helicopters circled overhead. Now word was coming over the transistor radios that the police had once more cleared Lincoln Park, using tear gas, which in addition to forcing the yips from the park, had gotten into drivers' eyes and stalled traffic on the highway. The crowds were moving through the streets stoning cars, and a group began to march towards Grant Park. More police were lined up before the Hilton. They were five deep in some places. They quietly moved in behind the park and on both sides of it. A police officer walked among the apprehensive reporters, suggesting they might better watch the scene from across the street. The convention adjourned. Buses carrying delegates were returning and the crowd, now numbering about 3,500, yelled at them, "Peace now"; "Join us, join us." First a few, then more, opened the bus windows and made the "V" sign at the crowd. There were cheers. "Join us, join us," went the chant. Fires were lit in the park. Now across the street in the hotel room lights were flashed on and off, giving the SOS signal. McCarthy youths began appearing at the windows, waving and calling out support. First one, then another came out on the street. "I didn't feel comfortable in that hotel with the pigs protecting us from you people," an Alabama challenge delegate said. "The real convention is in the streets," another said.

Although the gathering was pretty placid, with only a brief scuffle now and then, the police seemed increasingly edgy. At about 3 A.M. the first units of the Illinois National Guard were brought in. They got off their jeeps with rifles at the ready, and the police were marched off. The Guard commander, Brigadier-General Richard Dunn, tried to speak on his own microphone. But the crowd leaders suggested he come over and speak on theirs, instead. Dunn tried to do so, but was drowned out as Peter, Paul and Mary began singing, "If I Had a Hammer." Finally, Dunn was able to say that the National Guard didn't want to bother anyone. He retired to his jeep, which looked a little like a rabbit hutch, covered over with mesh wire for the commander's protection.

The insurrection was full-blown by Wednesday afternoon. Ten thousand people gathered at a band shell in the park, some distance from the hotel. When a youngster ran down the American flag, the police charged in swinging. One group of people wanted to go to the amphitheater, another to the Hilton. Both were blocked by troop movements which closed the bridges out of the park. To get out of the park, people walked north past the barricaded bridges. They milled around for a while, then seized upon one bridge which was still open to traffic, and blocked it. The police moved in, firing tear-gas barrages to break up the crowd. The gas spread back into the city, choking people in the streets and hotels. The demonstrators now split up and moved back through the different streets toward the Hilton, grouping finally on Michigan Avenue and marching on the hotel. Medics moved through the crowds, dampening handkerchiefs with water to fend off tear gas. Waving their hands in the "V" sign, chanting "Peace now, peace now," an enormous crowd marched on the hotel. The crowd came up against the police lines in front of the Hilton, milled around the edge of the hotel, held from below by the police and on the side by the military. It was about 8 P.M. Then the police charged, moving in skirmish line, columns, and two- and three-man groups. They hit the lines of marchers, clubbing down a man and then pulling him out for the arrest. A group to the south of the hotel fell back through stalled traffic before the police attack. The automobiles confused the officers and reduced the force of the attack. But suddenly 50 other officers burst out of a side street, hitting the march flank and driving the youngsters across the street against a wall. There they charged them, beating them indiscriminately.

A group gathered across from the hotel in the park. The police charged into it, beating people at will. They would pull them out into the street, fight them and then throw them into the paddy wagon. Others watching this from the Hilton grabbed anything they could find and threw it out the windows at the police.

The hotel was filled with nearly hysterical people, older women in faints, youngsters with blood streaming down their faces, girls crying.

At McCarthy's headquarters, on the Hilton's fifteenth floor, frenzied youths ripped up the sheets for bandages. The hotel manager was furious that his sheets were being torn and twice sent the police up to raid the McCarthy headquarters. The hotel management refused use of the hotel elevators to some people. The police sealed off the hotel and wouldn't let injured people enter.

Outside, the police continued forays into the crowd, beating and clubbing the people to make them disperse. The streets in front of the hotel were completely cut off. There was a no man's land around the side entrances where people darted in and out.

Vicious as this attack was, the demonstrators came back to Grant Park by midnight in large numbers. Thousands of people continued to gather there under the rifles of the troops, into the small hours of the morning. The lights flicked on and off in the hotel in support, but efforts to get the major candidates to come down and speak to the people ended in failure; Senator McCarthy wanted to go, but the Secret Service dissuaded him.

That night there was a new group of people there from the South

Side of Chicago—white youths—and they stood behind the police lines to support their boys. "Fruit," they yelled at a reporter wearing a checked coat. "Ya fuckin' coppa. Fruit." Long into the night, these two groups of Americans faced each other.

Following out their scheme to promote a continuing confrontation between growing numbers of people and the police—they figured that the Chicago officials would respond by bringing in more police and troops, and so make clear to all those looking on that Chicago was an armed camp and America was a police state—the radicals talked enthusiastically about little acts of violence, like a stink bomb in the hotel, or dirty words on some walls, to provoke the police and manipulate the liberal McCarthy youths into their own ranks. In effect, the idea was to simulate a little guerrilla war. By Wednesday night, it was clear that everyone—McCarthy youngsters, reporters, radicals, yips, well-to-do people walking their dogs, delegates to the convention, even some blacks—all sorts of people who had never heard of Tom Hayden or David Dellinger, were caught up in an insurrection in the streets. There were no real leaders. They came and went, sometimes carried out bleeding, sometimes arrested, sometimes off in a corner plotting. It made no real difference; to the crowds in the streets, it didn't matter who was at the microphone. Nobody manipulated these people. On Tuesday night they waved the Viet Cong flag and yelled, "Fuck you, LBJ." By Wednesday night, after they had been beaten by the Chicago police, held off by armed troops, gassed, they still came back to Grant Park in great numbers. At last they confronted the armed forces occupying the city, not with the Viet Cong flag, but with the American flag. Chicago smelled of revolution.

☐ MORALITY

The idea of a close connection between social organization and sexual repression may have been a new and disturbing insight when such works as Freud's *Civilization and its Discontents* and Lasswell's *Psychopathology and Politics* appeared in the early 1930s, but now it is a commonplace observation. Conservatives recognize accurately that an irreverent attitude toward social institutions goes hand in hand with an irreverent attitude toward traditional morality, and young rebels, recognizing with equal accuracy where their enemies are most tender, taunt the authorities with sexual symbols and dirty words.

Just as there have been organized protests to secure greater racial freedom and greater freedom of speech, there have been organized protests toward greater freedom of sexual behavior. In several major cities there are organizations working toward liberalization of laws affecting homosexuals, legalization of abortion, repeal of laws concerning sexual behavior between consenting adults. Of such organizations, undoubtedly the best-publicized is the San Francisco Bay area's Sexual Freedom League, some of whose protest activities are here described by Jack Lind.

THE SEXUAL FREEDOM LEAGUE

Jack Lind

On a bright, hot Saturday in August 1965, a young iconoclast from New York named Jefferson Poland strode into the chilly waters of San Francisco Bay accompanied by two girlfriends. The crowd of tourists and sun bathers in Aquatic Park cheered lustily; many shouted words of encouragement. The cause of the crowd's enthusiasm was plain: Poland and his friends were stark naked.

The event had been well publicized in advance and police were on the alert, but Sergeant John V. Kennedy, who was in charge of the detail, did not interfere. Either he was acutely embarrassed by the whole thing or he was myopic. "I can't see anything from here," he remarked softly. "I haven't seen a thing yet."

While Poland and the girls waded about in the water, pickets in the crowd circulated with banners carrying messages such as MAKE LOVE, NOT WAR; LOVE THY NEIGHBOR; LEGALIZE PROSTITUTION; WHY BE ASHAMED OF YOUR BODY? and BEING NUDE IS WHOLESOME. When Poland, lean and white, trudged out of the water with his two companions, Sergeant Kennedy's eyesight improved perceptibly and he went up and arrested all three on charges of swimming without proper attire at a public beach.

Poland and his friends—a petite brunette named Ina Saslow, who was living with him and supporting herself as a baby sitter, and an ample blonde named Shirley Einsiedel, a sometime bean picker— subsequently pleaded guilty to the charges in muncipal court. Poland served five weekends in jail and the girls were given suspended sentences.

It seemed a small price to pay for publicizing Poland's brain child, a loosely knit organization known as the Sexual Freedom League.

Since the historic wade-in at Aquatic Park, the League has become a highly articulate organization with a membership fluctuating between 100 and 200. The East Bay League, located in Berkeley, is the cornerstone of a movement now made up of 15 autonomous units

Jack Lind, "The Sexual Freedom League," PLAYBOY, November, 1966. Reprinted by permission.

around the country, mostly on university and college campuses.

The East Bay League is both the most active and, according to Poland, the sexiest of sex leagues in the country. Like its counterparts elsewhere, the East Bay group has a twofold purpose: the liberalization of laws pertaining to sex—abortion, prostitution, pornography—and the sheer, unadulterated enjoyment of sex.

"We believe," the League proclaims in a preamble to its "Statement of Position," "that sexual expression, in whatever form agreed upon between consenting persons of either sex, should be considered an inalienable human right. . . . Sex without guilt and restriction is good, pleasurable, relaxing, and promotes a spirit of human closeness, compassion and good will. We believe that sexual activity . . . has a wealth of potential for making life more livable and enjoyable . . ."

Poland started the first League in New York, but there were few members and little enthusiasm, so he went West to found a unit while studying at San Francisco State College. The group printed some literature and buttons, but the movement turned out to be too academic in its texture to attract much attention. As a friend wryly pointed out, "Sexual freedom has to be *implemented* to work."

Finally, Poland, who has from time to time supported himself by selling blood plasma (it beats selling whole blood in terms of income), moved across the Bay to the fertile fields of Berkeley, scene of Vietnam Day Committee demonstrations, the Free Speech Movement, and other manifestations of the free spirit.

Still, only a few staunch sexniks joined—until Poland staged the historic nude wade-in at Aquatic Park, which was copiously covered in the local press (the *San Francisco Chronicle,* which is the champion of topless and other developments on the cultural scene, ran a long, sympathetic piece on its front page). The wade-in gave the League just the impetus it needed and, for a while, enthusiastic adherents of free love stood in line to join.

From a narrow group of intellectually bent sensualists, the membership has grown to include various types of professionals. They are mostly, says Joseph Buch, the League's executive director and curator of membership files, people of the middle class—"young moderns." They have been liberated by the new morality and the pill. (There are no embarrassing pauses at an SFL party.) The average age of the members is 25.

"They are the type of people you are likely to find at an alumni club gathering," says Buch rather matter-of-factly. When the League was reorganized last summer because of leadership problems, Buch, a cerebral, articulate type with a penchant for tweeds and cords, was named to replace Richard Thorne, a pragmatic sensualist who, for a while, taught an amorphous course called History of Western Anti-Sensualism at Berkeley's Free University. Although weighted down by organizational matters and The Issues, Buch has no intention of de-emphasizing the corporeal aspects of sex.

"Hell, everybody involved likes to screw," he remarked recently.

As the group grows and furthers its efforts in disseminating information about sex and related matters, it often finds itself bogged down in the same procedural difficulties that beset other political and social groups. There are many arguments about procedures, committees and general structure; but it is still the only group whose membership application asks such diverse questions as "Are you interested in: mate swapping? picnics? public relations?"

In the beginning at the Berkeley chapter, under Thorne's stewardship, there were signs of sexual repressions and uncertainty, and gatherings joyously announced in invitations as nude parties were embarrassingly covered up during the early hours. "This is a nude party," a host would rather testily remind his guests as the evening wore on. He would then lead the way in helping a pretty young thing undress and by and by everybody was naked. From nudity to "expressive use of the body" was but a short jump and in no time couches, sofas and rugs became the scene of what one member described, with considerable satisfaction, as "a sheer undiluted sex orgy."

The nude party is less shrouded in inhibitions and uncertainty these days. The purpose is well defined in everybody's mind and the guests go at it zealously.

"The American people," Buch said recently, by way of introduction to a typical nude party, "are beginning to realize that there is more to sex than once a week with your wife in the missionary position. They are discovering that, despite the blandishments of advertising, one of the great leisure activities is *sex*. The Sexual Freedom League serves as a place where sexually liberated people can meet sexually—rather than having to look through the ads of the back pages of the tabloids."

At a nude party, sex is there for the asking—but you have to ask right.

"If a man wants to make it with a guest," explains Buch, "it depends on how he does it. If he comes up to a girl talking to a date or somebody else and says, 'Hi, I'm such and such, let's make it,' chances are she is going to look at him as if he just crawled out from under a rock."

One goes about establishing relations much as at any other social affair—except that the sexual interest is taken for granted in advance, and the chances of "making it" are infinitely greater. But there are, of course, "no guarantees," Buch warns.

That doesn't mean that all of the members accept the informalities. A young girl named Joan told of an experience she had at one of the first nude parties. "The party was kind of dull and I felt very uncomfortable and didn't undress. There had been some games and then a hypnotist tried to put a group into a trance, but things weren't going very well. Then one very pretty girl accommodated all of the men who hadn't made any contacts, and I thought that it would be wonderful to have a thousand men to choose from—all who wanted me. I wasn't ready to do it, but I couldn't help thinking about it. Then the hypnotist announced he was going to put us all into a deep trance, and we fell asleep. I vaguely remember being handled and moved about and I finally agreed to have intercourse with one of the men. Later I was told that I had been completely undressed and was crying and four different men had used me. I had been mumbling 'No, no, no.' Later, one of the men tried to convince me that I hadn't been insulted. That's not my idea of sexual freedom."

Many of those early problems have been solved by requiring that each male guest bring a female date to keep the odds even. Of course, both guests are free to make any new contacts they wish. As one might expect, the League has more male members than female at any given time. But the females are steady members, while the men are short-termers. Often a new male member will attend one or two parties without participating, "just to see what it's all about," and never show up again.

The setting of one recent typical nude party was a five-room apartment on the first floor of a stucco building on a pleasant tree-lined street on the fringe of the Berkeley campus of the University of California. The walls were buff-colored and empty, save for a couple of abstract paintings of no great merit. The décor was decidedly early Salvation Army—a blend of nonperiod chairs, an old sofa, a large couch covered with a purplish material and a gray patterned rug. (In the early days, the League had trouble finding hosts willing to hold nude parties in their homes. "The Social Committee," said an article in *Love,* the League's newsletter, "would like to plan more social gatherings but is hampered in its endeavors by a lack of facilities. . . . Members of the League have opened their minds and bodies but few have opened up their homes.")

There were about a dozen people in the living room of the stucco house, a few more men than women. A tall, lean man with a walrus mustache, dark hornrimmed glasses and wearing light corduroy pants and black turtle-neck sweater stood in a corner, cocktail glass close to chest, offering his expertise on Lyndon Johnson's failures in Vietnam to an earnest young man in white jeans and open shirt and a baby-faced blonde girl in tight green pants and matching blouse. The girl appeared bored with his ruminations and glanced around the room from time to time, hoping that somebody would rescue her.

In the dining room, a jovial round-faced chap in his mid-20s was regaling two couples with a story about a physician who had mistakenly prescribed an overdose of male hormones to a nymphomaniac. Suddenly, from out of nowhere, a pretty young thing in her early 20s, with closely cropped black hair and wearing only a bikini-type bottom, emerged. Her waist was slim and her breasts bobbed as she casually strode by the group at the dining-room table.

"I see the nudity is beginning," remarked a cherubic gentleman in a neat dark business suit, after casting a long look at the topless girl.

Shortly, one of the men stepped to a corner and deftly removed every shred of clothes, except for socks and loafers. "Why don't we go nude, too?" said a tweedy man to a sexy-looking girl he was talking to. "Everybody else seems to be." In short order, they both were.

The pace quickened and the volume of the hi-fi went up. One couple began to dance a mild version of the frug in the middle of the living-room floor. Shortly, another couple joined them. The rest of the guests appeared to pay no attention to them, although all four were stark naked. Some were drinking; others were talking in clusters, standing, or sitting on chairs or the couch.

"We play anything on the hi-fi," one of the guests remarked. "Jazz, blues, rock 'n' roll. Sometimes even Beethoven."

Another gentleman, who introduced himself as Herb (many League guests are first names only, often for fear of public identification,) and said he was an insurance salesman, was standing in the kitchen, nude, pouring himself a glass of wine from a gallon jug.

"It's funny," he mused, "how one's attitudes toward sex change after a few nude parties."

He pointed to a couple slouched, nude, on the couch in a corner of the living room. The man was cupping one of the girl's breasts in his hand as he pressed close to her.

"When I went to my first party," Herb went on, "I was frankly embarrassed and curious. When couples would start making love, on the rug or on the sofa, my eyes almost popped out of my head. I had never seen others make love before. Once I got used to it, I found it quite stimulating.

"Now it all seems so natural. Of course, you're still curious—after all, we are human and not robots—but there is no longer this intense, almost morbid curiosity about what other people are doing with each other at a party."

The couples on the floor were standing in warm embraces, swaying gently to the rhythms from the hi-fi. A girl was lounging on the sofa, drink in hand, gently, almost casually, fondling the erect penis of the dark-haired man sitting next to her. The turtle-neck expert on Vietnam was still holding forth, although the girl in green had been replaced by a dark man in briefs. The girl was nowhere to be seen.

The doorbell rang and the host, a rangy, bespectacled statistician who needed a haircut, went to the door and admitted two couples. After a few casual introductions, the four repaired to the kitchen, where one of the men began mixing drinks with a bottle of Scotch he had brought along.

"They are two married couples," volunteered a trim nude blonde, who strutted about the living room apparently looking for a suitable mate, "but I doubt that they are together tonight. I think the men came with each other's wives."

Buch explained afterward that this is not at all unusual. "Each married partner frequently shows up with somebody else. Maybe they started out from different places, maybe they just wanted to enlarge the party. There is no jealousy; I don't think there has to be.

"Nobody makes any bones about being married. Nobody in the League is ashamed of being married. In fact, it is a mark of some status. But nobody lets marriage interfere with their sex life." (In point of fact, about 85 per cent of the female members of the League are married, and most of them come to League functions with their spouses—although they frequently have sex with somebody else at a party.)

"The love-roses-and-marriage bit, the romanticized love, is a pretty sick aspect of love," Buch continued. "The religious setup of Western society teaches us to regard our wives as our possessions. Maybe it's a little silly to think of your wife or husband as chattel. Besides, often a man is involved in so many things that he is not really capable of giving his wife as much time as she, as a sexual being, deserves."

The apartment was now permeated with an aura of sensuality; interestingly, there was no longer much talk of sex. As one of the guests explained it: "Eventually, it can get to be boring to discuss the same subject with the same people all the time. It would drive me up the wall."

Most of the 20 or so persons in the apartment had drifted off. One couple was unabashedly engaged in lovemaking on the couch, others were fondling each other on the rug, several were in the two adjoining bedrooms. One paunchy gentleman still wearing his shorts was walking about rather aimlessly, obviously dispirited about not having made a contact and obviously trying not to be obvious about his curiosity and frustrations.

A pretty girl with long blonde hair drifted out to a small factional group in the kitchen. She pointed out the significant difference between this and other kinds of nudist groups: "Most nudist camps are really quite prudish. They have to use all that sunshine-and-health jazz as a justification for going nude—instead of just pure sensuality."

After a few more minutes of chitchat, she and one of the males in the kitchen moved on into one of the bedrooms, where a few moments later, the man could vaguely be seen through the open door on top of the girl. A stockily built man in his middle 30s brushed by the open door and peeked in. "Oh, pardon me," he said and turned around with an apologetic smile. He explained quite unemotionally that the girl was his wife and he certainly did not wish to intrude on her lovemaking.

From time to time, a couple would drift back into the living room. Some put on their clothes, thanked the host for a pleasant evening and left. By one A.M. the party was over.

"The striking thing about these parties," said Buch afterward, "is that they are really not very much different from any other social gathering."

That seems fairly accurate. SFL parties start slowly, like most ordinary cocktail parties. If most of the preliminary talk is about sex, it is not very different from the average penthouse bash. When normal cocktail parties loosen up, the liquor flows freer and the guests become more gregarious. Here the stimulation is of a different order, but the pace quickens in like manner. And while you can dig up strange histories of sexual trauma and disturbing adolescent experiences, there are probably quite similar tales told at the average PTA meeting.

As another member put it: "What we do is really no different from what many Congressmen do on their junkets or what fraternities do at their parties—except that we do it without shame or guilt or concealment. The only criterion for any sexual act is really, 'Do I want to do it? Does it hurt anyone else?' "

The intensity of the sensuality at parties varies from one to another, depending on in-group psychology and the personality of those present. Some are obviously trying to overcome deep-seated inhibitions and guilt complexes.

Others seem quite stable intellectually and emotionally, and they are consistent in word and deed. At a nude buffet dinner party, a lovely girl named Carol explained why she had joined the League: "I derive a lot of pleasure from having sex with men, but . . . after I sleep with a man, he will invariably develop a psychological dependence on me. I enjoy sex . . . and I consider any emotional involvement . . . an entirely undesirable side effect. I came to these parties hoping to meet men, enjoy sex with them, and then break off ties with them until perhaps the next party, so that there will be no possibility of . . . emotional hassle." Later Carol went upstairs and spent time with a few different men. Afterward she stood around watching the merrymaking of the others.

A more anxious attitude along the same lines was expressed by another girl, also quite attractive, named Shirley: "I might meet a young man I like at the party and go to bed with him. But I wouldn't want to do this with anyone I had met beforehand, and I would hope afterward that he would forget about me, unless perhaps we met at another nude party. That is, I would like to be two people, one person when I am at a nude party and another when I am leading my everyday life. I wouldn't want the things I did at the party to follow me . . ."

Shirley had some criticism about the parties themselves: "It often seems to me that there is no love present. People are merely playing games, engaging in exhibitionism, voyeurism. There are no guys or girls talking to each other, no groups of threes or fours; everyone seems intent on making someone or getting made."

A sociology student from Berkeley doing field research at the SFL parties had a more general theory about the motivations of the participants. "I used to wonder," he said, "why people would form groups like this when there are so many other opportunities to have sex. And why have it in public like this? I think the answer, especially for the girls, is that these are people who are stimulated and quite eager for sexual activity, but they condemn their own sociosexual behavior. They may be less socially adept than others and find it hard for a dinner conversation to develop into a roll in the hay, even if both parties are willing. At a nude party, all of the real and imagined barriers drop. Sexual intercourse becomes normal and acceptable, and some girls want to place themselves in a position where they have to have sex to go along with the crowd. I don't think this is deviant or perverted behavior. In many ways, it is the healthiest outlet for hyperactive or oversexed people to relieve their sexual problems."

The theory was given substantiation that same evening. A beautiful 19-year-old (girls that young are rarities at SFL gatherings) was attending her first party. She remained clothed and aloof from the goings on for most of the evening. Then she demonstrated her basic belief in sexual freedom by performing fellatio with one of the long-established male members. Afterward she remained as clothed and aloof as before, but she seemed more concerned with the activities of the others. Then that same male returned to prod her to undress and have intercourse with him. She refused, and he spent quite some time and energy accusing her of getting "kicks" from denying him. He then tried breaking her down with eloquent rhetoric about her glorious body and its capabilities. She seemed to be as aware of her capabilities as he, for she suddenly left him, strode over to another member who had obviously been scrutinized, proceeded to undress completely and tumble with her new friend.

The old hand never fully recovered from the loss of that pretty thing, even though there were many others around to kiss away his wounds. In fact, it is remarkable how good-looking most of the female League members are. The sociology student contributed some comments on this, too: "The females attending the parties vary from the average to the exceptionally well endowed. I'm sure that young ladies with less-than-average gifts are extremely reluctant to join." The same thought has been more profitably expressed by an advertisement for a local reducing salon that asks, "Are you ready for your first nude party?"

Another important observation that the student sociologist made concerned male physiology: "I've often heard that men don't get erections at nudist camps, because the atmosphere is intentionally sterile. Well, erections are the exception at nude parties, too. Of course, physical contact brings immediate results, but when just standing around, most men are relaxed in every sense."

Something else notably absent at nude parties are beards and beat types. The Berkeley activists and Telegraph Hill hipsters seem to regard the SFL as square and overregimented. One coffee-shop frequenter put the members down as "suburban wife swappers." A writer expressed a more general attitude that people who would join the League must be sexually "hung up."

The orgiastic nature of the SFL parties is by no means viewed with equilibrium by all those participating. Not long ago, *Love* dutifully printed a disclaimer from a disenchanted male member, who wrote:

How frightful it must be to go to an orgy expecting to be smothered with love and nothing happens except that you get pawed around a little. . . . I've been to orgies and they are always sad. Someone ends up crying or passing out drunk. . . . This is quite a comedown from the League's original spirit, when they first ventured forth with proud banners flying from erect penises. I'll be frank. I'm against sex under most conditions. Orgasm has a tendency to turn off friendship, tenderness and flowingness, while at the same time turning on possessiveness, jealousy and cantankerousness. You have no idea how many good relationships I have literally fucked away. Always there is guilt. Always there is "You made me do it" and "How can you still respect me?"

The League, this critic asserted, is clearly a place for men to "roll up a score." "It doesn't surprise me," he added gruffly, "that there are more men than women in the League."

A girl member of the League, an intense, young red-haired girl with an absorbing interest in sexual freedom, complained even more vociferously: "Frankly, I do not enjoy this kind of sex at all. Before you know it, there is nothing in the room but twenty-odd sweating bodies."

She was understandably depressed about her experiences at a nude party at which she was chased, during the course of an evening, by half a dozen strange men who considered her fair game.

"I had no empathy or feeling for any of them," she related. "Finally, I fled into a bedroom and plopped down on the bed—only to find a man in the bed who started pawing at me. I told him I didn't feel like it now and asked him to leave me alone."

She was obviously not being a gracious guest. "Then get out," snarled the enraged would-be swain, "this is my pad." The amative young man was, indeed, the owner of the apartment, and our red-haired ladyfriend beat a hasty retreat.

Love's editor, David Lichtenberg, a young and zealous Berkeley science student who has tried communal living under a kibbutzlike system and has dabbled in nonverbal communications programs sponsored by the Unitarian Church, sadly agreed with the male correspondent's criticism. "Some of the parties have been as you suggest," he said, but he felt confident that the rough spots would be smoothed out once the membership attained greater sexual maturity.

Love's editorial attitude is expressed by this statement from an early issue:

> Sex is an Art, the most fundamental of all the arts; like dancing, it is the expressive use of the body; like a play or novel, it is the use of conflict, suspense and the interaction of contrasting personalities; most of all it is like music.

When Richard Thorne was president of the East Bay League, he liked to put on sex games. His type of gamesmanship fell somewhat short of the standards set for games in other strata of society, yet some members complained that there weren't *enough* sex games at nude parties. (Buch thinks that games "smack of directedness and lack of imagination" and eschews them.)

A letter from a young wife in Marin County, who is studying for a master's degree in philosophy, to an officer of the League, sheds light on the games as well as on the attitude of married women who attend League functions with their husbands,

> Let me explain to you about Saturday night. I imagined it was obvious to you that neither Ron nor I were in our usual do-what-you-want-to-do-with-anybody mood. That was no accident, but it was our decision to stay pretty much together, since we enjoy each other's lovemaking and find it stimulating to watch sexual activities together. I see now, though, that this attitude is not one to maximize my pleasure, nor his. I found myself wanting to meet other people and perhaps do sexual things with them. He was content to just watch other couples on the bed. It would have been possible to separate, but I know there would have been reper-

cussions on his part. I found in the past that the only way I can help him not to be jealous is to assist him in developing a definite mental set before we go to a party. After this is done, he usually enjoys and encourages my lovemaking with other people. With this in mind, our attitude about the future will probably be much less sexually monogamous.

What also contributed to our leaving early was that I wanted to get some sleep Saturday night so I could stay up and study for a test on Monday. At first, I thought there would be quiet places to sleep at the party, but there was none.

One of the main attractions of the party to us, one that made us decide to spend the time going to Berkeley when we had a million things to do here, was the announcement of games, prizes and films. We expected some unique sex games and stag films.

A suggestion for future parties, by the way, might be to think up some new games to play. I know only two. One involves the male partners standing in line, with the females blindfolded and trying to guess who their partners are. The only part each girl is allowed to touch is the genital area (no trying on for size). I have no idea what the prizes would be, but I'm sure you'd come up with something.

The second game, and not quite as good, is for the guys and girls to squirt whipped cream on each other and then eat it off. This has interesting results.

You may or may not like the idea of games, but I think they are enjoyable diversions . . .

The prevalent attitude about past failures of games was expressed in a letter to *Love:* "People, mostly shadowy personalities, watched or participated, took what they wanted and slipped away. All feeling of total group communication was lost . . ."

One group that has been surprisingly absent from the fun and games has been the Berkeley police department. They have publicly stated a hands-off policy unless formal complaints are filed. And there has been only one full-scale raid, complete with plainclothesmen (but no noclothesmen), a midnight charge by camera-toting patrolmen popping flashbulbs, and all the other accouterments. In this case, a complaint had indeed been filed by a relative of the host; and the cops were looking specifically and only for minors who were drinking. They found none. More importantly, no arrests for sexual misbehavior were made, although some League activities are illegal under California law.

For the entire time the police were on the premises, one girl castigated them for not bringing dates and for ruining the male-female ratio. There was general confusion otherwise; no one was sure of his rights, nor did anyone want to reveal his name and address. Most of the members hastily dressed when the police arrived, but one young man stayed adamantly naked and he was left alone. When the little blitz was over, the party resumed; it was reported to have been one of the best in a long time.

Not all of the League's social affairs are *au naturel*. In fact, get-togethers are normally dressy affairs at which invited guests are urged to get acquainted and exchange views on sex and other pertinent matters. Nor, for that matter, are all affairs held indoors. Frequently, nude beach parties are held at Half Moon Bay, a stretch of which has long been the playground for other nude groups.

Not long ago, the League found an agreeably different setting for a social affair—a large ranch near San Francisco. While the ranch hands were tending cattle and horses, members of the League frolicked happily in and about the swimming pool in unencumbered nudity. From time to time, individual couples would drift off to patches of green under shady trees to practice, with crusading spirit, one of the avowed purposes of the League—the enjoyment of the art of sex.

Sometimes League members become confused and anxious about their goals and they turn to *Love*. It has, from time to time, run a lively column of advice to the sexlorn, conducted under the nom de plume Colette. The column offers a good deal of insight into the views and sexual appetites of the League's members.

"Dear Colette," an apprehensive girl member wrote recently, "after talking only a few hours with a man I met at a party, I had sex with him. I thought he liked me and expected he would call me again soon. He hasn't. Do you think that he has been fair?"

"It is very unwise," Colette responded, "to have sex with someone you've known only a few hours, unless you expect no more than an enjoyable sexual experience. If you want to see him again, call him. Why assume that maintaining the relationship is solely his responsibility?"

Another girl was faced with an equally painful problem. Would it, she asked, hurt her relationship with her husband if she had sex with an old boyfriend visiting from out of town? "Having several sexual relationships at the same time can be an enriching experience," wrote Colette, "if everyone involved is agreeable. Discuss your feelings with your husband and find our exactly how he feels about it.

Indicate to him that your love for him would not be affected if you had sex with Phil (the old boyfriend). Be sure that Phil understands how you feel so that he does not become jealous or suffer guilt."

Finally, the girl was advised that if she had sex with somebody else, her husband could scarcely be blamed for having his fun, too. "The problems that arise from multiple sexual relationships," averred Colette, "are usually caused by misunderstandings. Good luck!"

The philosophy of the League is fully—and ponderously—set forth in its published "Statement of Position" (the cover of which is adorned with an artful woodcut showing Adam and Eve about to make love in the Garden of Eden). The statement lashes out at Protestant ethics and a society rife with taboos, repressions, guilt complexes and antiquated sex laws. It specifically states the League's position on such social phenomena as:

Public nudity ("that nakedness excites others in an unwanted and prurient way and abets sex crimes is a myth"), young sex ("we believe that a sex organ in the hand of a child is more desirable than a toy machine gun"), pornography ("writing which focuses on sex does not need anything of 'redeeming social import' in order to justify such a focus on sex. Sex . . . is redeeming in and of itself"), abortions ("all laws and hospital regulations which restrict or deny such freedom should be repealed") and prostitution ("we believe that it is the prerogative of all persons to engage in sexual activity with all other consenting persons, free *or* for financial return").

Earlier this year, Thorne instituted a class in techniques of eroticism, a sort of academic 12-hour course, with demonstrations of sexual techniques. The new management of the League has scrapped it. "It is out, finished—as of now," Buch said recently. "All it succeeds in being is a big ego scene for the guy who is doing the demonstrations. The basic goal may be all right, but we're going to have to try to implement the idea in a more cerebral way. After all, the basic problems between man and wife are not the kind you need to demonstrate."

Since the reorganization of the League's top leadership last summer, the group has, in fact, taken on a somewhat intellectualized approach to sexual problems—although, Buch insists, not at the expense of the pure enjoyment of sex. He thinks it will strengthen the League immeasurably.

Under the new setup, members are organized in circles—each circle being a semiautonomous body represented on the League's executive committee, each with a membership that shares mutual interests in addition to sex itself. As of this writing, there were plans to organize a circle on eroticism and the arts, one on abortion problems, another on public relations and one on play reading. The young lady who conducts the Colette column, fearing that the play-reading circle, much like the one she had participated in in the Unitarian Church, might overlap with the eroticism-and-the-arts circle, suggested as an alternative that it might be a good idea to form a chess circle. The response was less than enthusiastic.

The purpose of the circles, explained Buch, is to get a dialog going among people who are interested in sexual liberality. But some people doubt that the Sexual Freedom League with its circles and nude parties can accomplish anything really significant in the way of sexual liberality and removal of repressions.

"Those who clamor the loudest are not really sexually free," says the Reverand David Baar, chaplain to the Bishop of the Episcopal Church in San Francisco, and an outspoken liberal. "Sexual freedom means that you retain your sexual identity and the ability to feel the sexual impulse in the face of confrontation with other people. Free sex isn't per se going to make people accept others any better and establish bonds with them. The ultimate object is not free love, but to be free to love."

Others, such as *Realist* editor Paul Krassner, take a lighter but no less serious view: "They (the SFL members) are a horny but consistent antidote to Norman Vincent Peale and Dear Abby. They are silly and I respect them."

☐ RELIGION

The churches, like the universities, have been caught offguard by the rapidity of the change in attitude toward constituted authority. As James A. Pike points out in *The Authority Crisis,* much of what has happened in the 1960s would have been unthinkable a decade ago. Pike, former Episcopal Bishop of California, is more than just a theorist in matters of protest—he has been a severe critic of official religious doctrines, once officially censured by his church's ruling body and four times the object of unsuccessful attempts to initiate heresy proceedings.

The churches have attempted to move with the changes, yet have balked when the changes seemed to be taking place too rapidly. The "rebellion" of the sisters of the Order of the Immaculate Heart of Mary—which brought them into a confrontation with church authority—was originally inspired by a papal exhortation toward renewal of values.

While there has been protest within the church, many religious leaders have gone out to lead civil rights marches and peace demonstrations. It is doubtful that any previous decade in American history could match the 1960s in the number of clergymen thrown into jail. One of the first great leaders of the modern civil rights movement was the Reverend Martin Luther King, Jr.; one of Dr. Benjamin Spock's co-defendants was the Reverend Sloan Coffin; and in Milwaukee a Catholic priest, Reverend James E. Groppi, was a leader in the fight for open housing.

THE AUTHORITY CRISIS

James A. Pike

Nowadays it's not what you are but what you say and do that counts. One of the rapid shifts of our times is the swift depreciation of status and titles as bases for acceptance of notions.

The change has reflected itself in every phase of society. Take the family. There was a time when most young people accepted something as sound or desirable because parents declared it so to be. Now, by and large, the cause-and-effect relation is reversed. Young people rate their parents' intelligence and good sense in terms of how smart and how sensible they consider their parents' words and actions to be. They may indeed respect their parents; but when they do, it is because their parents' words and deeds are assessed positively on their own merits.

The same is true of other institutions of our society. In the recollection of many of us, there was a time when the fact that the president of a college or university said something made it true for most of the enrolled listeners. Now, more and more such utterances are evaluated on their own merits and the speaker is accordingly assessed; less and less is recognition given to the speaker on the basis of his title with his utterance thus being automatically given credence.

. . . .

The ideas or factual statements of a clergyman, whether parson or primate, were once widely regarded as automatically true. These days having anything from "Rev." to "Most Rev." in front of his name does not produce the former almost Pavlovian response; rather, any reputation he may have for soundness rests upon the fact that a considerable number of things which he has been saying and doing have commended themselves to people in his flock, or beyond.

Nowhere has the development of the authority crisis been more evident than in the Roman Catholic Church during the last few years.

From pp. 25, 28-39 in IF THIS BE HERESY *by James A. Pike. Copyright © 1967 by James A. Pike. Reprinted by permission of Harper & Row, Publishers.*

The calling of Vatican Council II by Pope John XXIII can, in perspective, be seen as an effect as well as a cause. It is becoming increasingly evident that in this great Communion of Christians there was already an enormous amount of suppressed restiveness concerning manifold aspects of the Church's doctrinal and ethical teaching, structure and ministry, ways of worship, and practical operations. For many, no longer was it enough that the status quo rested upon the authority of Rome. So on reflection it now would seem apparent that beloved Pope John's then surprising major move toward opening up the whole situation was the only way to begin to ameliorate what would have surfaced before long anyway as an open crisis of authority.

Then, with the door to inquiry now at least ajar, the relatively free discussion of Bishops in Council—made public via the mass media—encouraged Roman Catholic thinkers (from theologians to journalists) to bring various other previously muffled issues even more out into the open. Before long almost everything was under challenge. The inauguration of more democratic policies—the adoption of the concept of the collegiality of bishops and its implementation through the forthcoming Synod, the organization of national conferences of bishops to exercise a considerable degree of "home rule," the formation of representative bodies on diocesan and parochial levels—represents more than the beginning of a reform in government; channels have now been provided for individuals, clergy and lay, to voice their queries about traditional positions and to propose alternatives. Meanwhile there has been a journalistic transition from "house organs" to a free press and the initiation of new lay-managed papers. The result: more intra-Church controversy is reflected in the pages of Roman Catholic papers and magazines than in all other church publications put together. And Roman Catholic authors have been turning out a spate of books offering candid appraisal and constructive criticism, far ahead in quantity, and often in quality, of critical writing on the part of non-Roman authors (which also, of course, has been on the increase).

The expression of such controversy is not only an effect but also a cause of increasing polarization in the Church between liberals and conservatives, or as they are now frequently called, "post-conciliar" Catholics and "Traditionalists." Obviously aware of the mounting tension, and possessing a more conservative temperament than John XXIII, Pope Paul has in the past year, in statement after statement, increasingly sought to restrain thrusts toward reform and slow up certain movements toward the fulfillment of *aggiornamento* in the doctrinal field.[1]

Not relevant at this point in our discussion is whether the Pope has been wrong or right in any given instance. What is significant, in terms of perceiving the general authority crisis, is the reception accorded these various declarations, and the correlative assessment of the Supreme Pontiff—in Roman Catholic papers and journals of opinion. A few examples will suffice.

His Holiness called a conference of learned scholars in several fields to "update" the Doctrine of Original Sin. In his greeting he reminded them that whatever they discussed or concluded must leave in the picture a single primal couple as the source of original sin. But after he had left, the group promptly proceeded to discuss the subject on the basis of the theory of polygenesis—a posture toward the subject taken for granted by scholars of the caliber of those assembled.

In an address lacking in specificity the Pope warned assembled representatives of the Jesuit Order throughout the world against dangerous trends within the Order. The result? Widespread bewilderment and rebuttal, but no signs of relaxation in the contribution to reform so notably being supplied to the Church by Jesuits.

His Holiness dispatched a strongly worded cautionary message to the Dutch hierarchy on the occasion of their first national conference. But the bishops have since put forth a bold new catechism for adults. It is without an Adam and Eve, a literal Virgin Birth, or a "limbo" for unbaptized children (Heaven is open to them). They left room for "conscientious" remarriage after divorce, left birth control by the best medical methods to the discretion of the couple, and no longer proclaimed the Atonement a "payoff," but rather an entering by us into the costly commitment of Jesus.[2] In connection with reforms in the teaching and practice in their own country the Dutch hierarchy

[1] But he has been impressively bold in other areas. Repeatedly he has pleaded for immediate steps for peace in Vietnam and has involved himself and his representatives in the effort. And Pope Paul's recent comprehensive analysis of the world's socioeconomic problems, in the Encyclical *Populorum Progressio,* was sufficiently liberal to be both criticized and praised by many outside and inside the Church as anti-capitalist and Marxist or "marxian."

[2] The approach is based on the challenge in Matt. 20:22b (A.V.): "Are ye able to drink of the cup that I shall drink of, and to be baptized with the baptism that I am baptized with?" and is parallel to the view of the Cross in the Statement of Faith of the United Church of Christ.

publicly stated that they wished no interference from the Curia, in-dicating pointedly that the Church of Holland did not seek to inter-fere in the affairs of the Church of any other country.[3]

Pleas from headquarters for a moratorium on discussion of the requirement of clerical celibacy have gone unheeded. Roman Catholic scholars and journalists have conducted several surveys of opinions of priests and of laymen; the results of such surveys have been given wide publicity within the Church; and discussion of the pros and cons of the topic have continued to abound in Roman Catholic pub-lications.

Last year the Sacred Congregation on Doctrine (successor to the Holy Office, itself successor to the Inquisition) instructed each national episcopal conference to report on the extent to which any of a long list of "heresies" were being taught within the Church in the given country, and what should be done about it. The French hierarchy's answer deplored the whole idea, declined to heresy-hunt, called for openness to new approaches to knowledge (to be treated as "sacred") and new foundations for doctrine and morals, seeing "enthusiastic overstatement" in so radical an enterprise not surprising —a stimulus and *not* to be stifled.

As is well known, Pope Paul has for some time had under con-sideration the matter of a change in the Church's teaching on birth control. During this period an increasing number of priests, including some theologians, have taken the position—publicly and in counseling —that the matter is up to the individual conscience of married couples since the Church's teaching on the subject is "doubtful." The bases stated for this claimed doubtfulness are (a) the fact that the subject has been under discussion with widely opposing views being presented (this would seem to be arguing in a circle!); (b) that an official Papal commission of representative clergymen and laymen was called upon to make a study of the whole question and has made its report, with most of them favoring change; and (c) that the Pope has the matter under consideration and has long been silent on it—some moral

---

[3] This is redolent of (but of course not identical with) the quite carefully delimited declaration—considering the temper of the times—of the bishops and proctors of the Convocations of Canterbury and York in 1534, which of-ficially marked the beginning of the first phase of the English Reformation: "That the Roman Pontiff hath not any greater authority (jurisdiction) bestowed on him by God in the Holy Scriptures in this realm of England than any other bishop." See Edward C. Rich, *Spiritual Authority in the Church of England* (New York: Longmans, Green & Co., 1953), p. 18.

theologians arguing that the longer the silence, the firmer the basis for the claim of dubiety: hence freedom of individual conscience. An obvious answer to the argument *sub silentio* would be to say something; and this is exactly what Pope Paul did last fall. He indicated that he was not ready to announce his final verdict but that meanwhile the question was *not* doubtful and that the previous negative teaching was in full force.

Here, as in the other illustrations, the point is not the merit of the matter but how this declaration of the Pope was received. First, the Pope's statement that the question was not doubtful was widely challenged, even in an article in the generally conservative *Our Sunday Visitor*. In effect commentators publicly said, How can he say something is not doubtful on which his own Commission has recommended a change, and which he, himself, is in the very process of weighing? For example, Father Albert Schlitzer, Chairman of the Department of Theology at Notre Dame, declared: "Many Catholics believe that there is still doubt, so it remains a personal choice. A good many theologians would question whether it is a matter of divine law at all. Many Catholics have already made up their minds, and will follow their decisions no matter what the Pope says in the future." Second, continued public comment in church publications and surveys providing indicators of the actual practice and attitudes of Roman Catholics would suggest that the Pope's declaration that the old teaching is still in force has had no marked effect. And the new Dutch catechism, mentioned above, which teaches precisely the opposite, was issued *after* the Pope's statement.

In 1953 in the Encyclical *Humani Generis,* Pope Pius XII decreed that the philosophy of St. Thomas Aquinas was to be permanently and everywhere accepted as the basis of doctrine; and this particular encyclical did the unusual thing of including an explicit assertion of its own infallibility. Now more and more Roman Catholic theologians not only depart from Thomism in their approaches, but openly disavow it and contradict it on given points or as a system. Yet not a single review or comment the author has seen on the volume most fully denying Thomistic metaphysics, Professor Leslie Dewart's *The Future of Belief,* has challenged it on the authority of Pope Pius XII's encyclical.

However, last winter when Cardinal Spellman called our military forces in Vietnam (Jews, unbelievers and all!) "soldiers of Christ" and urged peace through total victory, liberal commentators did point out the conflict of the Archbishop of New York's statement with the Pope's repeated and urgent calls for a negotiated peace. And, paradoxically enough, conservatives who, by and large, on other matters have been Traditionalist (hence "papalist") praised the Cardinal's position and ignored the Pope's. Here vividly displayed is the change all the examples above are meant to illustrate. *Why* did the liberals prefer the Pope's statement to the Cardinal's? Obviously not on a basis of authority. Rather it was simply because they found what one bishop said more in accord with their view of morals and of reality than they found the other bishop's position to be. And why did the conservatives support the Archbishop's position and despise the Pope's? For precisely the same reason!

Until recently Papal infallibility was viewed by many inside the Church and many more outside to be a block to ecumenism. But it is no longer a problem to the fore. It is abstractly in the picture, but it cannot be conceived of as having any practical relevance now that the papal *magisterium* is so obviously in question—and openly so, within the Roman Catholic Church itself. That the Pope himself is not unaware of this widely discussed authority crisis is evidenced by the noticeable increase this last year in the number of his authoritarian-sounding cautionary statements,[4] his inauguration of a Year of Faith (with rationale revealing his deep uneasiness), and his several addresses last Spring on the authority of the magisterium. For example, on April 7, 1967, in an address to the Italian bishops (though commentators saw it as directed to the Church elsewhere, e.g., Holland and the United States, since he said that the menacing developments "have not gone far in Italy"), Pope Paul said: "Something very strange and dolorous is happening, not only in the profane, unreligious, anti-religious mentality, but also in the Christian field, not excluding the Catholic camp, and often—almost by an inexplicable 'spirit of vertigo'—also among those who know and study the word of God." He referred to the alteration of the sense of the "unique and genuine faith," the most "radical aggressions against sacrosanct truths of our doctrine," and the questioning of "any dogma that does not please and that demands a humble homage of the mind to be received."

"One leaves out of consideration," he continued, "the unsubsti-

---

[4] "These 'go slow' warnings," according to Robert C. Doty, Rome correspondent for the *New York Times* (April 8, 1967, p. 8), "have been in a ratio of about 3 to 1 the 'let's get on with council reforms' speeches."

tutable and providential authority of the Magisterium; and one pretends to preserve the title of Christian reaching the extreme negation of any religious content. . . . It is up to us bishops . . . to take a stand" to combat the "cult of one's own person" and the spirit of disobedience to the Church that presents the peril of a "breaking up of doctrine"—which "some feel . . . is inevitable in the modern world." But in vain, this. When authority is gone, it's gone. Asserting authority authoritatively doesn't restore it.

It is out of neither bias nor favor that the authority crisis in one particular Church has been spelled out. It is the largest segment of Christendom, and what is happening therein obviously has a bearing on the rest of us. But also it is the Church in which a decade ago one would have least expected such a phenomenon. If sheer authority is not sufficient for unity of conviction in this Church, which had been assessed (too simplistically, it must now be granted) as monolithic, how likely is sheer authority to survive as the basis for certain belief in any other Church?

But lest so much attention in this regard to the Roman Catholic Church give the slightest impression either of prejudice or of myopia as to the operation of the same development elsewhere, now some examples relative to the Episcopal Church.

1. Our more modest version of the Vatican Council, the Lambeth Conference, convened decennially by the Archbishop of Canterbury, in 1920 solemnly declared any and every form of contraception to be sinful. Yet in the years which followed Episcopalians, with practically no pulpit or pastoral condemnation, engaged in birth control in higher percentages than members of most Churches; and from the ranks of the Episcopal Church came a relatively high proportion of leadership in the Planned Parenthood movement. In 1958 Lambeth conformed to the realities, declaring family planning to be a moral obligation.[5]

2. The Apostles' and Nicene Creeds are regularly recited in Prayer Book services, and the House of Bishops has from time to time issued Pastoral Letters (required to be read in all the Churches) as to their authoritative character. Yet fairly recent statistics show that, for example, only a minority of Church members now believe certain of the credal affirmations used as samples for the study made.

3. The controversy in the Episcopal Church of which the author has been made the focus also provides a telling illustration of the relationship

---

[5] In spite of this resolution (and the lack of opposition to its passage on the part of its own archbishop and bishops) the Province of the West Indies condemned contraception at its very next synod.

of ecclesiastical authority to the formation of convictions of those who make up the Church. Just as in all the previous illustrations in this chapter, the merits of the matter are not under discussion, nor even the fairness of procedures.

Last September a dozen bishops circulated a draft heresy present- ment among the episcopate, picking up only a dozen additional signatures out of a total of 190 bishops. However, since the concept of only three bishops is necessary to initiate the judicial proceedings and since the annual House of Bishops' meeting at Wheeling was but a month away, the Presiding Bishop persuaded the accusers to wait until consideration could be given to wisdom of a heresy trial in these times. Though three of an ad hoc committee of eight were among the accusers, the author's request for a hearing was unani- mously denied; and without any evidentiary process, the committee agreed on a report which, after very limited debate, the House adopted (with minor changes) by a considerable majority. The resolution was a censure of the author—not for heresy, but for conduct: in short, for rocking the boat. This satisfied the accusers; but the author, with the two required co-signers, initiated judicial proceedings—putting his mitre on the line.

From the vast amount of mail and various sermons and published statements throughout the country it would appear that the judgment of the House was not widely accepted throughout the Church. In fact, last January the Presiding Bishop (not yet having appointed the first of the required judicial bodies), in setting up an advisory com- mittee to study the basic issues (in response the author expressed himself as content that the Presiding Bishop delay further the called- for judicial action), admitted that the censure "had caused confusion and outright disagreement in the Church." This committee, in draw- ing up its report for the Presiding Bishop, will have had the benefit of a score of position papers from theologians, Anglican and non- Anglican, and personal consultation with four people, including the author. So it is likely that, whatever conclusions are reached, reasoned support for them will be included in the report. It is possible that the conclusions of the committee and of the Presiding Bishop may be such that an endorsement of the report by the House of Bishops at the Seattle General Convention this September would make it possible for the author and his two co-signers to withdraw the canoni- cal demand requiring the judicial process. But for our purposes here let us assume that the latter must proceed. In that case, should the trial stage be reached, full evidence would be adduced in an open hearing publicly reported.

Now involved here, actually and potentially, are three distinct types of processes, enabling us to assess fairly precisely *on what basis* people's convictions are reached within a Church today (not *what* conviction have been or might be reached or their soundness; neither is under consideration in this analysis).

The censure itself, in the first place—the fact of it and of its adoption by the bishops—was not the *cause* of assent or dissent in Church people. Rather, it was vice versa: laymen and clergy liked/disliked the censure, honored/dishonored the censuring bishops (or the minority who opposed the censure), depending on their own feelings toward the censured bishop and his teaching (and upon the degree of their sensitivity about due process).

On the other hand, the committee report may convince some because it includes supporting *reasons* for its action. These reasons—assuming plausibility—are more likely to persuade than the fact that a committee—talented as its members are, and the Presiding Bishop —as distinguished as is his primatial role, will have announced certain conclusions. (It is not likely that with today's mentality they will fare any better, in terms of authority-acceptance, than the Curia and the Papacy are faring these days!)

In the third place, a judicial outcome could be all the more persuasive to the laity and clergy, because in addition to reasoning, judicial opinions, and the like, there would be a full open airing of the *facts*. Yet, since it can be assumed that "the authority crisis" will by that time be still further advanced, it does not seem likely that many will have their doubts settled on the matter simply because a judicial body, official as it is, has announced a yea or nay.

Of the three processes outlined above, the first presented conclusions only. The second will present reasoning and conclusions. The third would involve facts plus reasoning plus conclusions.

In previous times, conclusions declared by any one of the three instrumentalities of the Church would have been widely accepted as the truth of the matter. Not so any more. The typical person in the Church today is likely to take what facts he knows and, using his own biases and the reasoning of the Church group involved, then form his own judgments of the stature of the members of each deciding body.

THE NUNS' REBELLION

Gail Cottman

Not long ago, some 500 Catholic parents met in a hall in San Pedro, and for a Christian gathering, it was marked by a singular absence of love and the turning of cheeks. In fact it was something of a donnybrook: "I never heard such shouting and screaming," recalled one survivor. The purpose of the meeting was to discuss the changes going on within the Order of the Immaculate Heart of Mary, many of whose members teach in local parochial schools.

The meeting started out in a dignified enough way, with an informative lecture by a young priest on the decree of Vatican Council II on the Adaptation and Renewal of Religious Life, but it soon degenerated. There were shouts from the audience of "I want my children to know about the Devil," and "I want them to learn the Ten Commandments." Television cameramen had a field day recording the action as angry parents yelled accusations at one another and at the sisters of IHM. "Do you know what the Immaculate Heart sisters are teaching?" cried one angry parent. "They're teaching that sexual intercourse before marriage is all right."

The meeting was only one incident in the dispute centering around the sisters of IHM and their current program of reexamining their way of life, and that dispute, in turn, is only one sign of the deep conflict which is going on between liberals and conservatives all over the Catholic world.

Los Angeles may be a long way from Rome, but it has somehow become one of the leading battlefields in the Catholic liberal-conservative conflict. "Here," writes *Times* religion editor Dan L. Thrapp, "the entire struggle of the great worldwide Roman Catholic Church within itself is present in microcosm, focused to a point."

The problem in Los Angeles, depending on where you stand, is caused either by the great numbers of liberal-minded Catholics, both lay and clergy, or it is caused by the conservative church authority—

Gail Cottman, "The Nuns' Rebellion," LOS ANGELES MAGAZINE, *March, 1968. Reprinted by permission.*

namely James Francis Cardinal McIntyre. Cardinal McIntyre's conspicuous resistance to change has won the Los Angeles Archdiocese the tag of "Fortress McIntyre" in some quarters. In recent years there have been repeated challenges to him from such individuals as the Rev. William DuBay; this time the challenge comes from a whole order of nuns. The sisters of IHM are—again, depending on where you stand—undermining the entire structure of the Catholic faith, or injecting into it a much-needed new dose of humanity and joy.

It all started last August, when 43 of the sisters—delegates elected from among the order's 560 members—met in the rustic lime-oak study of their retreat in Montecito. Dressed in the traditional long, navy blue habits of their order, they spent six weeks discussing basic values. The meeting was a response to the second Vatican Council in which Pope Paul had issued *Motu Proprio,* exhorting "all religious to examine and renew their way of life and toward this end, engage in wide-ranging experimentation in achieving this renewal." The response of the sisters to the Pope's recommendation was, to say the least, hearty, and the meeting of 500 agitated parents in San Pedro was only one of the reactions to their wide-ranging experimentation.

Out of the conference at Montecito came a 58-page document outlining some of the values the sisters felt needed greater emphasis and some of the specific ways they intended to go about their business in the future.

"We believe," the outline said, "that our direct and immediate participation in the temporal order calls for a new style of communal existence, one which will not rigidly separate us by customs, cloister or clothing from those we serve." It also called for the Church to "provide the opportunity for each sister to experience her own fulfillment as a person by adequate education."

In accordance with those general values, the following specific test proposals were adopted:

1. Sisters who are teaching without having completed their teaching credentials would be replaced and enrolled in universities until they complete their education.

2. Classrooms would be limited to 35 students.

3. Any sister who serves as a principal must be relieved of all teaching obligations.

4. Sisters are allowed to drop masculine religious names and reassume their family names.

5. Sisters may attend daily mass at their personal convenience and

pray "in a manner that is pleasing to them and God" instead of in regimented group ceremonies.

6. Personal dress is left to the discretion of each sister. ("No one style will be adopted, but sisters engaged in varying occupations may wear varying habits, suitable for their work.")

7. Sisters are free to pursue careers outside the Church. ("If one of our sisters has a special talent or interest, we will encourage her to pursue it. She might be a commercial artist, or a newspaperwoman, or a musician, or almost anything else. Whatever her talent, we will use it.")

8. Within the community house, sisters may democratically choose their own form of government.

The abandonment of the traditional nun's habit—this, like the others, a temporary experiment—has been the most conspicuous change. Along with the change of dress has come a monthly allowance of $20, and now the sisters, like most women, show a certain concern for their appearance. On Thursday nights, many have their hair washed and set at a nearby beauty college for the bargain price of 99 cents. Most of the clothes they wear are donated, but a few of the sisters have gone out bargaining in the local department stores. "A lot of businesswomen dress very well and can afford to wear a different dress every day," explained one sister. "We're trying to have nice clothes but not very many." The sister's own wardrobe, she reported, consists of two suits, a dress, and a blue shift.

With the change of clothes, there has also come a change in the style of life, particularly among the younger sisters of IHM. In the evenings they often gather around the television set in pajamas, or assemble in the recreation room for intense conversations, or, when the mood is on them, sessions of singing and guitar-playing. It is, by most standards, still a simple and uncluttered existence, but there is a gaiety about life at the old Immaculate Heart headquarters at Franklin and Western that tends to confound some of their religious colleagues. "I've figured out what's wrong with these people," remarked a Catholic educator after a visit to Immaculate Heart College. "They're laughing, the darn fools are laughing all the time."

In addition to experimenting with their own way of living, the sisters have experimented with new educational procedures. For example, the School of Education at Immaculate Heart College joined with the Western Behavioral Science Institute last year in a project of applying the techniques of group psychotherapy to education. The program, based on a plan for "self-directed change" developed by

Dr. Carl Rogers, a psychologist who has pioneered in the development of "non-directive" therapy techniques, brings students together for frank discussions of their problems—personal, sexual, family, educational, or whatever—in no-holds-barred encounter groups. Dr. Rogers sees this as a means of developing genuine communications skills, but shocked conservative parents view it as a "means of altering the personality structure of the individual."

Reaction to the sisters' experimentation in searching for new directions in their religious life has varied from uncritical praise to violent antagonism, some of which is so emotional as to convey that the Devil himself is holding office hours somewhere around Franklin and Western.

Much of the support for the sisters has come from within the Catholic world. Father Andrew Greeley, writing in *The Catholic Voice,* commented:

The Sisters of the Immaculate Heart are women on whose shoulders the mantle of progressive leadership sits very lightly. At a time when Catholic liberals feel honor bound to take everything, especially themselves with the most solemn possible seriousness, the Sisters of the Immaculate Heart resolutely refuse to fit the pattern. They can laugh at themselves as casually as they laugh at anything else; they are . . . casual, happy, laughing liberals and this is a rare, rare breed.

Father Greeley also pointed out an essential statistic about the order: At a time when the average age of most orders is increasing, a third of the sisters of Immaculate Heart are under 35.

Commonweal, another liberal Catholic publication, said in an editorial that "The whole approach is contemporary, American, and, of course, risky. The risks seem eminently worth taking."

There has, naturally, been opposition. Hardly suprising, one of the centers of the conservative reaction to IHM is located in Orange County. One of the leaders of this group is Paul Leininger, a public high school counselor, who contends that the sisters are "watering down the doctrines of the Church" and being "rebellious to Church authority."

"We feel the sisters are aiming at destroying their vocation and the whole concept of religious life," said Leininger's wife, another leader of the conservative group. "The sisters are products of a very permissive society and they're contaminating our children, teaching them in the name of religion ideas that are contrary to our beliefs. We cannot tolerate it."

In a recent interview the Leiningers and another member of the group—which is soon to affiliate with a national conservative organization called the National Federation of Laymen—accused the sisters of using "objectionable" textbooks. One example they cited was a book called *God Is for Real Men,* written by a Baptist prison chaplain named Carl Burke. The book, which attempts to translate the Ten Commandments into language which would be meaningful to the convicts, explains "Thou shalt not commit adultery" as "no whoring around," an exhortation which appeals to the Orange County group in principle but apparently not in wording.

They also objected to a short story entitled "An Individual at Bay," contained in the 11th and 12th grade textbook, *Christianity Today.* The story tells of a teenage boy's sexual experience, and Mrs. Leininger contends "there is no place for this in a high school religion class." A Los Angeles parent whose daughter attends an IHM school (IHM sisters do not, incidentally, teach in Orange County) defends the book. "Children," she maintains, "mature much faster today than when I was a teenager and the sisters are trying to fortify them for the problems they'll meet in our complex society." But Mrs. Leininger counters, "You should avoid impure things in order to avoid sin." And so goes the debate.

If the sisters had only stimulated discussion among the various elements of the Catholic world, their present position might not be particularly serious. But their course of religious and educational discovery has, of course, led them into a confrontation with Cardinal McIntyre—who is probably as conservative as the average Orange County Catholic and considerably more powerful. Although His Eminence does not have any direct authority over the order (he cannot simply order them to get back into their habits and stop messing around with hairdressers and group therapy), he does have authority over the parochial educational system within the arch-diocese. And the Cardinal has not, so far, shown any noticeable eagerness to join the sisters on the road to renewal. He has, in fact, forced a showdown—either they return to the "sanctity and reverence" of their former life or they won't staff the diocese's elementary and religious schools.

This cuts close to the heart of the whole issue, for the sisters of IHM, for all the talk of new careers, are mainly teachers, and the order's proposals for educational reforms are at least as important as their more-publicized experiments in dress. After the Montecito conference, the sisters asked the educational authorities to join with them in drawing up a written agreement which would incorporate their ideas for achieving "excellence in parochial schools"—the main idea being to raise the educational level of the teachers themselves.

For many years, IHM sisters have taught in parochial schools with less than the educational background that would have been required of them in the public school system: In a recent study conducted by the order, it was revealed that 39 per cent of the sisters instructing elementary school children and nine per cent of those teaching in high schools have neither college degree nor teaching credential.

For nuns to teach without degrees or credentials is not unusual; but it *is* unusual for an order of nuns to try to do something about the situation—and, in view of the tradition of obedience which is deeply ingrained in religious life, it is highly unusual for a group of nuns to make any demands upon their superiors. But IHM has clearly stated its seriousness of intention in the matter of working out new agreements in the schools where the sisters teach. "Where such mutual agreements cannot be reached," says Sister Anita Caspary, mother general of the order, "we will be forced to withdraw from such schools rather than perform a disservice to their students."

This statement was described as an "ultimatum" in a front page editorial of the Catholic Archdiocesan paper *The Tidings,* which stated that the sisters had "threatened to withdraw from the schools unless those in charge agree to certain changes. These changes involved far more than mere adjustments of curriculum or assignment of teachers. Far more important, they involved basic changes in the structure of religious life, which inevitably would affect their work in the schools." *The Tidings* editorial expressed its hope that the sisters would give up their crusade, return to the fold, and "be with us many years to come, in the spirit of their past tradition."

Meanwhile, keen eyes are watching this progressive experiment with hawkish scrutiny. "Time once spent in prayer is now spent in the beauty parlor," complains Mrs. Leininger; "the sisters are trying to look attractive and beautiful and this violates the spirit a religious has adopted for herself. If they want to live like we do, then let them leave the convent and get a job."

"A nun is free to live any way she wants but not with my money," adds Mrs. Loretta Tambourine, another of the Orange County conservatives. "You cannot make any excuse for going into an order and destroying it and that's what these nuns are doing. They say clothes don't make the woman, but from our observation of the IHM nuns, I would say the habit very definitely helped them remember who they were."

"I won't mention his name, but from the pulpit a priest pointed to the empty convent his parishioners paid for and said only two or three nuns were living there," says Mrs. Leininger, "the rest were living in apartments and commuting in sports cars."

On the other side a parent who supports the IHM experiment says: "My daughter was attending another Catholic school when she asked to be transferred to Immaculate Heart High School. They kept talking about love at the other school but at IHM they actually showed it. After a semester there, she literally came alive."

Says Maureen Tracy, an IHM college senior, "I always saw nuns as authority figures. I just knew the IHM nuns as people."

"They emphasize intelligent Catholicism," adds Pat Herman, assistant editor of *Comment,* the college newspaper. "The sisters humanized the Church and made it meet the needs of the people."

"An effort to hold back the change, such as Cardinal McIntyre seems intent on making, strikes me as being as foolish as trying to hold back the dawn," writes liberal John Cogley in *The Catholic Messenger.*

But Mrs. Diane Williams, a Northridge housewife, mother of three and a former IHM student, supports the Cardinal completely. "Our children have been told the Ten Commandments are out-dated," she claims. "I've taken my children out of Our Lady of Lourdes elementary school because I refuse to let the sister contaminate them." Her youngest son, a second grader, was removed and placed in public school because the sisters led the class in singing "We Shall Overcome," and "If I Had A Hammer," popular folk ballads which she feels are "associated with anarchy and civil disobedience and have no place being taught in elementary schools."

"Parochial schools are bought and owned by the people, not the sisters," she contends, "and the lack of respect they show for things that are sacred is shocking. Several years ago (December 1965) the children at Our Lady of Lourdes presented Christ's birth as a situation comedy, referring to Our Blessed Mother by her first name in complete lack of reverence."

And that one word—reverence—lies at the foundation of the whole dispute. The critics of IHM say the sisters are showing a lack of reverence for the traditions and authority of the Church, while the sisters and their supporters see themselves are being in a quest for the true meaning of Christianity and the real possibilities of human life.

As one sister proudly said, "we are in the middle of the city. We are two blocks from the Sunset Strip and a block from Hollywood Boulevard. There are cars; there are sirens; and there's dust and smog. We are very much a part of the world, making it expand and making it tender. We're free here to do the things we like to do and it feels good."

Sister Kelly, president of IHM college, summed up the order's new philosophy in her convocation address: "not only our own lives but the lives of almost everyone are much in need of fundamental change, change of mode, growing out of change of heart. We and the world need to grow up."

THE PLACE OF A PRIEST

James E. Groppi

Last year I was on the picket line in front of one of the schools of the black community of Milwaukee—the Dowe School. We were protesting because it was going to be predominantly black in a relatively short time. A newspaper reporter and a television camera-man from New York came up to me and said, "Father, what do your parishioners think about your activities?" I answered, "My parishioners are here on the picket line. In the paddy wagon over there they have just placed three of my parishioners. This is what my parishioners think of my activities. I am here because my parishioners are here, and I've always held that the place of a priest is with his people. I refuse to remain in the rectory and pray my breviary while my people are hungry, while my people are receiving third-rate educations, while my people are being relegated to second-ary status in this racist society."

Dr. Martin Luther King, Jr. once said, "This is not a struggle

James E. Groppi, "Open Housing: The Fight in the Streets," THE HUMANIST, *July/August, 1968. Reprinted by permission.*

between black and white. It is a struggle between right and wrong."
Every man who walks the face of the earth has an obligation to
get involved in the struggle for social justice and for human dignity
simply because all of us belong to the family of God. And unless a
man does get involved he becomes less and less human. The more
he becomes involved in the problems of his neighbor the more this
man grows in humanity and dignity. This is the reason why everyone
in this country today must become involved in the struggle of the
black man for equality.

Recently I have been receiving a great deal of publicity because
of my fight for fair housing in Milwaukee. I became involved because
there is an urgent need for housing on the part of the black community there. The population density of the black community is at
least four times greater than it is in any other city. There are 1,000
black families being removed from their homes through urban
development. There is no place for them to go. Discrimination, even
on the fringe areas of the city, is widely practiced. The rent is high.
One set of statistics presented by a Milwaukee sociologist showed
that the people of the black community are paying more rent per
square foot than whites are paying in one of the most affluent suburbs
of the city.

We established a Freedom House recently, our first one. The rent
was supposed to be 77 dollars per month. This seemed pretty good,
but the heating bill in the first Freedom House was something like
74 dollars per month during the winter months. There were no such
things as storm windows. Those houses, or homes, or whatever you
want to call them, were shacks in which the heat could not be kept
in. A family on welfare, a family in my own parish, lived in such a
house. They were living in a back-alley shack of five rooms. There
were 10 children in the family. The place was rat-infested. The only
means of heat in the house was a pot-bellied stove in the middle of
the dining room. It was something to walk into that house in the
middle of the winter and see those children with their coats on
huddled around that pot-bellied stove trying to keep warm. The
family broke up. The mother and the children had to go on welfare.
The Welfare Department tried to find a home for them, but the only
place it would refer me to were other slum dwellings.

When we began our fair-housing fight, the Mayor of Milwaukee
said that he was against any city fair-housing legislation. He said
that the affluent white people would move to the suburbs and we

would lose the tax money that we get from the white middle-class people living in the city now. I say that if they want to live in the suburbs, let them go. When they go, let them take their white gyp merchants and their liquor stores and everything else that they have brought into the black community as a means of bleeding black people. We'll build a fine community of our own. If whites want to come and live with us, that's fine. We have no objection to this. If a white man finds a home in the black community, he will become a part of our problems and part of our struggles.

If a black man wants to move into a white community, it seems to me that that is his business. I'll die for the black man's right to move. That is his personal right. What we are looking for is territorial expansion. Seventy-five per cent of the black people in Milwaukee are renters. The State Fair Housing Ordinance we have in Milwaukee right now covers only about 25 per cent of Wisconsin and does not reach the black man who is living in a state of poverty and who needs a place to rent at a reasonable rate. I feel that the black man has lost faith in the American system. He is losing hope. There is no way outside of the gun. We are told not to use the gun because we might get hurt, or killed. The black man says that he is dead anyway. He doesn't care.

We've had legislation in the past, and it was advancement. But we get a law and then it is never implemented. Or bills and laws are defeated. We've got one black Alderman in Milwaukee. Her name is Val Phillips. There are 19 white Aldermen. She presented her Fair-Housing Bill four times, and four times it was defeated. During one of the instances when she presented her Bill, the community rallied behind her. We filled the Council chambers, and man after man got up before the microphone and told the Common Council about the immorality of discrimination and the necessity for fair-housing legislation. After we got finished, we went home, and the next day the Common Council defeated the Bill 19 to 1.

We waited until summer, and then we went to the last Common Council meeting. We told them not to adjourn but to deal with the housing issue and to deal with it now. The Common Council voted to ignore us and adjourned for the summer. One week later Milwaukee exploded into a so-called riot. The Mayor called it a riot, but my Youth Council called it a social revolution.

I call the young men who participated in that fight "freedom fighters." I compare them to the Hungarian freedom fighters in

Europe. In the past Americans have looked at individuals who were oppressed, and when they rose behind their leaders to struggle against the oppressors, we were thrilled. We remember Patrick Henry and his, "Give me liberty or give me death!"

But when the black man resorted to that same technique because he had used every other means, we looked at him and said, "Hoodlum!" I won't even argue the morality of the violence of the black man living in poverty. We must talk of violence only as a technique or a strategy. The United States can spend billions of dollars every month killing innocent individuals in Vietnam and then can turn around and say, "Now black man, don't you use this technique!" To me that is sheer hypocrisy.

We waited a few months, and then we began our demonstrations in Milwaukee. We decided to march on the South Side, an all-white, predominantly Polish-Catholic area. A symbolic bridge called the Sixteenth Street Viaduct was chosen by the Commandos, who protect the Youth Council, for their march. They decided to march across the bridge for fair housing.

We marched and the bottles flew. And the rocks flew. And firecrackers. And then we heard, "Blacks, go back to Africa." And then a rather modern chant, "E-I-O, Father Groppi has got to go!" Soon we came to a park, where we held a very short rally. Then we tried to march back again on the sidewalk because we didn't want to break the law, but a police officer said that we had to march in the street or be killed. The next night we were going to march again. I called the Mayor's office and asked for protection. He refused.

We marched again that night. There were white men there with their kids, shouting, "Nigger lover, nigger lover, go back to Africa!" Fathers and mothers standing right there with their kids and spitting at us, throwing everything, grabbing bottles. The crowd got so big that we just couldn't march any further. They streamed out into the roads. The policemen formed a line in front of us, but the crowds pushed the policemen back. The policemen threw tear gas bombs. It's a funny thing about tear gas, when it's thrown at "them," we get it, too. One of the members of the Special Assignment Squad said, "We'll get a squad car and go get school buses. We've got to get out of here or someone will get killed."

Lawrence Friend, who was then Chairman of the Youth Council, said, "Look, we asked for protection and you wouldn't give it to us.

Now, we're going to that park. If we all get killed, we all get killed, but we're going to exercise our right to freedom of speech." We marched to the park, and the whole crowd regathered and encircled us, and the demonstrators sat down and began to talk to them. I never thought that we were going to get out of the South Side alive that night, and I shouted as loud as I could, "We still sing, 'We shall overcome'." Someone exploded a bomb near me, which blew the purse held by a girl sitting next to me to pieces. It also burned her arm. She was taken away in an ambulance, and we were harassed all the way home. Another tear gas attack was held. We marched across the bridge, and when we got to our own homes, were were tear gassed.

Some of the Youth Council members were disturbed by the police and shouted words to them. Before we knew it, the tear gas was flying across the street at Freedom House, and the policemen took out their high-powered rifles and shot them off in the air. Later they claimed that there was a sniper inside Freedom House, but there was no sniper there, only a mother and some of her kids.

The tear gas bomb that was thrown into Freedom House was so hot that it started a fire there. We were waiting for the fire engines to come. Finally they came—no siren, lights off. We saw the house burn and saw the house next door catch fire. The next day the Mayor issued a Proclamation banning all marches.

We decided that instead of a march we would have a meeting in front of Freedom House, on our own property. When I got there that night the police were already throwing our young men and women into the paddy wagon. I said, "What's going on?" One of the police officers who had been following me nightly for three months said, "This is an unlawful assembly! If you go near that house, you will be arrested!" But we went on to Freedom House, and the people began to gather. They gathered on the Freedom House property, on the property next door, and on the properties across the street. And that is where we conducted our rally. The police arrested 58 people that night for practicing their right of freedom of assembly and freedom of speech.

We had a rally in a church the next night, and the issue was not only fair housing but the right to freedom of speech. What angered us most of all was the Mayor of Milwaukee. When violence flared in the black community, he immediately brought in the National Guard, and he placed the entire city under a curfew. We couldn't get out of our houses. We couldn't do anything. If you tried to go out on the sidewalk, a National Guardsman would come pointing a machine gun at you.

We marched the night afterward. During that walk about 150 of us were arrested. Everyone I knew was in jail. The most conservative people in our parish. Whites and blacks, all in jail! Not only that, they were in jail with their children! When I was carried to the paddy wagon, I went limp, not resisting. It took four policemen to carry me. The policeman who had me by the foot was digging his fingernails into my foot, and I thought he must be getting some kind of sadistic pleasure out of this. He kept digging his fingers into my foot. I got into the wagon, and I was sitting on someone's lap. It was pretty crowded in there. I said, "What's that policeman's name?" The policeman who was in my end of the wagon said, "That's for me to know and for you to find out!" I found out when I got downtown. I spent that night in jail. The next morning I was taken to the District Attorney's office and was charged with violation of the Mayor's Proclamation, resisting arrest, and battery. The police officer who was digging his fingers into my foot said that I had kicked him so hard in the chest that he lost his breath, and had to go to the emergency section of Mt. Sinai Hospital for chest X-rays.

The next night we had a rally. We marched again, and the Police Department again attacked us. Again the police shoved me in the paddy wagon. Another fellow was brought in, a young man who had spent four years in the Air Force. His head was split open and the blood was all over his face and on his shirt, and the police officer started to curse him and called me a "white nigger." As we pulled away, the police officer shouted, "Shoot those dirty black bastards. Kill the niggers."

I was taken downtown again. I was surprised that this time the only charge filed against me was for disobeying the Proclamation.

Right now we are still marching. The Milwaukee Common Council voted down the Fair-Housing Bill. They voted to put it on a referendum. White people can live and move wherever they want in this country. In Milwaukee we are now going to determine by vote whether the black people will also have that right.

I have a very fine black friend, a priest, and he was talking down South one day to a group of sisters. He said, "Sisters, why don't you integrate your hospital?" "Oh, Father, we can't do that," one said. "We got a letter from the Ku Klux Klan. They said that if we integrate this hospital, we are all going to be killed." Father Patterson looked at her and said, "Sister, that would be wonderful."

We must be martyrs for the sake of unity. We must fight for equality, brotherhood, human dignity, and the eradication of the caste system in this country.

☐ THE PSYCHOLOGY OF PROTEST

One of the reasons that protests so seldom produce true dialogue is that authorities fail consistently to understand the character and motivations of protesters. The standard concepts of "payoffs" utilized in the social sciences are seldom adequate to explain why protest movements start and how they gain momentum, and all discussions tend to be dominated by an image of protesters as angry, misfit, bearded youths. Too, there is a widely-held assumption that "hippie" and "protester" are more or less interchangeable terms.

Actually, there is evidence of great differences between the two. The hippies described in Lewis Yablonsky's recent study [1] are dedicated dropouts preoccupied with their own internal spiritual voyages, and most of them are inclined to dismiss social protests as futile ego games. Undoubtedly there is some crossing-over between hippies

[1] Lewis Yablonsky, *The Hippie Trip* (New York: Pegasus, 1968).

and student protesters, but it is a complex and instable alliance. According to Kenneth Keniston, the common public conception of student protesters is badly distorted—the campus activist is a far different breed from either the hippie or the alienated delinquent youth.

Abraham Maslow, whose studies of self-actualizing people have introduced new values into psychology, argues that the standard concepts of motivation are too limited—that behavior usually described as "idealistic" is in fact a necessary function of the human organism.

Nat Hentoff explores another dimension of the psychology of protest, and argues that the burden for true dialogue rests not with the authorities but with the protesters; and sociologist David O. Arnold raises some questions concerning the relation between protest and violence.

THE SOURCES OF STUDENT DISSENT

Kenneth Keniston

The apparent upsurge of dissent among American college students is one of the more puzzling phenomena in recent American history. Less than a decade ago, commencement orators were decrying the "silence" of college students in the face of urgent national and international issues; but in the past two or three years, the same speakers have warned graduating classes across the country against the dangers of unreflective protest, irresponsible action, and unselective dissent. Rarely in history has apparent apathy been replaced so rapidly by publicized activism, silence by strident dissent.

This "wave" of dissent among American college students has been much discussed. Especially in the mass media—popular magazines, newspapers, and television—articles of interpretation, explanation, depreciation, and occasionally applause have appeared in enormous numbers. More important, from the first beginnings of the student civil rights movement, social scientists have been regular participant-observers and investigators of student dissent. There now exists a considerable body of research that deals with the characteristics and settings of student dissent (see Lipset and Altbach, 1966; Block, Haan, and Smith, forthcoming; Katz, 1967; Peterson, 1968 for summaries of this research). To be sure, most of these studies are topical (centered around a particular protest or demonstration), and some of the more extensive studies are still in varying stages of incompletion. Yet enough evidence has already been gathered to permit tentative generalizations about the varieties, origins, and future of student dissent in the 1960's.

In the remarks to follow, I will attempt to gather together this evidence (along with my own research and informal observations) to provide tentative answers to three questions about student dissent today. First, What is the nature of student dissent in American

Condensed from pp. 297-325 in YOUNG RADICALS: NOTES ON COMMITTED YOUTH, © *1968, by Kenneth Keniston. Reprinted by permission of Harcourt, Brace & World, Inc.*

colleges? Second, What are the sources of the recent "wave of protest" by college students? And third, What can we predict about the future of student dissent?

Dissent is by no means the dominant mood of American college students. Every responsible study or survey shows apathy and privatism far more dominant than dissent (see, for example, *Newsweek,* 1965; Katz, 1965; Reed, 1966; Peterson, 1966; Block, Haan, and Smith, forthcoming). On most of our twenty-two hundred campuses, student protest, student alienation, and student unrest are something that happens elsewhere, or that characterizes a mere handful of "kooks" on the local campus. However we define "dissent," overt dissent is relatively infrequent and tends to be concentrated largely at the more selective, "progressive," and "academic" colleges and universities in America. Thus, Peterson's study of student protests (1966) finds political demonstrations concentrated in the larger universities and institutions of higher academic caliber, and almost totally absent at teachers' colleges, technical institutes, and non-academic denominational colleges. And even at the colleges that gather together the greatest number of dissenters, the vast majority of students—generally well over ninety-five per cent—remain interested onlookers or opponents rather than active dissenters.

Partly because the vast majority of American students remain largely uncritical of the wider society, fundamentally conformist in behavior and outlook, and basically "adjusted" to the prevailing collegiate, national, and international order, the small minority of dissenting students is highly visible to the mass media. As I will argue later, such students are often distinctively talented; they "use" the mass media effectively; and they generally succeed in their goal of making themselves and their causes highly visible. Equally important, student dissenters of all types arouse deep and ambivalent feelings in non-dissenting students and adults—envy, resentment, admiration, repulsion, nostalgia, and guilt. Such feelings contribute both to the selective overattention dissenters receive and to the often distorted perceptions and interpretations of them and their activities. Thus, there has developed through the mass media and the imaginings of adults a more or less stereotyped—and generally incorrect—image of the student dissenter.

The "stereotypical" dissenter as popularly portrayed is both a Bohemian and a political activist. Bearded, be-Levi-ed, long-haired, dirty, and unkempt, he is seen as profoundly disaffected from his society, often influenced by "radical" (Marxist, Communist, Maoist, or Castroite) ideas, as experimenter in sex and drugs, unconventional in his daily behavior. Frustrated and unhappy, often deeply maladjusted as a person, he is a "failure" (or as one U.S. Senator put it, a "reject"). Certain academic communities like Berkeley are said to act as "magnets" for dissenters, who selectively attend colleges with a reputation as protest centers. Furthermore, dropouts or "nonstudents" who have failed in college cluster in large numbers around the fringes of such colleges, actively seeking pretexts for protest, refusing all compromise, and impatient with ordinary democratic processes.

According to such popular analyses, the sources of dissent are to be found in the loss of certain traditional American virtues. The "breakdown" of American family life, high rates of divorce, the "softness" of American living, inadequate parents, and, above all, overindulgence and "spoiling" contribute to the prevalence of dissent. Brought up in undisciplined homes by parents unsure of their own values and standards, dissenters channel their frustration and anger against the older generation, against all authority, and against established institutions.

Similar themes are sometimes found in the interpretations of more scholarly commentators. "Generational conflict" is said to underlie the motivation to dissent, and a profound "alienation" from American society is seen as a factor of major importance in producing protests. Then, too, such factors as the poor quality and impersonality of American college education, the large size and lack of close student-faculty contact in the "multiversity" are sometimes seen as the latent issues around which students are organized. And still other scholarly analysts, usually men now disillusioned by the radicalism of the 1930's, have expressed fear of the dogmatism, rigidity, and "authoritarianism of the Left" of today's student activists.

These stereotyped views are, I believe, incorrect in a variety of ways. They confuse two distinct varieties of student dissent; equally important, they fuse dissent with maladjustment. There are, of course, as many forms of dissent as there are individual dissenters; and any effort to counter the popular stereotype of the dissenter by pointing to the existence of distinct "types" of dissenters runs the risk of oversimplifying at a lower level of abstraction. Nonetheless, it seems to me useful to suggest that student dissenters generally fall somewhere along a continuum that runs between two ideal types—first,

the political activist or protester, and second, the withdrawn, culturally
alienated student.

The activist.   The defining characteristic of the "new" activist is
his participation in a student demonstration or group activity that
concerns itself with some matter of general political, social, or ethical
principle. Characteristically, the activist feels that some injustice has
been done, and attempts to "take a stand," "demonstrate," or in
some fashion express his convictions. The specific issues in question
range from protest against a paternalistic college administration's
actions to disagreement with American Vietnam policies, from indignation at the exploitation of the poor to anger at the firing of a
devoted teacher, from opposition to the Selective Service laws which
exempt him but not the poor, to—most important—outrage at the
deprivation of the civil rights of other Americans.

The initial concern of the protester is almost always immediate,
ad hoc, and local. To be sure, the student who protests about one
issue is likely to feel inclined or obliged to demonstrate his convictions on other issues as well. But whatever the issue, the protester
rarely demonstrates because his *own* interests are jeopardized, but
rather because he perceives injustices being done to *others* less fortunate than himself.

The anti-ideological stance of today's activists has been noted by
many commentators. This distrust of formal ideologies (and at times
of articulate thought) makes it difficult to pinpoint the positive social
and political values of student protesters. Clearly, many current
American political institutions like *de facto* segregation are opposed;
clearly, too, most students of the New Left reject careerism and
familism as personal values. In this sense, we might think of the
activist as (politically) "alienated." But this label seems to me
more misleading than illuminating, for it overlooks the more basic
commitment of most student activists to other ancient, traditional,
and creedal American values like free speech, citizen's participation
in decision-making, equal opportunity and justice. Insofar as the
activist rejects all or part of "the power structure," it is because
current political realities fall so far short of the ideals he sees as
central to the American creed. And insofar as he repudiates careerism
and familism, it is because of his implicit allegiance to other human
goals he sees, once again, as more crucial to American life. Thus,
to emphasize the "alienation" of activists is to neglect their more basic
allegiance to creedal American ideals.

One of these ideals is, of course, a belief in the desirability of political and social action. Sustained in good measure by the successes of the student civil rights movement, the protester is usually convinced that demonstrations are effective in mobilizing public opinion, bringing moral or political pressure to bear, demonstrating the existence of his opinions, or, at times, in "bringing the machine to a halt." In this sense, then, despite his criticisms of existing political practices and social institutions, he is a political optimist. Moreover, the protester must believe in at least minimal organization and group activity; otherwise, he would find it impossible to take part, as he does, in any organized demonstrations or activities. Despite their search for more truly "democratic" forms of organization and action (e.g., participatory democracy), activists agree that group action is more effective than purely individual acts. To be sure, a belief in the value and efficacy of political action is not equivalent to endorsement of prevalent political institutions or forms of action. Thus, one characteristic of activists is their search for new forms of social action, protest, and political organization (community organization, sit-ins, participatory democracy) that will be more effective and less oppressive than traditional political institutions.

The culturally alienated. In contrast to the politically optimistic, active, and socially concerned protester, the culturally alienated student is far too pessimistic and too firmly opposed to "the System" to wish to demonstrate his disapproval in any organized public way. His demonstrations of dissent are private: through non-conformity of behavior, ideology, and dress, through personal experimentation and, above all, through efforts to intensify his own subjective experience, he shows his distaste and disinterest in politics and society. The activist attempts to change the world around him, but the alienated student is convinced that meaningful change of the social and political world is impossible; instead, he considers "dropping out" the only real option.

The recent and much-publicized emergence of "hippie" subcultures in several major cities and increasingly on the campuses of many selective and progressive colleges illustrates the overwhelmingly apolitical stance of alienated youth. For although hippies oppose war and believe in interracial living, few have been willing or able to engage in anything beyond occasional peace marches or apolitical "human be-ins." Indeed, the hippie's emphasis on immediacy, "love," and "turning-on," together with his basic rejection of the traditional values of American life, inoculates him against involvement in long-range activist endeavors like education or community organization, and even against the sustained effort needed to plan and execute demonstrations or marches. For the alienated hippie, American society is beyond redemption (or not worth trying to redeem); but the activist, no matter how intense his rejection of specific American policies and practices, retains a conviction that his society can and should be changed. Thus, despite occasional agreement in principle between the alienated and the activists, co-operation in practice has been rare, and usually ends with activists accusing the alienated of "irresponsibility," while the alienated are confirmed in their view of activists as moralistic, "up-tight," and "un-cool."

What I have termed "alienated" students are by no means a new phenomenon in American life, or for that matter in industrialized societies. Bohemians, "beatniks," and artistically inclined undergraduates who rejected middle-class values have long been a part of the American student scene, especially at more selective colleges; they constituted the most visible form of dissent during the relative political "silence" of American students on the 1950's. What is distinctive about student dissent in recent years is the unexpected emergence of a vocal minority of politically and socially active students. Much is now known about the characteristics of such students, and the circumstances under which protests are likely to be mounted.

A large and still growing number of studies, conducted under different auspices, at different times, and about different students, present a remarkably consistent picture of the protest-prone individual (Aiken, Demerath, and Marwell, 1966; Flacks, 1967; Gastwirth, 1965; Heist, 1965, 1966; Lyonns, 1965; Somers, 1965; Watts and Whittaker, 1966; Westby and Braungart, 1966; Katz, 1967; and Paulus, 1968). For one, student protesters are generally outstanding students; the higher the student's grade average, the more outstanding his academic achievements, the more likely it is that he will become involved in any given political demonstration. Similarly, student activists come from families with liberal political values; a disproportionate number report that their parents hold views essentially similar to their own, and accept or support their activities. Thus, among the parents of protesters we find large numbers of liberal Democrats, plus an unusually large scattering of pacifists, socialists, et cetera. A disproportionate number of protesters come from Jewish families; and if the parents of activists are religious, they tend to be concentrated in the more liberal denominations—Reform Judaism, Unitarianism, the Society of Friends, et cetera. Such parents are reported to have high ethical and political standards, regardless of their actual religious convictions.

As might be expected of a group of politically liberal and academically talented students, a disproportionate number are drawn from professional and intellectual families of upper-middleclass status. For example, compared with active student conservatives, members of protest groups tend to have higher parental incomes, more parental education, and less anxiety about social status (Westby and Braungart, 1966). Another study finds that high levels of education distinguish the activist's family even in the grandparental generation (Flacks, 1967). In brief, activists are not drawn from disadvantaged, status-anxious, underprivileged, or uneducated groups; on the contrary, they are selectively recruited from among those young Americans who have had the most socially fortunate upbringings.

The basic value commitments of the activist tend to be academic and non-vocational. Such students are rarely found among engineers, future teachers at teachers' colleges, or students of business administration (see Trent and Craise, 1967). Their over-all educational goals are those of a liberal education for its own sake, rather than specifically technical, vocational, or professional preparation. Rejecting careerist and familist goals, activists espouse humanitarian, expressive, and self-actualizing values. Perhaps because of these values, they delay career choice longer than their classmates (Flacks, 1967). Nor are such students distinctively dogmatic, rigid, or authoritarian. Quite the contrary, the substance and style of their beliefs and activities tend to be open, flexible, and highly liberal. Their fields of academic specialization are non-vocational—the social sciences and the humanities. Once in college, they not only do well academically, but tend to persist in their academic commitments, dropping out *less* frequently than most of their classmates. As might be expected, a disproportionate number receive a B.A. within four years and continue on to graduate school, preparing themselves for academic careers.

Survey data also suggest that the activist is not distinctively dissatisfied with his college education. As will be noted below, activists generally attend colleges that provide the best, rather than the worst, undergraduate education available today. Objectively then, activists

probably have less to complain about in their undergraduate educations than most other students. And, subjectively as well, surveys
show most activists, like most other American undergraduates, to be
relatively well satisfied with their undergraduate educations (Somers,
1965; Kornhauser, 1967). Thus, dissatisfaction with educational fail-
ings of the "impersonal multiversity," however important as a rally-
ing cry, does not appear to be a distinctive cause of activism.

In contrast to their relative satisfaction with the quality of their
educations, however, activists *are* distinctively dissatisfied with what
might be termed the "civil-libertarian" defects of their college administrations. Furthermore, activists tend to be more responsive than
other students to deprivations of civil rights on campus as well as
off campus, particularly when political pressures seem to motivate
on-campus policies they consider unjust. The same responsiveness
increasingly extends to issues of "student power": *i.e.,* student participation and decisions affecting campus life. Thus, bans on controversial
speakers, censorship of student publications, and limitations on off-
campus political or social action are likely to incense the activist, as
is arbitrary "administration without the consent of the administered."
But it is primarily perceived injustice or the denial of student rights
by the administration—rather than poor educational quality, neglect
by the faculty, or the impersonality of the multiversity—that agitates
the activist.

However we define his characteristics, one activist alone cannot
make a protest: the characteristics of the college or university he
attends have much to do with whether his protest-proneness will ever
be mobilized into actual activism. Politically, socially, and ideologi-
cally motivated demonstrations and activities are most likely to occur
at certain types of colleges; they are almost unknown at a majority of
campuses.

In order for an organized protest or related activities to occur,
there must obviously be sufficient *numbers* of protest-prone students
to form a group, these students must have an opportunity for *inter-
action* with each other, and there must be *leaders* to initiate and mount
the protest. Thus, we might expect—and we indeed find—that protest
is associated with institutional size, and particularly with the congregation of large numbers of protest-prone students in close
proximity to each other. More important than sheer size alone, however, is the "image" of the institution: certain institutions selectively
recruit students with protest-prone characteristics. Specifically, a repu-

tation for academic excellence and freedom, coupled with highly selective admissions policies, will tend to congregate large numbers of potentially protesting students on one campus. Thus, certain institutions do act as "magnets" for potential activists, but not so much because of their reputations for political radicalism as because they are noted for their academic excellence. Among such institutions are some of the most selective and "progressive" private liberal-arts colleges, major state universities (like Michigan, California at Berkeley, and Wisconsin) that have long traditions of vivid undergraduate teaching and high admissions standards (Lipset and Altach, 1966), and many of the more prestigious private universities.

Once protest-prone students are on campus, they must have an opportunity to interact, to support one another, to develop common outlooks and shared policies—in short, to form an *activist subculture* with sufficient mass and potency to generate a demonstration or action program. Establishing "honors colleges" for talented and academically motivated students is one particularly effective way of creating a "critical mass" of protest-prone students. Similarly, inadequate on-campus housing indirectly results in the development of off-campus protest-prone subcultures (e.g., co-op houses) in residences where student activists can develop a high degree of ideological solidarity and organizational cohesion.

But even the presence of a critical mass of protest-prone undergraduates in an activist subculture is not enough to make a protest without leaders and issues. And, in general, the most effective protest leaders have not been undergraduates, but teaching assistants. The presence of large numbers of exploited, underpaid, disgruntled and frustrated teacher assistants (or other equivalent graduate students and younger faculty members) is almost essential for organized and persistent protest. For one, advanced students tend to be more liberal politically and more sensitive to political issues than are most undergraduates—partly because education seems to have a liberalizing effect, and partly because students who persist into graduate school tend to be more liberal to start than those who drop out or go elsewhere. Furthermore, the frustrations of graduate students, especially at very large public universities, make them particularly sensitive to general problems of injustice, exploitation, and oppression. Teaching assistants, graduate students, and young faculty members also tend to be in daily and prolonged contact with students, are close enough to them in age to sense their mood, and are therefore in an excellent position to lead and organize student protests. Particularly at institutions which command little institutional allegiance from large numbers of highly capable graduate students (Lipset and Altbach, 1966) will such students be found among the leaders of the protest movement.

Finally, issues are a necessity. In many cases, these issues are provided by historical developments on the national or international scene, a point to which I will return. But in some instances, as at Berkeley, "on-campus" issues are the focus of protest. And in other cases, off-campus and on-campus issues are fused, as in the recent protests at institutional cooperation with draft-board policies considered unjust by demonstrating students. In providing such on-campus issues, the attitude of the university administration is central. Skillful handling of student complaints, the maintenance of open channels of communication between student leaders and faculty members, and administrative willingness to resist public and political pressures in order to protect the rights of students—all minimize the likelihood of organized protest. Conversely, a university administration that shows itself unduly sensitive to political, legislative, or public pressures, that treats students arrogantly, ineptly, condescendingly, hypocritically, or, above all, dishonestly, is asking for a demonstration.

Thus, one reason for the relative absence of on-campus student protests and demonstrations on the campuses of private, non-denominational "academic" colleges and universities (which recruit many protest-prone students) probably lies in the liberal policies of the administrations. As Cowan (1966) notes, liberal students generally attend non-restrictive and "libertarian" colleges. Given an administration and faculty that support or tolerate activism and student rights, student activists must generally find their issues off-campus. The same students, confronting an administration unduly sensitive to political pressures from a conservative board of regents or state legislature, might engage in active on-campus protests. There is also some evidence that clever administrative manipulation of student complaints, even in the absence of genuine concern with student rights, can serve to dissipate the potentialities of protest (Keene, 1966).

Among the institutional factors often cited as motivating student protest is the largeness, impersonality, atomization, "multiversitification," et cetera, of the university. I have already noted that student protesters do not seem distinctively dissatisfied with their educations. Furthermore, the outstanding academic achievements and intellectual motivations of activists concentrate them, within any college, in the courses and programs that provide the most "personal" attention: honors programs, individual instruction, advanced seminars, and so forth. Thus, they probably receive relatively *more* individual attention and a *higher* caliber of instruction than do non-protesters. Furthermore, protests generally tend to occur at the best, rather than the worst, colleges, judged from the point of view of the quality of undergraduate instruction. Thus, despite the popularity of student slogans dealing with the impersonality and irrelevance of the multiversity, the absolute level of educational opportunities seems, if anything, positively related to the occurrence of protest: the better the institution, the more likely demonstrations are.

Nor can today's student activism be attributed in any direct way to mounting academic pressures. To be sure, activism is most manifest at those selective colleges where the "pressure to perform" (Keniston, 1965b) is greatest, where standards are highest, and where anxieties about being admitted to a "good" graduate or professional school are most pronounced. But, contrary to the argument of Lipset and Altbach (1966), the impact of academic pressure on activism seems negative rather than positive. Protest-prone students, with their superior academic attainments and strong intellectual commitments, seem especially vulnerable to a kind of academic professionalism that, because of the enormous demands it makes upon the student's energies, serves to cancel or preclude activism. Student demonstrations rarely take place during exam periods, and protests concerned with educational quality almost invariably seek an improvement of quality, rather than a lessening of pressure. Thus, though the pressure to perform doubtless affects *all* American students, it probably acts as a deterrent rather than a stimulus to student activism.

What probably does matter, however, is the *relative* deprivation of student expectations (see Brown, 1967). A college that recruits large numbers of academically motivated and capable students into a less than first-rate education program, one that oversells entering freshmen on the virtues of the college, or one that reneges on implicit or explicit promises about the quality and freedom of education may well produce an "academic backlash" that will take the form of student protests over the quality of education. Even more important is the gap between expectations and actualities regarding freedom of student expression. Stern (1966) has demonstrated that most entering freshmen have extremely high hopes regarding the freedom of speech and action they will be able to exercise during college: most learn the real facts quickly, and graduate thoroughly disabused of their illusions. But since activists, as I have argued above, are particularly responsive to these issues, they are apt to tolerate disillusion less lightly, and to take up arms to concretize their dashed hopes. Compared to the frustration engendered by disillusionment regarding educational quality, the relative deprivation of civil libertarian hopes seems a more potent source of protests. And with regard to both issues, it must be recalled that protests have been *fewest* at institutions of low educational quality and little freedom for student expression. Thus, it is not the absolute level either of educational quality or of student freedom that matters, but the gap between student hopes and institutional facts.

Even if a critical mass of interacting protest-prone students forms in an institution that provides leadership and issues, student protests are by no means inevitable, as the quiescence of American students during the 1950's suggests. For protests to occur, other more broadly cultural factors, attitudes, and values must be present. Protest activities must be seen as meaningful acts, either in an instrumental or an expressive sense; and activists must be convinced that the consequences of activism and protest will not be overwhelmingly damaging to them. During the 1950's, one much-discussed factor that may have militated against student activism was the conviction that the consequences of activism and protest (black-listing, FBI investigations, problems in obtaining security clearance, difficulties in getting jobs) were both harmful to the individual and yet extremely likely. Even more important was the sense on the part of many politically conscious students that participation in left-wing causes would merely show their naïveté, guillibility, and political innocence without furthering any worthy cause. The prevailing climate was such that protest was rarely seen as an act of any meaning or usefulness.

Today, in contrast, student protesters are not only criticized and excoriated by a large segment of the general public, but—more crucial—actively defended, encouraged, lionized, praised, publicized, photographed, interviewed, and studied by a portion of the academic community. Since the primary reference group of most activists is not the general public, but rather that liberal segment of the academic world most sympathetic to protest, academic support has a disproportionate impact on protest-prone students' perception of their own activities. In addition, the active participation of admired faculty members in protests, teach-ins, and peace marches, acts as a further incentive to students (Kelman, 1966). Thus, in a minority of American colleges, subcultures have arisen where protest is felt to be both an important existential act—a dignified way of "standing up to be counted"—and an effective way of "bringing the machine to a halt," sometimes by disruptive acts (sit-ins, strikes, et cetera), more often by calling public attention to injustice.

An equally important if less tangible "cultural" factor is the broad climate of social criticism in American society. As Parsons (1951, 1960), White (1961), and others have noted, one of the enduring themes of American society is the pressure toward "universalism," that is, an increasing extension of principles like equality, equal opportunity, and fair protection of the law to all groups within the society (and in recent years, to all groups in the world). As affluence has increased in American society, impatience at the slow "progress" of non-affluent minority groups has also increased, not only among students, but among other segments of the population. Even before the advent of the student civil rights movement, support for racial segregation was diminishing. Similarly, the current student concern for the "forgotten fifth" was not so much initiated by student activists as it was taken up by them. In this regard, student activists are both caught up in and in the vanguard of a new wave of extension of universalism in American society. Although the demands of student activists usually go far beyond the national consensus, they nonetheless reflect (at the same time that they have helped advance) one of the continuing trends in American social change.

A contrasting but equally enduring theme in American social criticism is a more fundamental revulsion against the premises of industrial—and now technological—society. Universalistic-liberal criticism blames our society because it has not yet extended its principles, privileges, and benefits to all: the complaint is injustice and the goal is to complete our unfinished business. But alienated-romantic criticism questions the validity and importance of these same principles, privileges, and benefits—the complaint is materialism and the goal is spiritual, aesthetic, or expressive fulfillment. The tradition of revulsion against conformist, anti-aesthetic, materialistic, ugly, middle-class America runs through American writing from Melville through the "lost generation" to the "beat generation" and has been expressed concretely in the Bohemian subcultures that have flourished in a few large American cities since the turn of the century. But today the power of the romantic-alienated position has increased: one response to prosperity has been a more searching examination of the technological assumptions upon which prosperity has been based. Especially for the children of the upper middle class, affluence is simply taken for granted, and the drive "to get ahead in the world" no longer makes sense for students who start out ahead. The meanings of life must be sought elsewhere, in art, sentience, philosophy, love, service to others, intensified experience, adventure—in short, in the broadly aesthetic or expressive realm.

Whatever the most plausible explanation of the socio-cultural sources of activism, the importance of prevailing attitudes toward student protest and of the climate of social criticism in America seems clear. In the past five years a conviction has arisen, at least among a minority of American college students, that protest and social action are effective and honorable. Furthermore, changes in American society, especially in middle-class child-rearing practices, mean that American students are increasingly responsive to both the universalistic and romantic critique of our society. Both strands of social criticism have been picked up by student activists in a rhetoric of protest that combines a major theme of impatience at the slow fulfillment of the creedal ideals of American society with a more muted minor theme of aesthetic revulsion at technological society itself. By and large, activists respond most affirmatively to the first theme, and alienated students to the second; but even within the student protest movement, these two themes coexist in uneasy tension.

In interviewing student activists I have been impressed with how often they mention some world-historical event as the catalyst for their activism—in some cases, witnessing via television of the Little Rock demonstrations over school integration, in another case watching rioting Zengakuren students in Japan protesting the arrival of President Eisenhower, in other cases, particularly among Negro students, a strong identification with the rising black nationalism of recently independent African nations.

Several factors help explain this sensitivity to world events. For one, modern means of communication make the historical world more psychologically "available" to youth. Students today are exposed to world events and world trends with a speed and intensity that has no historical precedent. Revolutions, trends, fashions, and fads are now world-wide; it takes but two or three years for fashions to spread from Carnaby Street to New York, New Delhi, Toyko, Warsaw, Lagos, and Lima. In particular, students who have been brought up in a tradition that makes them unusually empathic, humanitarian, and universalistic in values may react more intensely to exposure via television to student demonstrations in Japan than to social pressures from their fellow seniors in Centerville High. Finally, this broadening of empathy is, I believe, part of a general modern trend toward the *internationalization of identity*. Hastened by modern communications and consolidated by the world-wide threat of nuclear warfare, this trend involves, in vanguard groups in many nations, a loosening of parochial and national allegiances in favor of a more inclusive sense of affinity with one's peers (and non-peers) from all nations. In this respect, American student activists are both participants and leaders in the reorganization of psycho-social identity and ideology that is gradually emerging from the unique historical conditions of the twentieth century (Lifton, 1968).

A small but growing number of American students, then, exhibit a peculiar responsiveness to world-historical events—a responsiveness based partly on their own broad identification with others like them throughout the world, and partly on the availability of information about world events via the mass media. The impact of historical events, be they the world-wide revolution for human dignity and esteem, the rising aspirations of the developing nations, or the war in Vietnam, is greatly magnified upon such students; their primary identification is not their unreflective national identity, but their sense of affinity for Vietnamese peasants, Negro sharecroppers, demonstrating Zengakuren activists, exploited migrant workers, and the oppressed everywhere. One of the consequences of security, affluence, and education is a growing sense of personal involvement with those who are insecure, non-affluent and uneducated.

Are we likely to produce (a) more protest-prone personalities? (b) more institutional settings in which protests are likely? (c) a cultural climate that sanctions and encourages activism? and (d) a historical situation that facilitates activism? To three of the questions (a, b, and d), I think the answer is a qualified yes; I would therefore expect that in the future, if the cultural climate remains the same, student activism and protest would continue to be visible features on the American social landscape.

Consider first the factors that promote protest-prone personalities. In the coming generation there will be more and more students who come from the upper middle class, highly educated, politically liberal, professional backgrounds from which protesters are selectively recruited (Michael, 1965). Furthermore, we can expect that a significant and perhaps growing proportion of these families will have the universalistic, humanitarian, equalitarian, and individualistic values found in the families of protesters. Finally, the expressive, permissive, democratic, and autonomy-promoting atmosphere of these families seems to be the emerging trend of middle-class America: older patterns of "entrepreneurial-authoritarian" control are slowly giving way to more "bureaucratic-democratic" techniques of socialization (Miller and Swanson, 1958). Such secular changes in the American family would produce a growing proportion of students with protest-prone personalities.

The growing size of major American universities, their increasing academic and intellectual selectivity, and the emphasis on "quality" education (honors programs, individual instruction, greater student freedom)—all seem to promote the continuing development of activist subcultures in a minority of American institutions. The increasing use of graduate-student teaching assistants in major universities points to the growing availability of large numbers of potential "leaders" for student protests. Admittedly, a sudden increase in the administrative wisdom in college deans and presidents could reduce the number of available "on-campus" issues; but such a growth in wisdom does not seem imminent.

In sharp contrast, a maintenance of the cultural climate required for continuation of activism during the coming years seems far more problematical. Much depends on the future course of the war in Vietnam. Continuing escalation of the war in Southeast Asia will convince many student activists that their efforts are doomed to ineffectuality. For as of mid-1967, anti-war activism has become the primary common cause of student protesters. The increasing militancy and exclusivity of the Negro student civil rights movement, its emphasis on "Black Power" and on grass-roots community-organization work (to be done by Negroes) is rapidly pushing white activists out of civil rights work, thus depriving them of the issue upon which the current mood of student activism was built. This fact, coupled with the downgrading of the War on Poverty, the decline of public enthusiasm for civil rights, and the increasing scarcity of public and private financing for work with the underprivileged sectors of American society, has already begun to turn activists away from domestic issues toward an increasingly single-minded focus on the war in Vietnam. Yet at the same time, increasing numbers of activists overtly or covertly despair of the efficacy of student attempts to mobilize public opinion against the war, much less to influence directly American foreign policies. Continuing escalation in Southeast Asia has also begun to create a more repressive atmosphere toward student (and other) protesters of the war, exemplified by the question, "Dissent or Treason?" Already a movement of activists back to full-time academic work is apparent.

Thus, the war in Vietnam, coupled by the "rejection" of white middle-class students by the vestigial black Civil Rights Movement is producing a crisis among activists, manifest by a "search for issues" and intense disagreement over strategy and tactics. At the same time, the diminution of support for student activism tends to exert a "radicalizing" effect upon those who remain committed activists—partly because frustration itself tends to radicalize the frustrated, and partly because many of the less dedicated and committed activists have dropped away from the movement. Furthermore, most activists find it difficult to turn from civil rights or peace work toward "organizing the middle class" along lines suggested by alienated-romantic criticisms of technological society. On the whole, activists remain more responsive to universalistic issues like peace and civil rights than to primarily expressive or aesthetic criticisms of American society. Furthermore, the practical and organizational problems of "organizing the middle class" are overwhelming. Were the student movement to be forced to turn away from universalistic issues like civil rights and peace to a romantic critique of the "quality of middle-class life," my argument here implies that its following and efficacy would diminish considerably. Were this to happen, observations based on student activism of a more "universalistic" variety would have to be modified to take account of a more radical and yet more alienated membership. Thus, escalation or even continuation of the war in Vietnam, particularly over a long period, will reduce the likelihood of student activism.

Yet there are other, probably more permanent, trends in American culture that argue for a continuation of activism. The further extension of affluence in America will probably mean growing impatience over our society's failure to include the "forgotten fifth" in its prosperity: as the excluded and underprivileged become fewer in number, pressures to include them in American society will grow. Similarly, as more young Americans are brought up in affluent homes and subcultures, many will undoubtedly turn to question the value of monetary, familistic, and careerist goals, looking instead toward expressive, romantic, experiential, humanitarian, and self-actualizing pursuits to give their lives meaning. Thus, in the next few decades, barring a major world conflagration, criticisms of American society will probably continue and intensify on two grounds: First, that it has excluded a significant minority from its prosperity, and, second, that affluence alone is empty without humanitarian, aesthetic, or expressive fulfillment. Both of these trends would strengthen the climate conducive to continuing activism.

Finally, protest-promoting pressures from the rest of the world will doubtless increase in the coming years. The esteem revolution in developing nations, the rise of aspirations in the impoverished two-thirds of the world, and the spread of universalistic principles to other nations—all of these trends portend a growing international unrest, especially in the developing nations. If young Americans continue to be unusually responsive to the unfulfilled aspirations of those abroad, international trends will touch a minority of them deeply, inspiring them to overseas activities like the Peace Corps, to efforts to "internationalize" American foreign policies, and to an acute sensitivity to the frustrated aspirations of other Americans. Similarly, continuation of current American policies of supporting anti-Communist, but often repressive, regimes in developing nations (particularly regimes anathema to student activists abroad) will tend to agitate American students as well. Thus, pressures from the probable world situation will support the continuance of student protests in American society.

In the next decades, then, I believe we can foresee the continuation, with short-range ebbs and falls, of activism in American society. Only if activists were to become convinced that protests were ineffectual or social action impossible is this trend likely to be fundamentally reversed. None of this will mean that protesters will become a majority among American students; but we can anticipate a slowly growing minority of the most talented, emphatic, and intellectually independent of our students who will take up arms against injustice both here and abroad.

In the future, the tension between the romantic-alienated and the universalistic-activist styles of dissent will probably increase. I would anticipate a growing polarization between those students and student groups who turn to highly personal and experiential pursuits like drugs, sex, art, and intimacy, and those students who redouble their efforts to change American society. In the past five years, activists have been in the ascendant, and the alienated have been little involved in organized political protests. But a variety of possible events could reverse this ascendancy. A sense of ineffectuality, especially if coupled with repression of organized dissent, would obviously dishearten many activists. More important, the inability of the student protest movement to define its own long-range objectives, coupled with its intransigent hostility to ideology and efficient organization, means that *ad hoc* protests are too rarely linked to the explicit intellectual, political, and social goals that alone can sustain prolonged efforts to change society. Without some shared sustaining vision of the society and world they are working to promote, and frustrated by the enormous obstacles that beset any social reformer, student activists would be likely to return to the library.

How and whether this tension between alienation and activism is resolved seems to me of the greatest importance. If a growing number of activists, frustrated by political ineffectuality or a mounting war in Southeast Asia, withdraw from active social concern into a narrowly academic quest for professional competence, then a considerable reservoir of the most talented young Americans will have been lost to our society and the world. The field of dissent would be left to the aliented, whose intense quest for *personal* salvation, meaning, creativity, and revelation dulls their perception of the public world and inhibits attempts to better the lot of others. If, in contrast, tomorrow's potential activists can feel that their demonstrations and actions are effective in molding public opinion and more important, in effecting needed social change, then the possibilities for constructive change in post-industrial American society are virtually without limit.

A THEORY OF METAMOTIVATION:
THE BIOLOGICAL ROOTING
OF THE VALUE-LIFE

Abraham H. Maslow

Self-actualizing individuals (more matured, more fully-human), by definition, already suitably gratified in their basic needs, are now motivated in other higher ways, to be called "metamotivations."

By definition, self-actualizing people are gratified in all their basic needs (of belongingness, affection, respect, and self-esteem). This is to say that they have a feeling of belongingness and rootedness, they are satisfied in their love needs, have friends and feel loved and love-worthy, they have status and place in life and respect from other people, and they have a reasonable feeling of worth and self-respect. If we phrase this negatively—in terms of the frustration of these basic needs and in terms of pathology—then this is to say that self-actualizing people do not (for any length of time) feel anxiety-ridden, insecure, unsafe, do not feel alone, ostracized, rootless, or isolated, do not feel unlovable, rejected, or unwanted, do not feel despised and looked down upon, and do not feel deeply unworthy, nor do they have crippling feelings of inferiority or worthlessness.

Clearly we must make an immediate distinction between the ordinary motives of people below the level of self-actualization— that is, people motivated by the basic needs—and the motivations of people who are sufficiently gratified in all their basic needs and therefore are no longer motivated by them primarily, but rather by "higher" motivations. It is therefore convenient to call these higher motives and needs of self-actualizing persons by the name "meta-needs" and also to differentiate the category of motivation from the category of "metamotivation."

All such people are devoted to some task, call, vocation, beloved work ("outside themselves").

Condensed from Abraham H. Maslow, "A Theory of Metamotivation," JOURNAL OF HUMANISTIC PSYCHOLOGY, Fall, 1967. Reprinted by permission.

In examining self-actualizing people directly, I find that in all cases, at least in our culture, they are dedicated people, devoted to some task "outside themselves," some vocation, or duty, or beloved job. Generally the devotion and dedication is so marked that one can fairly use the old words vocation, calling, or mission to describe their passionate, selfless, and profound feeling for their "work." We could even use the words destiny or fate. I have sometimes gone so far as to speak of oblation in the religious sense, in the sense of offering oneself or dedicating oneself upon some altar for some particular task, some cause outside oneself and bigger than oneself, something not merely selfish, something impersonal.

In the ideal instance, inner requiredness coincides with external requiredness, "I want to" with "I must."

I often get the feeling in this kind of situation that I can tease apart two kinds of determinants of this transaction (or alloying, fusion, or chemical reaction) which has created a unity out of a duality, and that these two sets of determinants can and sometimes do vary independently. One can be spoken of as the responses within the person, e.g., "I love babies (or painting, or research, or political power) more than anything in the world. I am fascinated with it. . . . I am inexorably drawn to . . . I need to . . ." This we may call "inner requiredness" and it is felt as a kind of self-indulgence rather than as a duty. It is different from and separable from "external requiredness," which is rather felt as a response to what the environment, the situation, the problem, the external world calls for or requires of the person, as a fire "calls for" putting out, or as a helpless baby demands that one take care of it, or as some obvious injustice calls for righting. Here one feels more the element of duty, or obligation, or responsibility, of being compelled helplessly to respond no matter what one was planning to do, or wished to do. It is more "I must, I have to, I am compelled" than "I want to."

In the ideal instance, which fortunately also happens in fact in many of my instances, "I want to" coincides with "I must."

This ideal situation generates feelings of good fortune and also of ambivalence and unworthiness.

This model also helps to convey what is difficult to communicate in words, that is, their sense of good fortune, of luck, or gratuitous grace, of awe that this miracle should have occurred, of wonder that they should have been chosen, and of the peculiar mixture of pride fused with humility, of arrogance shot through with the pity-for-the-less-fortunate that one finds in lovers.

Of course the possibility of good fortune and success also can set into motion all sorts of neurotic fears, feelings of unworthiness, counter-values, Jonah-syndrome dynamics, etc. These defenses against our highest possibilities must be overcome before the highest values can be wholeheartedly embraced.

At this level the dichotomizing of work and play is transcended; wages, hobbies, vacations, etc., must be defined at a higher level.

And then, of course, it can be said of such a person with real meaningfulness that he is being his own kind of person, or being himself, or actualizing his real self. An abstract statement, an extrapolation out from this kind of observation toward the ultimate and perfect ideal would run something like this: This person is the best one in the whole world for this particular job, and this particular job is the best job in the whole world for this particular person and his talents, capacities, and tastes. He was meant for it, and it was meant for him.

Of course, as soon as we accept this and get the feel of it, then we move over into another realm of discourse, i.e., the realm of being, of transcendence. Now we can speak meaningfully only the language of being ("The B-language," communication at the mystical level, etc.). For instance, it is quite obvious with such people that the ordinary or conventional dichotomy between work and play is transcended totally. That is, there is certainly no distinction between work and play in such a person in such a situation. His work is his play and his play is his work. If a person loves his work and enjoys it more than any other activity in the whole world and is eager to get to it, to get back to it after any interruption, then how can we speak about "labor" in the sense of something one is forced to do against one's wishes?

It is my strong impression that the closer to self-actualizing, to full-humanness, etc., the person is, the more likely I am to find that his "work" is metamotivated rather than basic-need-motivated. For more highly evolved persons, "the law" is apt to be more a way of seeking justice, truth, goodness, etc., rather than financial security, admiration, status, prestige, dominance, masculinity, etc. When I ask the questions: Which aspects of your work do you enjoy most? What gives you your greatest pleasures? When do you get a kick out of your work? etc., such people are more apt to answer in terms of intrinsic values, of transpersonal, beyond-the-selfish, altruistic satisfactions, e.g., seeing justice done, doing a more perfect job, advancing the truth, rewarding virtue and punishing evil, etc.

These intrinsic values overlap greatly with the B-values, and perhaps are identical with them.

I feel it desirable to use my description of the B-values, not only because it would be theoretically pretty if I could, but also because they are operationally definable in so many different ways. That is to say, they are found at the end of so many different investigative roads, that the suspicion arises that there is something in common between these different paths, e.g., education, art, religion, psychotherapy, peak-experiences, science, mathematics, etc. If this turns out to be so, we may perhaps add as another road to final values, the "cause," the mission, the vocation, that is to say, the "work" of self-actualizing people. (It is also theoretically advantageous to speak of the B-values here because of my strong impression that self-actualizing, or more fully-human, people show, *outside* their calling, as well as in it and through it, a love for and satisfaction in these same values.)

Or, to say it in another way, people who are reasonably gratified in all their basic needs now become "metamotivated" by the B-values, or at least by "final" ultimate values in greater or lesser degree, and in one or another combination of these ultimate values.

In another phrasing: self-actualizing people are not primarily motivated (i.e., by basic needs); they are primarily metamotivated (i.e., by metaneeds = B-values).

This introjection means that the self has enlarged to include aspects of the world and that therefore the distinction between self and not-self (outside, other) has been transcended.

These B-values or metamotives are, therefore, no longer *only* intrapsychic or organismic. They are equally inner and outer. The metaneeds, insofar as they are inner, and the requiredness of all that is outside the person are each both stimulus and response to each other. And they move toward becoming indistinguishable, that is, toward fusion.

This means that the distinction between self and not-self has broken down (or has been transcended). There is now less differentiation between the world and the person because he has incorporated into himself part of the world and defines himself thereby. He becomes an enlarged self, we could say. If justice or truth or lawfulness have now become so important to him that he identifies his self with them, then where are they? Inside his skin or outside his skin? This distinction comes close to being meaningless at this point because his self no longer has his skin as its boundary. The inner light now seems to be no different than the outer light.

Certainly simple selfishness is transcended here and has to be defined at higher levels. For instance, we know that it is possible for a person to get more pleasure (selfish? unselfish?) out of food through having his child eat it than through eating it with his own mouth. His self has enlarged enough to include his child. Hurt his child and you hurt him. Clearly the self can no longer be identified with the biological entity which is supplied with blood from his heart along his blood vessels. The psychological self can obviously be bigger than its own body.

Just as beloved people can be incorporated into the self, become defining characteristics of it, so also can beloved causes and values be similarly incorporated into a person's self. Many people, for instance, are so passionately identified with trying to prevent war, or racial injustice, or slums or poverty, that they are quite willing to make great sacrifices, even to the point of risking death. And very clearly, they don't mean justice for their own biological bodies alone. Something personal has now become bigger than the body. They mean justice as a general value, justice for everyone; justice as a principle. Attack upon the B-values is then also an attack upon any person who has incorporated these values into his self. Such an attack becomes a *personal* insult.

To identify one's self with the highest values of the world out there means, to some extent at least, a fusion with the non-self. But this is true not only for the world of nature. It is also true for other human beings. That is to say that the most highly valued part of such a person's self, then, is the same as the most highly valued part of the self of other self-actualizing people. Such selves overlap.

There are other important consequences of this incorporation of values into the self. For instance, you can love justice and truth in the world or in a person out there. You can be made happier as your friends move toward truth and justice, and sadder as they move away from it. This is easy to understand. But supposing you see yourself moving successfully toward truth, justice, beauty, and virtue? Then of course you may find that, in a peculiar kind of detachment and objectivity toward oneself, for which our culture has no place, you will be loving and admiring yourself, in the kind of healthy self-love that Fromm has described. You can respect yourself, admire yourself, take tender care of yourself, reward yourself, feel virtuous, love-worthy, respect-worthy. You may then treat yourself with the responsibility and otherness that, for instance, a pregnant woman does, whose self now has to be defined to include not-self. So also may a person with a great talent protect it and himself as if he were a carrier of something which is simultaneously himself and not himself. He may become his own guardian, so to speak.

The full definition of the person or of human nature must then include intrinsic values, as part of human nature.

If we then try to define the deepest, most authentic, most constitutionally based aspects of the real self, of the identity, or of the authentic person, we find that in order to be comprehensive we must include not only the person's constitution and temperament, not only anatomy, physiology, neurology, and endocrinology, not only his capacities, his biological style, not only his basic instinctoid needs, but also the B-values, which are also *his* B-values. (This should be understood as a flat rejection of the Sartre type of arbitrary existentialism in which a self is created by fiat.) They are equally part of his "nature," or definition, or essence, along with his "lower" needs, at least in my self-actualizing subjects. They must be included in any ultimate definition of "the human being," or of full-humanness, or of "a person." It is true that they are not fully evident or actualized (made real and functionally existing) in most people. And yet, so far as I can see at this time, they are not excluded as potentials in any human being born into the world.

These intrinsic values are instinctoid in nature, i.e., they are needed (a) to avoid illness and (b) to achieve fullest humanness or growth. The "illnesses" resulting from deprivation of intrinsic values (metaneeds) we may call metapathologies. The "highest" values, the spiritual life, the highest aspirations of mankind are therefore proper subjects for scientific study and research. They are in the world of nature.

I wish now to advance another thesis, which comes also from (unsystematized and unplanned) observations on the contrasts between my subjects and the population in general. It is this: I have called the basic needs instinctoid or biologically necessary for many reasons but primarily because the person *needs* the basic gratifications in order to avoid illness, to avoid diminution of humanness, and, positively stated, in order to move forward and upward toward self-actualization or full-humanness. It is my strong impression that something very similar holds true for the metamotivations of self-actualizing people. They seem to me to be also biological necessities in order (a) negatively, to avoid "illness" and (b) positively, to achieve full-humanness. Since these metamotivations are the intrinsic values of being, singly or in combination, then this amounts to contending that the B-values are instinctoid in nature.

These "illnesses" (which come from deprivation of the B-values or metaneeds or B-facts) are new and have not yet been described as such, i.e., as pathologies, except unwittingly, or by implication, or as by Frankl, in a very general and inclusive way, not yet teased apart into researchable form. In general, they have been discussed through the centuries by religionists, historians, and philosophers under the rubric of spiritual or religious shortcomings, rather than by physicians, scientists, or psychologists under the rubric of psychiatric or pychological or biological "illnesses" or stuntings or diminutions.

I will call these "illnesses" (or, better, diminutions of humanness) "metapathologies" and define them as the consequences of deprivation of the B-values either in general or of specific B-values.

The metapathologies of the affluent and indulged young come partly from deprivation of intrinsic values, frustrated "idealism," from disillusionment with a society they see (mistakenly) motivated only by lower or animal or material needs.

This theory of metapathology generates the following easily testable proposition: I believe that much of the social pathology of the affluent (already lower-need-gratified) is a consequence of intrinsic-value-starvation. To say it in another way: much of the bad behavior of affluent, privileged, and basic-need-gratified high school and college students is due to frustration of the "idealism" so often found in young people. My hypothesis is that this behavior can be a fusion of continued search for something to believe in, combined with anger at being disappointed. (I sometimes see in a particular young man total despair or hopelessness about even the *existence* of such values.)

Of course, this frustrated idealism and occasional hopelessness is partially due to the influence and ubiquity of stupidly limited theories of motivation all over the world. Leaving aside behavioristic and positivistic theories—or rather non-theories—as simple refusals even to see the problem, i.e., a kind of psychoanalytic denial, then what is available to the idealistic young man and woman?

Not only does the whole of official nineteenth-century science and orthodox academic psychology offer him nothing, but also the major motivation theories by which most men live can lead him only to depression or cynicism. The Freudians, at least in their official writings (though not in good therapeutic practice), are still reductionistic about all higher human values. The deepest and most real motivations are seen to be dangerous and nasty, while the highest human values and virtues are essentially fake, being not what they seem to be, but camouflaged versions of the "deep, dark, and dirty." Our social scientists are just as disappointing in the main. A total cultural determinism is still the official, orthodox doctrine of many or most of the sociologists and anthropologists. This doctrine not only denies intrinsic higher motivations, but comes perilously close sometimes to denying "human nature" itself. The economists, not only in the West but also in the East, are essentially materialistic. We must say harshly of the "science" of economics that it is generally the skilled, exact, technological application of a totally false theory of human needs and values, a theory which recognizes only the existence of lower needs or material needs.

How could young people not be disappointed and disillusioned? What else could be the result of *getting* all the material and animal gratifications and then *not being happy,* as they were led to expect, not only by the theorists, but also by the conventional wisdom of parents and teachers, and the insistent gray lies of the advertisers?

What happens then to the "eternal verities"? to the ultimate truths? Most sections of the society agree in handing them over to the churches and to dogmatic, institutionalized, conventionalized religious organizations. But this is also a denial of high human nature! It says in effect that the youngster who is looking for something will definitely *not* find it in human nature itself. He must look for ultimates to a non-human, non-natural source, a source which is definitely mistrusted or rejected altogether by many intelligent young people today.

The end-product of such surfeit conditions is that material values have come more and more to dominate the scene. In the result, man's thirst for values of the spirit has remained unquenched. Thus the civilization has reached a stage which virtually verges on disaster. (E. F. Schumacher)

I have focused on the "frustrated idealism" of the young here because I consider it to be a hot research topic today. But, of course, I consider all metapathologies in anybody to be also "frustrated idealism."

THEM AND US:
ARE PEACE PROTESTS
SELF-THERAPY?

Nat Hentoff

On a Sunday morning toward the end of January, twenty-three people rose during a high mass at St. Patrick's Cathedral in New York. They unfurled posters showing a maimed Vietnamese child. They and their posters were bundled up so quickly by forewarned police that only a few of the worshipers in the Cathedral knew what was going on. Many later found out, of course, through the extensive newspaper and television coverage.

Had the demonstrators not been rushed out by the police, their intent had been to leave anyway in protest against Cardinal Spellman's Christmas declaration that "the war in Vietnam is a war for civilization."

I knew about the planned interruption of the mass some days before. In characteristically liberal fashion, I sent a few dollars for the bail fund. But the event continued to trouble me as I began to wonder whether this kind of demonstration—and many other kinds involving various sectors of the peace movement—did not actually increase

Originally published in EVERGREEN REVIEW, *Vol. II, No. 48. Copyright © by Evergreen Review, Inc., 1967.*

divisions between "them" and "us." Whom were the demonstrators talking to? If to the Catholics in the Cathedral, what less effective way is there to persuade them of their complicity in what is happening in Vietnam than by interrupting an occasion that is sacred to them? The context is hardly one for rational dialogue. If the intent was to speak to all those who would see or read about the demonstration, what actually was the effect on *them?* In all likelihood, their reaction was one of resentment and anger. Instead of the issue being focused on Vietnam, attention had been directed to the demonstrators and their manner of demonstration.

With all respect for, and some envy of the particular qualities of courage which enabled the twenty-three to do what they did, I would suggest that their act's essential effect was to make *them* feel relevant, to make *them* feel that some of their guilt as Americans had been atoned for by this witness. I am all for self-therapy, but if that's what it is, let us call it that.

The conviction used to be—and still is in some areas of the peace and post-civil-rights movements—that demonstrations have to exacerbate because only in that way can full attention be drawn to injustice. Dead rats were thrown in front of city halls. Rush hour traffic was stalled. Young people chained themselves to pillars in front of court buildings. And nothing very much happened as a result. Nothing happened because those demonstrations made it easier for the bystander—the *moyen* citizen—to separate himself from the activists and their concerns. The idea was to speak truth to power. But the mayors and the governors and the legislators, seeing no real counter-power behind the few demonstrators, ignored them. And the *moyen* citizen, who also feels himself impotent to affect change even if he wanted to, regarded the activists as so different in kind from him that the thought of ever possibly allying himself with them was inconceivable. (Even if such a thought could have stirred in any case.)

These days, there is a thrust among black people to mount more of their demonstrations in their own neighborhoods as a means not only of underlining injustices—bad ghetto schools, for instance, which are not accountable to the parents—but also of using the demonstrations to mobilize other black people. That direction makes sense. If there is ever to be sufficient counter-power from the ghettos, there has to be recruitment and organization, and demonstrations can be one way to mobilize. If, however, there are not further plans to keep up the pressure and to construct feasible alternatives—ways of real community participation in the schools, for example—the initial impetus to get together is quickly lost.

But what of those of us who do want to speak to, to persuade, the citizenry at large to end the war in Vietnam? What of those who want to amass sufficient political pressure so that this country's resources can be directed at the cities, at creating new jobs, at establishing a guaranteed annual income? Simply demonstrating in the old ways—peacefully or abrasively—won't do it. The twenty-three at St. Patrick's Cathedral did not, I expect, make many converts. Nor did the members of the San Francisco Mime Troupe a few years ago when they suddenly put on a free anti-war performance in a San Francisco public park. Lenny Bruce, observing the occasion, shook his head. "The people in the park," he said, "didn't *ask* for this. They didn't come here for this. And so they're turned off, not on."

I would suggest that one reason the old ways of demonstrating continue to be held onto is that most of "us" have never tried role reversal, have never tried to imagine being one of "them," have no idea of what worries them, motivates them. We see them as a homogeneous, passive mass that can be moved, if at all, the way one would move clay. Or rather, the way one would mold clay. We want to shape them, direct them. The I-thou relationship of Buber doesn't enter at all. And so we few continue to stand on one side of the divide, and all of "them" are on the other. We are encapsulated, and they are encapsulated.

Consider, for instance, how naturally and inevitably we of more or less similar goals congregate together. I don't know, I literally don't know, a single political conservative, let alone a member of the John Birch Society. And, in fact, if I were not a journalist, I would know very few different kinds of people. I would be limited, as most people are, to the peripheral relationships of an office or institution and to a few after-hours friends of roughly consonant tastes and values. Of course, we huddle together for comfort. And there are some who make their islands as small as possible, sometimes consisting only of a wife and children.

How to break through? First, there has to be the desire to, and then the opportunity. And before the desire, there has to be the recognition that there are individuals making up that passive mass of "them." To begin that recognition, I would suggest a remarkable book, Studs Terkel's *Division Street: America* (Pantheon). The book consists of conversations by Terkel with some seventy people in and around Chicago. A more diversified range of people than most of us ever get a chance to know. They are of a wide variety of backgrounds, vocations, temperaments. Most are "ordinary," as we might regard them, but each is, of course, unique. (How seldom we who want to change society and mankind ever really consider the uniqueness of everyone in the society to be changed. We too have our categorical assumptions about the poor, the cops, the right-wingers, the administrators of the power structure, the politicians, the Midwesterners, the general. And they of us. And so there *cannot* be any communication. Categories do not communicate.)

Wisely, Terkel eliminated from the book clergymen, college professors, journalists, and writers of any kind. "I felt," he explained, "that their articulateness and literacy offered them other forums. They had created their own books; my transcribing their attitudes would be nothing more than self-indulgence. It was the man of inchoate thought I was seeking rather than the consciously articulate."

I will not try to summarize seventy different lives and life styles, but *Division Street: America* does make clear how deep the sense of loss of community is among many otherwise widely different members of "them." It makes clear how powerless *they* feel. Or most of them. It reveals in all kinds of people a yearning to communicate, to relate, to be an organic part of a neighborhood, a city. But they don't know how.

In the *New York Times,* Tom Wicker distilled how most of "us" feel. Intellectuals, for example, protesting against the war in Vietnam. We suffer, he says, "the malaise beyond dissent." And that is "the fear that dissent does not matter any more; that only action counts; but that no one really knows what action to take. More and more, twentieth-century man crouches like an old woman on her stoop, pointing her rusty shotgun at the oncoming expressway, knowing all the time that in the end the bulldozer will go through."

And "they" feel that way too. A thirty-five-year-old mother of six, a Catholic, says in *Division Street: America:* "This morning when I went to work there was a red brick building. When I came home, the building wasn't there. It was flattened. I can't decide whether it's all for the good. All I know is there's a feeling of loss, a lot of things leaving us."

A seventy-five-year-old widow: "I can't understand, and never will, what gives the few men the right to hold all our lives in the palm of their hand? What right have they got, what God-given right have they got? Just to press the button and say you've had it. And you think of your own son, who's just starting to live, and all these kids. Is it really freedom for them they're seeking?"

As if in answer, a middle-aged woman who owns a tavern: "Most that disturbs me today is when I talk to some of my neighbors, none of them, they don't like this Vietnam going on, but here's where they say, 'What's the use? Who are we? We can't say nothing. We have no word. We got the President. We elected him. We got congressmen in there. They're responsible. Let them worry. Why should I worry about it?' It's already pounded into them, you're just a little guy, you vote and you're through, it won't do no good anyhow."

"There is a coldness to our time," says an architect. A woman in her sixties, living in a public housing project: "I don't like all this steel and glass that's going up straight. It don't look very warm or homey. I know they are inside, but they just don't look that way from the outside. It makes the city look cold, I think. People are moving to get away from people. I don't like the way we're going."

Some, of course, have accepted the coldness. A swinger and part-owner of a bar: "I don't bother anybody and I don't like anybody to bother me. If I were walkin' down the street and they were robbin' a bank, the guy would walk out and say, 'Hi Gene, how are you?' And if I knew him or didn't know him, I'd say, 'Hi, how are you?' And as long as he didn't step on my foot while I was walkin' by the bank, let him do what he wants to do. It's none of my goddamn business . . . I'm pleasant, get along, courteous."

And that reminded me of a letter I received from a girl at Pembroke College, a New Left activist: "There are in fact few real ogres on the scene. One sees the world being killed off by nice, generous, courteous, kind people."

And yet there are many more throughout the book who, though resigned to the coldness, have not accepted it. Impotent, they dream of community. A thirty-five-year-old housewife, with no political ideology, in an "ordinary" neighborhood: "The greatest day of my life was the day I went to see a Pete Seeger concert. I think he's good. But to me the greatest thrill that I got was the fact that there were that many people together that felt a certain way. And I've never been in a crowd where everybody felt that way. And yet at the same time, how come. . . . You could read in the paper that so many people felt like you do, yet you could never yourself meet anybody that feels the same way."

A John Bircher: "I've lived in a wilderness all my life." A nineteen-year-old, a loner, who works in a supermarket while going to college: "I love life. I only wish some of it would come my way." A girl, who has been drinking since she was twelve and is a frequent user of marijuana, ends a poem: "If I am for myself alone/ What am I?" A fifty-three-year-old cop: "I'd like to take up something else if I can. Be able to enter—this sounds sort of corny—more of a community life, in a smaller community where you participated more, you know. *In doing something."*

My point in all this is that because we do not know "them," we do not recognize how great a sense of waste of life, of spirit, does exist beyond our own islands. There are many who could be activated to work for change in their neighborhoods, in their cities, if they felt a *possibility* of enough others coming together with them. And there are more than the polls reveal who are deeply disquieted by the war but feel isolated as well as impotent. I do not want to sound ingenuous. Many of "them" have dropped out and make it as best they can in isolation. But others who are isolated do not want to be.

How can they begin to feel that their lives can have greater dimension, that they can have a say in what happens to them and their neighborhood and their city? Not by us parading among them. One way, as yet a very small beginning of a way, is being discovered by the young community organizers who live among the people for whom they're trying to be catalysts. One is in this book, a member of JOIN (Jobs or Income Now), a subsidiary of Students for a Democratic Society, which works among poor Appalachians transplanted to Chicago. The young woman in JOIN says: "We've recently discovered we're not getting anywhere with the door-to-door technique. . . . Somehow this is not working because we're not friends with these people, we're not part of their lives; as one guy put it, maybe getting drunk with these guys on Saturday night (would help).

"Now," she continues, talking of her child, "I just take Sarah on my arm and just go up and have coffee with the lady down the block and talk about her son, who she's afraid is going to be a delinquent. And I just have coffee with another lady and we talk about what it's like back home. Not just gripes they have, something wholly unrelated, personal. At meetings, we have country music."

And in Newark, a member of the SDS-initiated Newark Community Union became a teacher there, in the neighborhood in which he lives. His methods—trying to overturn the school dictum of substituting discipline for interest—drew him into conflict with the bureaucracy, and he has been fired. Now he and some parents are working on their own school, which will be certified by the state as a private school. He has found an organic way of relating to that community.

And in other cities throughout the country, there are young teachers—hardly enough of them yet—who are trying to give children and their parents a sense of themselves and a sense of the possibility of community. And not only in poor neighborhoods.

Meanwhile there are peace activists who are beginning to realize that if there is to be an end to this country's militarism, large *ad hoc* parades and demonstrations are not going to be nearly effective enough. Instead, roots have to be grown in as wide a variety of neighborhoods as possible. My own feeling is that there's a wide scope of potentiality for young peace activists, not yet anchored to a job or a particular neighborhood of those like themselves. Their role in "the movement" could be to become part of different kinds of neighborhoods, get to know as many of their neighbors as they can, and like the young woman from JOIN, find out who each of them is—as individuals, not as manipulatable subjects for proselytization.

I don't expect those of "us" in our thirties and forties and beyond to spread out and live among "them," but the young can, and I hope a sizable number will. Meanwhile there are other ways of bridging the divide between "them" and "us." In New York City last year, the Committee of the Professions started an experimental community action project based on meetings in apartments throughout the city for which the Committee provided speakers. Several thousand people, most of whom had never taken part in a demonstration, or even thought of the possibility, became involved in over a hundred meetings. From those meetings, block clubs and community organizations were formed which began work on other issues besides peace. Now the Committee of the Professions is trying to establish "a network of neighborhood political groups that would span the city and which could provide the basis for concerted political and educational activity." And most of these neighborhoods, it should be emphasized, are largely populated by "them."

There must be other ways of bridging the division, and I'd welcome any ideas readers of this article have. In the meantime, of course, there will be need for demonstrations. If, for instance, the draft-resistance movement among college students grows to the point at which sizable numbers of them are arrested, they will need support; and demonstrations—if large enough—can be part of that support. And if only to keep a sense of community alive among those already converted to an end to militarism, massive demonstrations . . . are important.

But if we are ever to break through our own encapsulation and if "they" are to release themselves from *their* isolation, the I-thou relationship will have to become the normative principle of more and more movements for change. At this very late time in this administered society, afflicted by "the malaise beyond dissent," the only way out—simplistic and corny as it may sound—is the individual. An architect in *Division Street: America* notes that "the doctrine of the announced idea" won't make it. No matter how many placards proclaim MAKE LOVE, NOT WAR. The only thing that will make it is: "man must listen to man himself talking."

The late A. J. Muste was, as usual, prescient when he wrote in 1952: "Precisely on that day when the individual appears to be utterly hopeless, to 'have no choice,' when the aim of the 'system' is to convince him that he is helpless as an individual and that the only way to meet regimentation is by regimentation, there is absolutely no hope save in going back to the beginning. The human being . . . must exercise the choice which is no longer accorded him by society. (It is a choice) which, 'naked, weaponless, armourless, without shield or spear, but only with naked hands and open eyes,' he must create again. He must understand that this naked human being is the one *real* thing in the face of the machines and the mechanized institutions of our age."

He must also understand that there are other naked human beings who would like a chance to believe they can exercise that choice. And that they are to be found in places not yet familiar to the peace agitators and those others who want to stop and then redirect the machinery. And that it makes much more sense to talk to them in their bars or schools than to rise up in isolated protest in the middle of St. Patrick's Cathedral.

THE AMERICAN WAY OF DEATH: THE ROOTS OF VIOLENCE IN AMERICAN SOCIETY

David O. Arnold

When Senator Robert F. Kennedy was shot, U.N. Secretary-General U Thant wired Mrs. Kennedy that he found it "incomprehensible . . . that in the great nation of the United States violence should continually jeopardize the lives of the society's finest men" and Governor Richard Hughes of New Jersey stated that he found the shooting "unbelievable." Had this been America's first assassination of the decade I would have no quarrel with these remarks. As it was, these men simply echoed similar statements made by others under similar circumstances over the last few years. How could it happen that John F. Kennedy could be fatally shot? Or Medgar Evers? Or Martin Luther King? Or even American Nazi leader George Lincoln Rockwell?

Assassination in America today is not incomprehensible or unbelievable. Those who claim it is are either mouthing platitudes, being amazingly blind and naive, or deliberately covering up or obscuring a fact of American life that reflects deep structural defects in the society.

Assassination and other forms of political violence by private citizens is not an anomaly in America today. We cannot dismiss it as the action of lunatics; to do so would be merely to hide our ignorance behind the labels of psychiatry. Rather, such killings are an understandable response to several developments of 20th century America. If we are to avoid losing more of our great men we must recognize this and work to correct the underlying causes of assassinations. Morning-after press statements or Fourth of July speeches won't do it. Gun laws are part of what is needed, but by themselves can have only little effect. Assassinations and similar acts of violence are, unfortunately, not contrary to the American way of life; they are

David O. Arnold, "The American Way of Death: The Roots of Violence in American Society," INSTITUTE OF GOVERNMENT AND PUBLIC AFFAIRS, U.C.L.A., *June, 1968. Reprinted by permission.*

totally in accord with some of the most basic aspects of that way of life.

This analysis should not be expected to fit all the details of any particular assassination or assassin. It is an attempt to spell out some of the causes that operate in a greater or lesser degree in many assassins, and to some degree in all of us.

Blaming many of our social ills on "aiienation" has become commonplace in recent years. Analyses which do this tend to suffer from two major flaws. First, alienation is often used as a diffuse, undefined *ad hoc* label. Only an alienated person would do X; Y did X, therefore Y is alienated. Second, the linkage is not made explicit between the alienation and the social ill supposedly caused by it. Even if we agree that Y is alienated, why did Y choose X as a solution?

More concretely, I argue that American society breeds certain sorts of alienation for certain reasons. And that violence against other human beings—especially against public figures and most especially against political figures—is a natural outgrowth of certain central aspects of American society.

Sociologists have conducted hundreds of studies of alienation. So many, in fact, that other sociologists have written dozens of articles and books attempting just to sort out the various types of alienation which the studies have tried to measure. A man can be alienated from his job, his family, or his community, or from his country, its political system or its economic system, and so on, ad infinitum. He can manifest this alienation in the form of normlessness, meaninglessness, self-estrangement, misanthropy, and so on. But in spite of all this we can speak meaningfully of something called alienation, because within any given individual or group a relationship does exist between the various forms of alienation. Viktor Frankl has written a book about *Man's Search for Meaning.* Eric Berne, in *Games People Play,* speaks of our need for figurative "strokes" from other people. In *The Adjusted American,* Snell and Gail Putney claim that what we need is verification and expansion of our self-image, both from others and from activity. And earlier in the century Thorstein Veblen wrote of an "instinct of workmanship." Whatever their differences, these writers agree that man needs to lock-in to something that seems to have meaning and that by having meaning bestows meaningfulness on the person himself. Lacking this he senses a gap and is alienated, perhaps even from himself, seeing himself-as-he-is as separated from himself-as-he-should-be.

This alienation, this lack of meaning, can occur in relation to his job, family, or country. Finding meaning in one relationship can to some degree make up for a lack in another. For some people meaningful family relationships make less important, jobs or political situations that would otherwise be alienating. Meaning might be found in tilling the land or painting, which would replace other relationships. Or religion, a meaningful relationship to God, might give a man the validation he needs. But no one can entirely replace the others. Political alienation may be relatively insignificant to a man with a meaningful job, a chance to create, a family, or a god that makes sense. But alienation from the political system may still be there, like a latent ulcer, waiting to give him trouble at the slightest excuse.

If we look beyond the newspaper headlines and the radio and TV commentators the sources of alienation, particularly of political alienation in this country are not really hard to locate. In the last 200 years America has grown like Topsy; it is now packed with more than 200,000,000 people and saddled with institutions that were originally shaped in slower-moving and less-crowded centuries. Today the primary political feeling of the average American is impotence. He feels he, as an individual, can have little if any impact on the political system which does exercise an ever-increasing power over him. And for the most part his feeling is accurate: the individual citizen in this country counts for almost nothing politically. Rarely is any legitimate way open for him to influence his country—one which offers a reasonable possibility of success.

We deify the voting process, yet with even "close" races being won by thousands of votes the man casting his ballot is partaking of an activity that is 90 per cent ritual and 10 per cent hope. He can contribute to the party or candidate of his choice, but since even local campaigns require astronomical sums even the businessman or professional can achieve little more than a tax deduction by his contribution. Petitions and letters face the same difficulty: amid the hundreds of thousands one alienated American makes little difference. As often as not a letter to his congressman is answered by a form letter, which makes it clear that even the congressman's mail boy has not bothered to read past the constituent's opening sentence.

All this is not the fault of callous congressmen, money-hungry campaign managers or an unjust voting system. Rather it is merely one of the results of natural escalation: the population explosion and the increased complexity and segmentalization of all phases of our society (and especially of our government) have increased the distance between the governing and the governed.

When polite, legitimate forms of political action fail to give the individual a feeling of accomplishment he turns to the impolite yet legitimate forms: peaceful demonstrations, picket lines, marches, and the like. And if the participant doesn't examine the results too closely such activity may for a time quiet down that gnawing alienation, and perhaps even convince him that his life can indeed have meaning. But on closer examination, it usually turns out that the main effect of the activity has been on the activists themselves, in deceptively countering their alienation. The 1963 march on Washington was proclaimed a success because many people came, not because it changed anything. Picket lines and boycotts rarely achieve more than token success. The only people who benefit from most large demonstrations are the policemen who earn overtime pay for protecting America from Americans.

When even impolite yet legitimate forms of protest fail they are invariably followed by illegitimate forms such as civil disobedience, riots, assassinations, and guerrilla warfare. Some of these are rational from the standpoint of the goals sought, some are not. But that is not the point. The point is that in their alienation people try whatever is at hand in desperate attempts to validate their existence in a society that says they don't count.

Why is it violent action to which people turn? Granted, many do not turn to violence, but instead live out their lives in quiet desperation, or perhaps escape into drugs, television, alcohol, or pulp fiction. But it is not hard for Americans to turn to violence as a solution to their alienation. What is surprising is not that we have assassinations, but that we have so few. Ours is a violent society. It was born out of a violent revolution which took place after petitions to the king and acts of civil disobedience proved to be of no avail. And our society has been violent ever since. From infancy we are taught that while the creation of life is obscene, the violation of life is laudable. When a society uses, condones, and even glamorizes violence as a way to solve its problems, why do we express surprise when its members show they have learned their lessons well? We go around the world using violence to force countries like Vietnam and the Dominican Republic to do our bidding, and blackmail other countries with the threat of similar violence. Internally we arm our "peace officers" with instruments of violence and tell them it is proper to destroy human life in order to protect material goods. In Watts, in Detroit, and in Newark, most of the victims were killed not by blacks but by whites—by whites with uniforms, guns, and bullets bought with tax dollars that properly spent could have eliminated many of the underlying causes of these riots. When the mayor of one of America's great cities, a man dubbed by his constitutents "shoot-to-kill Daley," tells Chicago's police force that a man seen carrying a molotov cocktail or taking a TV set from a store should be shot down in cold blood, do we really have to ask why private citizens also turn to violence?

If it were only official violence that we condoned its influence on the individual would be bad enough. But we glorify all violence. Bonnie and Clyde, who were so bloodthirsty that the real professionals in their occupation looked down their noses at them, have become public heroes. Instead of finding people who bear any resemblance to Bonnie and Clyde changing their names, faces, or clothes, we find other people flocking to the stores to attire themselves in the "Bonnie and Clyde look" and advertisers of everything from cars to shoe polish using the Bonnie and Clyde image to promote their products.

In summary, then, the situation is this. The structure of American society today is such that large numbers of its citizens are alienated and lack adequate ways to feel that their lives have real meaning. This creates a problem, and one of the solutions our society suggests is violence. Obviously, therefore, speeches deploring violence can have no effect. Neither can governmental commissions whose recommendations, if they call for more than speeches, are ignored. What we need to do, and I am not certain it can be accomplished, is to reduce the underlying social causes of alienation and to stop giving our citizens a lifetime of training for violence. I have no "answer" for how this double task can be fulfilled. I can merely suggest a few directions to which we might start giving more thought and in which we might start moving before we lose another Kennedy or King.

The under-30 generation has lost faith in representative democracy. The choice of candidates rarely provides meaningful alternatives and even when it seems to, once a man is in office his program rarely bears much resemblance to his platform. Perhaps we need to seek ways to re-establish participatory democracy in the U.S. One possibility might be to reduce the importance of state government, turn the national government into more of an information gathering and disseminating unit, and place as many governmental functions as possible in the hands of local communities. This would put government closer to the individual but has a number of drawbacks. For instance, increasing the strength of local government would disenfranchise the more mobile members of the population and allow an entrenched plurality in a community to impose its will on others. Unless a way could be found to overcome such shortcomings they might well outweigh the advantages.

Another possibility to be explored is increasing grass roots involvement at all levels of government. The example of TVA, the Tennessee Valley Authority, deserves examination. However, we must avoid the examples of many of the public housing and slum improvement commissions, which are set up with the assumption that the people the commissions are to help are too stupid to know what they want; thus the commissions are staffed with middle-class whites who do not live in and are not involved in the communities to be served.

We might also consider the possibility of extending participatory democracy beyond the political realm. Why can't we have democracy in the economic system? Maximizing profit as a basis for deciding what, and what quality to produce may have been justifiable in the 19th century but the time has come to re-think many of our assumptions. We have become victims of a cult of efficiency, with quality, old-fashioned craftsmanship, and satisfaction for both producer and consumer falling by the wayside. We need desperately to bring man back in.

These comments concern the problem that America has given its members. In addition to eradicating the problem we need to do something about the faulty solution that has been offered. We need somehow to end our glorification of violence. The first step will have to be recognizing and admitting that we have indeed been glorifying it. We have to stop hiding behind the "this hurts me more than it hurts you" sort of hypocrisy. We claim we abhor war; we say we deplore riots, assassinations, and other forms of violence. But our deeds repeatedly make liars of us. We must face up to the issue if we are to deal with it.

The second step is less clear. After we admit that we have this disease, how do we cure it? We need to give serious attention to how we can shift our values. Until we find violence between man and man truly repugnant we will continue to surround ourselves with it.

Maybe legislation can help. Perhaps if we stop worrying about magazines that show human life in its natural state and books that say "fuck" and start worrying about magazines that show human life destroyed and multilated and books that say "kill," we can improve matters.

Maybe education can help. Let us stop giving our children war toys, comic books about violence, and TV stories about war. Let us get the militarists and their ROTC out of our high schools and colleges. Or at least balance the curriculum with courses about ending hate and violence.

Maybe . . . maybe. These may not work. Or, they may backfire. What we should not do is drive our violent urges underground. We have to keep them in sight so we can cure them. I don't have the cure at my fingertips. But the 200 million of us have accomplished almost everything else we have set out to do. If we really set out to become a non-violent society, I strongly believe that we can do it.

12994F
P